Computing Research & Innovation (CRINN) Vol 2 October 2017

Computer & Mathematical Sciences
Computer Network & Data Communications
Information Technology & System Sciences

By:

Faculty of Computer & Mathematical Sciences
Universiti Teknologi MARA
Perlis Branch, Malaysia

http://crinn.conferencehunter.com/openconf.php

ISBN: 978-1-387-00704-2

FOREWORD

CRINN (Computing Research and Innovation), Volume 2, October 2017, is a compilation of peer-reviewed research papers, technical and concept papers and innovations among the academicians from Faculty of Computer and Mathematical Sciences, Universiti Teknologi MARA, Perlis Branch and other universities from all over Malaysia. CRINN also serves as a sharing center for every faculty members and others to share their research findings, experiences and innovations.

This volume comprises a selection of 38 scholarly articles from Mathematical Sciences, Computer Sciences, Computer Network, Information Technology and System Sciences fields. I would like to take this opportunity to thank and congratulate the authors for their contributions. My congratulations are also extended to the editors for putting together the contributions into a cohesive and readable form.

Dr Rizauddin Saian
Head
Faculty of Computer and Mathematical Sciences
Universiti Teknologi MARA
Perlis Branch
MALAYSIA

TABLE OF CONTENTS

SECTION I: COMPUTER &MATHEMATICAL SCIENCES

SECTION II: COMPUTER NETWORK & DATA COMMUNICATIONS

SECTION III: INFORMATION TECHNOLOGY & SYSTEM SCIENCES

Article	Title	Page No.

Article	Title	Page No.

SECTION I:

COMPUTER
&
MATHEMATICAL
SCIENCES

Article 1

Assigning Examination Invigilator's Schedule Problem: An Approach of Programming Techniques Using Simple Sequential Assignment

Jamal Othman, Naemah Abdul Wahab, Rozita Kadar, Saiful NizamWarris
Department of Computer and Mathematical Sciences,
Universiti Teknologi MARA Pulau Pinang Branch, Malaysia

Abstract
Preparation of examination invigilation schedule is a tedious and challengingtasks. It is impossible to satisfy all invigilators or proctors with the invigilation schedules prepared. The examination committees have to analyze and thoroughly checks all constraints submitted by the invigilators. Formerly, the process of assignments and deciding the best slot for invigilation will usually take a couple of weeks and all these processes are done manually. This paper proposes a programming technique using simple sequential approach to assign the invigilators on the proper examination slot without any conflicts or clashes aligned with the list of constraints and parameters. This simple tools or systems has been developed to help the examination committee to reduce the time taken for invigilation schedule preparation, avoid erroneous of incorrect assignment of invigilators and increase the satisfaction amongst invigilators with the invigilation schedule assigned. However, this tool is only a supplementary support in invigilation assignment process and the manual changes by considering human touch factors are still considered to produce friendly and empathy worthy invigilation schedules.

Keywords: Invigilators, Invigilation, Sequential Techniques

Introduction

One of the main operations of any university is examination. Most universities setup special unit under the Department of Academic Affairs to manage the examination operations. Universiti Teknologi MARA (UiTM) for example, runs an independent department or section to manage all examination operations, which is connected to all faculties, centers and campuses. Basically, the examination department manages the printing and packaging of question papers, distribution of examination package to faculties, centers or campuses, preparation of examination schedules,determination of examination venues and assignment of invigilators(UiTM, 2016).

ISBN: 978-1-387-00704-2

Gaspero et al. (2003)has statedthat the university timetabling problem includes the preparation of lectures and examination scheduling which allocate to the number of rooms, consisting of lecturers or tutors, administrative staffs and students in a specified duration of time. Furthermore, ahead of the schedule preparations, the constraints as predetermined are filtered and verified as soft and hard constraints to minimize the lecturer's and student's workload. Carter & Laporte(1997)has mentioned, generally, for the preparation of examination scheduling in tertiary education, it involves large number of constraints, highly considered constraints and complex multiple combination of constraints.Several applications have been developed to generate the class and examination scheduling by using special techniques such as mathematical modeling(Sagir & Ozturk, 2010), constructive heuristic approach(Kahar & Kendall, 2010), particle swarm based hyper-heuristic approach(Ahmed, Sajid, Ali, & Bukhari, 2011), bender's partitioning(Sarin, Wang, & Varadarajan, 2010)and graph coloring framework(Mohamed, Mushi, & Mujuni, 2013).

Experts have introduced several approaches to perform an efficient, accurate and establish the best solution to solve complex and large problem of examination or class scheduling(Chunbao & Nu, 2012). Furthermore, the existence of big data evolution has coincidently influence and increase the complexity of timetabling system. The happinessindex of timetable becomes the highest priority of timetabling schedule regardless of the complexity of the system. The systems cannot promise fulfilling 100% of users' satisfactions, nevertheless, complying with 70% of happinessindex isconsidered successful.

This paper will focus on the preparation of invigilation examination schedules amongst invigilators at UiTM Pulau Pinang Branch, Malaysia. The scope of invigilators comprises the lecturers, administrative staff, invigilators assistant and part-timers. The parameters and constraints are determined as required data for the invigilation processing. The hard and soft constraint

ISBN: 978-1-387-00704-2

are determined and prioritized to optimize the complexity of invigilation assignments.

An algorithm has been developed to generate the invigilation assignment reports,taking into consideration all approved parameters and constraints. This algorithm has been tested to several sets of data for testing and it has continuously been applied on real data since January 2016 examination session until the current session of examination. The programming language used is the Java Programming language. Figure 1 illustrates the records extraction process from the text file and automated records generation process subsequently intoMicrosoft Access.

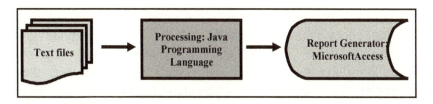

Figure 1: The Framework of Invigilation Timetabling Systems

Prior Practices of Invigilation Assignment

In the pastpractices, most of the invigilation duties preparation will be managed by the examination committee which approximately consists of 10 members. The committee will be concentrating on the invigilation duties preparation after the examination placement of venue is completed. Once the examination placement is verified and accepted, the committee will be requesting data such as the list of invigilators, ratio of invigilator to the number of candidates or capacity of the examination rooms, records of examination from the first day until the final day of examination together with the examination venue which has been placed and list of constraints. All this data are needed by the committee and the preparation will consume more than 1 week together with the validation and verificationprocesses before the letter ofappointment can be distributed to each invigilator.

ISBN: 978-1-387-00704-2

All these processes are done manually by examination committee. Most of the examination committee members are lecturers that are busy with other commitments besides teaching and doing research work. Furthermore, several members of examination committee are also holding administrative position such as program coordinator or head of department. With the time constraint and workloads, this is one of the reasonsfor some cases in the invigilation assignmentthe committees are unable to take into account the hard constraints as requested by the invigilators. Similarly mentioned byHanum, Romliyah, & Bakhtiar(2015), the manual system fails to consider the hard constraints and the invigilators are unhappy with the invigilation dutiesreceived.

Related paper which has mentioned byCowling, Kendall and Hussin(2002)from the survey has observed that most of invigilators are not satisfied with their timetables and they requested the scheduler or examination committee to do a thorough work on invigilation assignment duties. Other desirable factor such as the human touch or personal preferences is also considered as one of the element during the assignment of invigilation duties. Most of the examination committee members work accordingly to the standard operating procedure (SOP) as stated, determined and standardized by the committee. We believe that the personal preferences will be look over thoroughly if the examination committee has ample time to amend the invigilation assignment duties.

Table 1 shows the total changes or invigilators replacement after the manual assignment of invigilation duties amongst invigilators. This data has been collected from Examination Unit at Permatang Pauh Campus, UiTM Pulau Pinang Branch.

ISBN: 978-1-387-00704-2

Table 1: Total Changes of Invigilation Duties according to Examination Session

	Examination Session			
	Jan 2013	Mar 2013	Jun 2013	Dis 2013
Total Invigilation	578	1096	624	1290
Total request to change or amend the invigilation duties	153	245	148	301
Percentages of changes	26.47	22.36	23.72	23.33

Based on the above table, it shows that although the examination committee members have spent almost two weeks to prepare the invigilation duties, howeverthe percentage of changes are still more than 20%. The suggested algorithm is expected to decline the percentage of changes andincrease the invigilators satisfaction.

Assignment Model for Invigilation Schedule
Examination Management Systems (EMS) has been developed and consistingof four (4) main modules including the Examination Placement module, Printing & Packaging of Question Papers module, Assignment of Invigilation Duties module and Examination Operation module. This paper will concentrate on the discussion of Assignment of Invigilation Duties amongst invigilators.

The process of assigning of invigilation duties amongst invigilators will be performed after the examination placement is completed. EMS requires the following data for assignment of invigilation duties:

- List of invigilators or proctors. The invigilators including the academic staffs either the permanent staffs, contract staffs, part-timers or part-time full-timers (PTFT). Besides that, the administrative staffs and invigilators assistant (outsiders) will be appointed to assist the invigilation at the examination hall which requires many invigilators.

ISBN: 978-1-387-00704-2

	KAMPUS	JAWATAN	NAMA	BIDANG	KULTI/JABATA	LEVEL
5						
12	P	PENSYARAH	MOHD HAPIZ BIN MAHAIYADIN (DR)	ACIS	ACIS	0
13	P	PENSYARAH	MOHD MARBAWI BIN TAHA (DR)	ACIS	ACIS	0
14	P	PENSYARAH	ROSHAIMIZAM BIN SUHAIMI	ACIS	ACIS	0
15	P	PENSYARAH	ZAITON BINTI DIN	ACIS	ACIS	0
16	P	PROF MADYA	HOE FOO TERNG (PM) (DR)	APB	APB	0
17	P	PENSYARAH MUDA (K	NUR DARINA BINTI IBRAHIM	APB	APB	0

Figure 2: List of Invigilators

- The examination records from the first day until the final day of examination including the venue of examination that has been assigned to each course.

14	1	27/03/2017	ISNIN	PAGI	9:00 AM	11:00 AM	S	EC110	ELC151	PEC1102A1/2	24	DEWAN BESAR
15	1	27/03/2017	ISNIN	PAGI	9:00 AM	11:00 AM	S	EC110(27)	ELC151	PEC1102B1/2	28	DEWAN BESAR
16	1	27/03/2017	ISNIN	PAGI	9:00 AM	11:00 AM	S	EC110	ELC151	PEC1102C1/2	24	DEWAN BESAR
17	1	27/03/2017	ISNIN	PAGI	9:00 AM	11:00 AM	S	EE110(15)	ELC151	PEE1102A1/2	20	DEWAN BESAR
18	1	27/03/2017	ISNIN	PAGI	9:00 AM	11:00 AM	S	EE111	ELC151	PEE1112A1/2	29	DEWAN BESAR
19	1	27/03/2017	ISNIN	PAGI	9:00 AM	11:00 AM	S	EE111(31)	ELC151	PEE1112B1/2	32	DEWAN BESAR
20	1	27/03/2017	ISNIN	PAGI	9:00 AM	11:00 AM	S	EE111	ELC151	PEE1112C1/2	31	DEWAN BESAR
21	1	27/03/2017	ISNIN	PAGI	9:00 AM	11:00 AM	S	EE111(1)/	ELC151	PEE1122A1/2	30	DEWAN BESAR

Figure 3: Examination Records

Furthermore, EMS requires parameter setting for invigilators either will be appointed as invigilator (represents as index 1) or not invigilating (represent as index 0). Moreover, additional parameter setting such as number of invigilation duties during weekends or weekdays and fairness dissemination of invigilation duties amongst invigilators is manually determined.

KAMPUS	JAWATAN	NAMA	BIDANG	KULTI/JABAT	LEVEL	WDAY S(K)	WEND S(K)	WDAYS (PK + PwB)	WENDS (PK + PwB)	TOTAL INVIGIL ATIONS
P	PENSYARAH KANAN	WAN ANISHA BINTI WAN MOHAMMAD	JSKM	JSKM		1	0	0	1	0	1
P	PENSYARAH	MUNIROH BT HAMAT	JSKM	JSKM		1	0	0	1	0	1
P	PENSYARAH	NORSHUHADA BINTI SAMSUDIN	JSKM	JSKM		1	0	0	1	0	1
P	PENSYARAH	SHARIFAH SARIMAH BINTI SYED ABDULLAH	JSKM	JSKM		1	0	0	1	0	1
P	PENSYARAH	SITI BALQIS BINTI MAHLAN	JSKM	JSKM		1	0	0	0	1	1
P	PENSYARAH	WAN NUR SHAZIAYANI BINTI WAN MOHD ROSL	JSKM	JSKM		1	0	0	0	1	1
P	PENSYARAH	ZURAIRA BINTI LIBASIN	JSKM	JSKM		1	0	0	0	1	1
P	PENSYARAH KANAN	CHE HASLINA BINTI ABDULLAH (DR)	ACIS	ACIS		1	0	0	1	0	1
P	PENSYARAH KANAN	NORHASIDAH BINTI A. BAKAR	ACIS	ACIS		1	1	0	0	0	1

Figure 4: Assignment of total invigilation duties parameter to invigilators

ISBN: 978-1-387-00704-2

Constraints of invigilators are also needed if there are any exceptions of invigilation duties either constraints on partial duration or full duration of examination week. Besides that, special request to avoid invigilating at certain examination venues are also considered.

	A Kampus	B Nama Staf	C Index
2	J4	SITI NOORAIN BINTI ZULKIFLY	2
3	J4	SITI NOORAIN BINTI ZULKIFLY	4
4	J4	SITI NOORAIN BINTI ZULKIFLY	6
5	J4	SITI NOORAIN BINTI ZULKIFLY	8
6	J4	SITI NOORAIN BINTI ZULKIFLY	10
7	J4	SITI NOORAIN BINTI ZULKIFLY	12
8	J4	SITI NOORAIN BINTI ZULKIFLY	14
9	J4	SITI NOORAIN BINTI ZULKIFLY	16
10	J4	SITI NOORAIN BINTI ZULKIFLY	18
11	J4	SITI NOORAIN BINTI ZULKIFLY	20
12	J4	SITI NOORAIN BINTI ZULKIFLY	22
13	J4	SITI NOORAIN BINTI ZULKIFLY	24
14	J4	SITI NOORAIN BINTI ZULKIFLY	26
15	J4	SITI NOORAIN BINTI ZULKIFLY	28
16	J4	SITI NOORAIN BINTI ZULKIFLY	30
17	J4	SITI NOORAIN BINTI ZULKIFLY	32
18	J4	SITI NOORAIN BINTI ZULKIFLY	34
19	J4	SITI NOORAIN BINTI ZULKIFLY	36
20	J4	SITI NOORAIN BINTI ZULKIFLY	38
21	J4	SITI NOORAIN BINTI ZULKIFLY	40
22	J4	SITI NOORAIN BINTI ZULKIFLY	42
23	J4	MOHD HANAFIE BIN YASIN	11
24	J4	MOHD HANAFIE BIN YASIN	12
25	J4	MOHD HANAFIE BIN YASIN	13
26	J4	MOHD HANAFIE BIN YASIN	14

Figure 5: Constraints of examination date

	A Kampus	B Nama Pengawas	C Tempat Peperiksaan
2	J4	NOOR RAIFANA BINTI AB RAHIM	DP 1/3
3	J4	NOOR RAIFANA BINTI AB RAHIM	DP 2/4
4	J4	DR MAHFUZA MOHAMMED ZABIDI	DP 1/3
5	J4	DR MAHFUZA MOHAMMED ZABIDI	DP 2/4
6	J4	ZURRIATI BINTI MOHD ALI (DR.)	DP 1/3
7	J4	ZURRIATI BINTI MOHD ALI (DR.)	DP 2/4
8	J4	ROHAYA BINTI SULAIMAN	DP 1/3
9	J4	ROHAYA BINTI SULAIMAN	DP 2/4
10	J4		
11	J4		
12	J4		
13	J4		
14	J4		
15	J4		
16	J4		
17	J4		
18	J4		

Figure 6: Constraints of examination venue

The last constraint is the list of courses and the lecturer's name. EMS avoids the invigilators invigilating the course that he or she taught.

ISBN: 978-1-387-00704-2

9	J4	S	EH110	CHE111	J4EH1102A	25	SHARIFAH IZIUNA BINTI SAYED JAMALUDIN
10	J4	S	EH110	CHE111	J4EH1102B	22	SHARIFAH IZIUNA BINTI SAYED JAMALUDIN
11	J4	S	EH110	CHE111	J4EH1102C	22	SALMI NUR AIN BINTI SANUSI
12	J4	S	EH110	CHE111	J4EH1102D	25	SHARIFAH IZIUNA BINTI SAYED JAMALUDIN
13	J4	S	EH110	CHE121	J4EH1101A	37	NOR FADILAH BINTI MOHAMAD / AHMAD RAFIZAN BIN MOHAMAD DAUD (DR)
14	J4	S	EH110	CHE135	J4EH1104A	34	MUHAMMAD IMRAN BIN ISMAIL
15	J4	S/SML/	EH110	CHE135	J4EH1104B	36	MUHAMMAD IMRAN BIN ISMAIL
16	J4	S	EH110	CHE135	J4EH1104C	34	MUHAMMAD IMRAN BIN ISMAIL

Figure 7: List of lecturer's name for each subject or course

Basically, the process of assigning the invigilators will consider the following factors as shown in Figure 8.

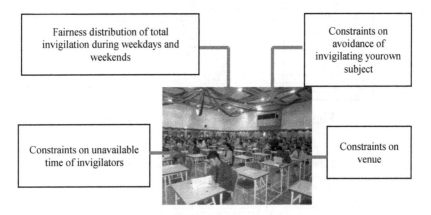

Figure 8: List of constraints considered in the process of assigning the invigilation duties

As shown in Figure 8, the constraints are divided into two types of constraints which the major constraints that are classified as hard constraints and the minor constraints which are categorized as soft constraints. Fairness distribution of invigilation during weekdays or weekends and constraints of unavailable time are considered as hard constraints, while the remaining constraints are categorized as soft constraints. The hard constraints will be the main priority while running the assignment of invigilation duties. The soft constraints will be considered as secondary or optional if the output of invigilation assignment is acceptable and satisfied. Otherwise, the soft constraints will be ignored. In

ISBN: 978-1-387-00704-2

otherwords, the system will ignore the invigilators request in minor cases such as the invigilator invigilating their own subject or the invigilator is appointed as the chief invigilator for all invigilation or the invigilator has to invigilate in afternoon session only.

An algorithm has been developed to consider the hard and soft constraints as shown in Figure 9. The lists of examination records are extracted from an array list and the invigilators name will be determined sequentially from the array list of invigilators name. Each invigilator has been assignedto the total invigilation during weekdays or weekends and the algorithm will ensure that the total invigilation assigned is alignedto the parameter that has been determined. If the condition is fulfilled, the next step is to determine the assigned invigilators on that particular time slot has the same unavailable slot constraints, invigilating their own subjects and venues that should be omitted. If any of the constraints emerge, the selected invigilator will be rejected, the total number of invigilation assigned will remain the same and the next invigilators from the invigilators name array list will be establish.

This process continues until all examination records are successfully assigned with the invigilators name. The process of assigning the invigilators used the sequential techniques which the name of invigilators are retrieved sequentially from an array list until all invigilators are successfully assigned without any conflicts with the list of constraints. The following figure shows the model of algorithm for assignment of invigilation duties for each invigilator.

```
for(a=0;a<totExamRecords;a++)
{for (b=0; b<totInvigilator;b++)
    {stringtempName = invglatorName[b];
        inttotInvglation = ttlInvglation[b];
        if (totInvglation>ttlAlreadyAssign[b])
        {     assignNamed[a] = tempName;
            ttlAlreadyAssign[b]++;
        }
        for (c=0;c<totConstraintList;c++)
        {     inttempIndex = constraintIndex[c];
```

ISBN: 978-1-387-00704-2

```
if((tempIndex==examIndex[a])&&(tempName==constraintName[c]))
                {       assignNamed[a] = NIL;
                        ttlAlreadyAssign[b]--;
                        break; }
          }
        for (d=0;d<totVenueConstraint;d++)
        {       stringtempVenue = constraintVenue[d];
                if((tempVenue    ==    examVenue[a])&&(tempName    ==
lectName[d]))
                {       assignNamed[a] = NIL;
                        ttlAlreadyAssign[b]--;
                        break; }
        }
        for (e=0;e<totListSubject;e++)
        {stringtempSubject = subjectName[e];
            if((tempSubject==examSubject[a])&&(tempName==lecturerT
eachName[e]))
             {  assignNamed[a] = NIL;
                ttlAlreadyAssign[b]--;
                break; }
        }
}
}
```

Figure 9: Algorithm for invigilators assignment of invigilation duties

The following figure shows the list of examination records that successfully assigned the invigilators name.

```
M-TransactionWithInvigilators - Notepad
File  Edit  Format  View  Help
1   27/03/2017  ISNIN  PAGI  9:00  AM  11:00  AM  S  HM111  ELC151  MHM1112B  24  DB  MAZLAN BIN SALLEH   K
1   27/03/2017  ISNIN  PAGI  9:00  AM  11:00  AM  S  MC110  ELC151  MMC1102A  30  DB  SHARMIZAH BINTI ABU HASSAN (DR) PK(P)
1   27/03/2017  ISNIN  PAGI  9:00  AM  11:00  AM  S  MC110  ELC151  MMC1102B  32  DB  NUR AINA NABILAH BINTI MOHD FARIS   PP
1   27/03/2017  ISNIN  PAGI  9:00  AM  11:00  AM  S  MC110  ELC151  MMC1102C  33  DB  MUHAIZAM BINTI ROSTAM AFFENDI  PP
1   27/03/2017  ISNIN  PAGI  9:00  AM  11:00  AM  S  HM111(3)/MC110(31)/  ELC151  MMC1102D  34  DB  SITI HAMIZAH BINTI BAHAMAN
1   27/03/2017  ISNIN  PAGI  9:00  AM  11:00  AM  S  HM111(1)/MC110(31)/  ELC151  MMC1102E  32  DB  ISMAIL BIN YUSOFF   PwB(P)
1   27/03/2017  ISNIN  PAGI  9:00  AM  11:00  AM  S  MC110  ELC151  MMC1102F  30  DB  BUSHRA BINTI MOHD ZAKI  PwB(P)
1   27/03/2017  ISNIN  PAGI  9:00  AM  11:00  AM  S  MC110  ELC151  MMC1102G  34  DB  FARRAH BINTI OTHMAN   PwB(P)
1   27/03/2017  ISNIN  PAGI  9:00  AM  11:00  AM  S  MC110  ELC151  MMC1102H  30  DB  NOR HALAWAH BINTI AHMAD PwB(P)
1   27/03/2017  ISNIN  PAGI  9:00  AM  11:00  AM  S  MC110  ELC151  MMC1102J  28  DB  KHAIRUNNISA BINTI ABD SAMAD   PwB(P)
1   27/03/2017  ISNIN  PAGI  9:00  AM  11:00  AM  S  MC110  ELC151  MMC1102K  30  DB  NOOR HAFIZA BINTI ISMAIL   PwB(PTFT)
1   27/03/2017  ISNIN  PAGI  9:00  AM  12:00  PM  S  PD002(24)/PD003(1)/  MAT037  MPD0021A  25  DS  NANI SHUHADA BINTI SEHAT
1   27/03/2017  ISNIN  PAGI  9:00  AM  12:00  PM  S  PD002(20)/PD003(2)/  MAT037  MPD0021B  22  DS  IRWANI HAZLINA BTE ABD. SAMAD
1   27/03/2017  ISNIN  PAGI  9:00  AM  12:00  PM  S  PD002(23)/PD003(2)/  MAT037  MPD0021C  25  DS  SITI NURAISHAH BINTI SCHAHARUM
1   27/03/2017  ISNIN  PAGI  9:00  AM  11:00  AM  S  AD118  ELC150  M3AT1102A  1  DS  SUZZANA BINTI OTHMAN   PwB(P)
1   27/03/2017  ISNIN  PAGI  9:00  AM  11:00  AM  S  MC110  ELC151  MMC1102L  32  DS  ROZAIHA BINTI AB MAJID  PwB(P)
1   27/03/2017  ISNIN  PAGI  9:00  AM  11:00  AM  S  MC111  ELC151  MMC1112A  26  DS  KHAIZIE SAZIMAH BINTI AHMAD   PwB(P)
1   27/03/2017  ISNIN  PAGI  9:00  AM  11:00  AM  S  MC111  ELC151  MMC1112B  24  DS  NIL   V
1   27/03/2017  ISNIN  PAGI  9:00  AM  11:00  AM  S  AC110  ELC151  MAC1102A  23  DTS  AKMAL BIN ADANAN   K
1   27/03/2017  ISNIN  PAGI  9:00  AM  11:00  AM  S  AC110  ELC151  MAC1102B  25  DTS  AZAHARI BIN KHALIP   PK(P)
```

Figure 10: Text file of examination records with invigilators name

ISBN: 978-1-387-00704-2

Testing and Findings

The algorithm has been tested for several semester using the real set of examination records. The algorithm has almost 94% successfully assigned the invigilators name on the requested time slots. There are no issues of invigilation clashes which refer to the incidents of the same invigilator is assigned to invigilate at the same time slot but at different places. All constraints and parameters that have been identified earlier for each invigilator are properly assigned as required. Approximately5%to 9% of the total examination records found as nil since the algorithm fails to identify the required invigilators. Those nil records will be assigned manually by the members of examination committee. This manual assignment will take less than 1 hour.

A simple survey has been conducted to calculate the total changes of invigilation duties amongst invigilators after the Examination Management Systems (EMS) is implemented.The following table indicates the percentage of invigilation duty changes of four (4) examination sessions in 2016 at UiTM Pulau Pinang Branch.

Table 2: Total Changes of Invigilation Duties according to Examination Session

	Examination Session			
	Jan 2016	Mar 2016	Jun 2016	Dis 2016
Total Invigilation	625	1287	702	1358
Total request to change or amend the invigilation duties	94	184	86	227
Percentages of changes	15.04	14.30	12.25	16.72

The above table shows the percentage of invigilation duty changes dropped to almost 6% to 7% as compared to Table 1. The changes of invigilation duty are unavoidable because most of the invigilators have other important commitment such as unexpected or ad-hoc responsibility and urgent personal matters.

ISBN: 978-1-387-00704-2

Nevertheless, the examination committee members are happy because they do not need to spend several days to prepare the invigilation duties. Now, EMS helps them to reduce the workloads and amendments process took less than 2 hours. Furthermore, the examination committees have ample time to consider those special preferences and human touch factors. Formerly the assignment of invigilation duties has taken up 3 to 5 days excluding adjustments of invigilators invigilation schedules.

Conclusion

In conclusion, the algorithm as introduced in this paper has improved the satisfaction level of invigilation duties assignment amongst invigilators. The soft constraints as mentioned in this paper require some room forimprovement and modification to the algorithm because they are still volatile. The soft constraint is inefficient whenever the situation such as the number of unavailability time slot (hard constraint) is huge. The algorithm fails to identify suitable invigilator if the hard constraint records exceed300. In order to reduce the number of constraint records, the examination committee needs to filter the application of examination exception.

Furthermore, the algorithm needs to consider other aspects such as avoiding the muslim invigilators invigilating on Fridays afternoon session and preventing the non-muslim invigilators to be on duty on Sunday morning session. Those requests which are considered as personal preferenceswill only be given as special attention by examination committee after the assignment of invigilation duties are completed by the EMS. The examination committee will try to fulfill all requests from each invigilator with the aims to produce friendly invigilation duties. More soft constraints will be introduced and the existing algorithm will be enhanced continuously to produce a more comprehensive invigilation schedule.

Comparing with the previous manual method of invigilation duties assignments in 2013, it can be observed that the required time for the assignments has declined from a few days to a single

ISBN: 978-1-387-00704-2

day. EMS fulfilled the optimum results as needed by the examination committees and Examination Unit.

References

Ahmed, A., Sajid, A., Ali, M., & Bukhari, A. H. S. (2011). Particle Swarm Optimizatin Based Hyper-Heuristic For Tackling Real World Examinations Scheduling Problem. *Australian Journal of Basic and Applied Sciences, 5,* 1406–1413.

Carter, M. W., & Laporte, G. (1997). Recent developments in practical course timetabling. In *International Conference on the Practice and Theory of Automated Timetabling* (pp. 3–19). Springer.

Chunbao, Z., & Nu, T. (2012). An intelligent, interactive & efficient exam scheduling system (IIEESS v1. 0). *Proceeding of the Practice and Theory of Automated Timetabling (PATAT), Norway,* 437–450.

Cowling, P., Kendall, G., & Hussin, N. M. (2002). A survey and case study of practical examination timetabling problems. In *PATAT* (pp. 258–261).

Di Gaspero, L., Schaerf, A., Cadoli, M., Slany, W., & Falaschi, M. (2003). Local Search Techniques for Scheduling Problems: Algorithms and Software Tool. Forum.

Hanum, F., Romliyah, M. A., & Bakhtiar, T. (2015). Exam invigilators assignment problem: a goal programming approach. *Applied Mathematical Sciences, 9*(58), 2871–2880.

Kahar, M. N. M., & Kendall, G. (2010). The examination timetabling problem at Universiti Malaysia Pahang: Comparison of a constructive heuristic with an existing software solution. *European Journal of Operational Research, 207*(2), 557–565.

Mohamed, A. S., Mushi, A. R., & Mujuni, E. (2013). An Examination Scheduling Algorithm Using Graph Coloring–the case of Sokoine University of Agriculture.

Sagir, M., & Ozturk, Z. K. (2010). Exam scheduling: Mathematical modeling and parameter estimation with the Analytic Network Process approach. *Mathematical and Computer Modelling, 52*(5), 930–941.

Sarin, S. C., Wang, Y., & Varadarajan, A. (2010). A university-timetabling problem and its solution using Benders' partitioning—a case study. *Journal of Scheduling, 13*(2), 131–141.

UiTM. (2016). Examination Procedures Manual, Academic Assessment Division of UiTM.

ISBN: 978-1-387-00704-2

Article 2

Integration of Ontology and UML Class-Based Modelling for Knowledge Representation

Rozita Kadar
School of Computer Sciences,
Universiti Sains Malaysia, Pulau Pinang, Malaysia
Faculty of Computer and Mathematical Sciences,
Universiti Teknologi MARA Pulau Pinang Branch, Malaysia

Sharifah Mashita Syed-Mohamad, Putra Sumari
School of Computer Sciences,
UniversitiSains Malaysia, Pulau Pinang Branch, Malaysia

Nur 'Aini Abdul Rashid
Department of Computer Sciences,
College of Computer & Information Sciences,
Princess Nourahbint Abdulrahman University, KSA.

Abstract
Program comprehension is an important process carried out involving much effort in software maintenance process. A key challenge to developers in program comprehension process is to comprehend a source code. Nowadays, software systems have grown in size causing increase in developers' tasks to explore and understand millions of lines of source code. Meanwhile, source code is a crucial resource for developers to become familiar with a software system since some system documentations are often unavailable or outdated. However, there are problems exist in understanding source codes, which are tricky with different programming styles, and insufficient comments. Although many researchers have discussed different strategies and techniques to overcome program comprehension problem, only a shallow knowledge is obtained about the challenges in trying to understand a software system through reading source code. Therefore, this study attempts to overcome the problems in source code comprehension by suggesting a suitable comprehension technique. The proposed technique is based on using ontology approach for knowledge representation. This approach is able to easily explain the concept and relationship of program domain. Thus, the proposed work will create a better way for improving program comprehension.

Keywords: *Program Comprehension, Knowledge Based, Information Extraction, Visualization, Ontology.*

ISBN: 978-1-387-00704-2

Introduction
Nowadays, software is developed iteratively and incrementally, which results in rapid evolution of software system. Besides, with today's rapid growth in system size and complexity, software maintainers are facing tremendous comprehension challenges driven by the need to maintain software system (Tiarks&Röhm, 2013; Carvalho, 2013; Yazdanshenas and Moonen, 2012). One of the key challenges faced by novice software maintainer is to comprehend the software system being maintained. Program comprehension is one of the major activities in software maintenance that mainly takes place prior maintaining process (Rajlich and Gosavi, 2004). Furthermore, software maintainers assigned with changing a large software system spend much effort on program comprehension to gain the knowledge on the system that needs to employ the changes (Corley et al., 2012).

Program comprehension can be very time-consuming due to the lack of proper documentation where some estimate that up to 50% of software maintenance effort is spent on understanding the software system maintained (Roongruangsuwan and Daengdej, 2010; SWEBOK, 2004; Guzzi et al., 2011; Xu, 2005), whereas 41.8% of the total effort is in reading and understanding program (Normantas and Vasilecas, 2013).

Hence, this work proposed the source code metadata extraction process and represented it in a form of ontology. The findings of this work are demonstrated as part of knowledge representation. This work focuses on Object-Oriented Programming. Meanwhile, the research questions are on how to design rules used to extract metadata from source code. The goal of this study is to facilitate novice developers to comprehend a program while performing maintenance tasks. This goal can be specifically achieved through the following objectives: to propose an extraction rules used to extract source code metadata. The expected contributions of this work are: the rules to extract source code metadata as the knowledge representation.

ISBN: 978-1-387-00704-2

The paper is organised as follows. The next section reviews the previous studies by comparing the techniques in this area. The following section discusses the propose work. The conclusion of this study is presented in the final section.

Related Work

Ontology fragment is an approach used to improve program comprehension (Wilson, 2010). In populating ontology, the source code should be analysed through a process of information extraction, which is a process to obtain the information in a source code and display it in a different view. The retrieved information from the source code should be stored in a standard form of information. It will go through a process using an ontological approach. At present, the ontology is used in many fields to represent knowledge and to provide a formal way to define a concept. Use of ontology includes to support program understanding (Wilson, 2010). Bohnet et al. (2008) proposed a technique of retrieving source code information and then visualising various characteristics of the execution information to gain insight on how features are built on the code. Developers provide a scenario as an input that triggers a feature of interest in the system, whereas the output is presented to the developers using advanced visualisation views. This approach has been compared to a tool called grep with the result showing that developers are able to locate the concept of interest in less than half an hour without having prior knowledge about the system.

Similarly, Abebe & Tonella (2010) introduced an approach that extracts concepts from source codes by applying Natural Language Process (NLP) techniques where the identifiers of program elements are extracted and candidate sentences that use those identifiers are formed. Some of the sentences that do not follow certain rules were eliminated, while the remaining sentences were used as an input for creating ontology that captures the concepts and relations of the source code. A preliminary evaluation revealed that using information from ontology concept can improve the accuracy of query, allow

ISBN: 978-1-387-00704-2

developers to formulate queries that are more precise and can reduce the search space.

Petrenko et al. (2008) developed a feature location technique based on grep and ontology fragments. The ontology fragments stored partial domain knowledge about a feature. The hypothesis of this approach is that ontology fragments help developers to formulate queries and guide the investigation of their results, which would increase the effectiveness of the feature location.

The tool used to support the management of the ontology fragment is called Protégé. Wilson (2010) extended Petrenko et al. (2008) approach by introducing a systematic approach for formulating queries based on ontology fragments, which represents partial knowledge about the system. This approach has allowed the developers to formulate a query based on terms presented in the ontology fragment. A preliminary evaluation involving four developers to perform concept location on the Mozilla and Eclipse systems revealed that a small and partial knowledge about the system is sufficient for successfully locating a concept in the code. This approach is relevant to Petrenko et al. (2008) approach, but the main difference is that the former approach automatically generates the ontology, whereas the latter approach is manually generated by developers.

Meng et al. (2006) proposed a technique to program comprehension using ontology and description logic. As a part of the technique, they adopted a new interactive story metaphor to represent the interactions between users and comprehension process. The comprehension process can be viewed as authoring an interactive narrative between users and systems towards completing a specific goal. Developers have mapped between program comprehension process model and story model. The advantage of using story metaphor is that it provides an interactive context to guide comprehension process.

ISBN: 978-1-387-00704-2

The Integration Rules of Ontology and UML Class-based Modelling

In general, ontology development is divided into two main phases: specification and conceptualisation. The goal of specification phase is to acquire informal knowledge on the domain while the goal of conceptualisation phase is to organise and structure the obtained knowledge. The processes taken in developing the proposed program ontology that consists of three phases are illustrated in Fig. 1. Nonetheless, this article only discusses the first phase, which is the integration process of ontology and UML class-based modelling.

Ontology is used to define sets of concept describing the domain knowledge and allow for specifying classes by rich and precise logical definitions. The basic idea of developing ontology for software system is to provide an artefact consisting both code knowledge and domain knowledge, with which software maintainers can understand the features of source code. Ontology includes the concepts, relationships and instances to describe the **specific** domain of concern.

Concepts are referred to a category that is also known as a class. A series of concepts represents the topics or characters in the domain ontology; relations show the connection between concepts and used to describe the association between concepts when considering a specific concept, which is also called an attribute; while instances describe a series of concepts and relationships with specific knowledge. Instances in ontology are the values of attribute of the class that describe necessary properties. Instances will also inherit all attributes or relationships of their class.

ISBN: 978-1-387-00704-2

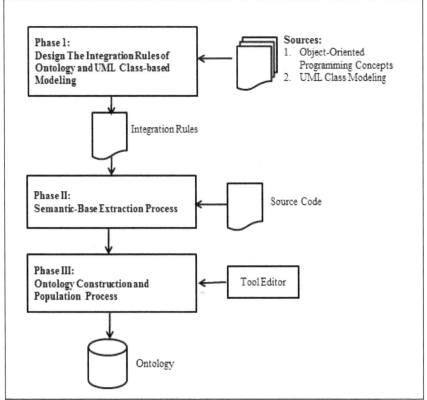

Figure 1: A Framework of Ontology Development

The proposed approach was used to extract an ontological point of view for software system by integration utilising the ontology and UML class-based modelling. Due to the similar features shared by both UML class diagram and ontology, class diagram was used to aid in populating code ontology (Table 1).

UML class has the following features that make it possible to be transformed in the form of ontology.

Definition 1 A UML class diagram is a tuple, $C = \{C|\ C = (C_N, C_A,\ C_M,\ C_R)\}$ where C_N represents the name of class in UML class diagram, C,C_A is the list of attributes associated with this particular class, C,C_M is a set of methods for defined class, C,

ISBN: 978-1-387-00704-2

whereas C_R describes the different types of relation that can exist between any pair of classes in the UML class diagram, C.

Definition 2 An attributes in UML class diagram is a tuple $C_A = \{A|A=(A_n, A_t, A_v, A_d)\}$ where A_n is an attribute name, A_t is an attribute type, A_v is an attribute visibility (Public, Protect or Provate) and A_d is an attribute default value if given.

Definition 3 A set of methods in UML class diagram is a tuple $C_M = \{M|M=(M_n, M_t, M_v)\}$ where M_n is the name of the method, M_t is the method type and M_v is the visibility of the method.

Definition 4 A relationship between classes in UML class diagram is a tuple, $C_R = \{R|R=(R_t, R_c, R_r)\}$ where R_t is the type of relationship (Association, Composition, Aggregation or Generalization), R_c is the cardinality specified for the source class and R_r defines the target class with which the source class is connected.

A set of class diagram ontology described above are the complete structure of class diagram, which contains 4-tuples where the first concept is the class name, CN. The other element is concept of attribute, CA, where attribute name ∋ An, attribute type ∋ At, attribute visibility ∋ Av and attribute default ∋ Ad. The concept method defines a set of methods in class diagram and describe as method name ∋ Mn, method type ∋ Mt and method visibility ∋ Mv.

The concepts relations described in the ontology were defined as relation type ∋ Rt, relation cardinality ∋ Rc and relation between classes ∋ Rc. All elements can be described as attribute type or method type = {numeric, string, NULL}, visibility of attribute and method = {public, private, protected}. Meanwhile, the relationship type = {aggregation, composition, association, generalisation}. The relationship cardinality = {0..*, 1..*, 0..1, 1} was used to describe the quantitative relationship between classes given by specifying minimum and maximum cardinalities.

Hence, a set of transformation rules was proposed to populate ontology from a UML class diagram. On the other hand, it is believed that class diagram also has semantics representation,

ISBN: 978-1-387-00704-2

which is somehow implicitly preserved. Thus, ontology could be used to recover the semantics for class diagram.

Table 1: Concepts Similarity of UML Class and Ontology Model

Concept Similarity	Similarity Description
CS1	UML class denotes a set of objects with common features, while concept in ontology also does the same thing.
CS2	UML class has hierarchical structure, while hierarchical structure is basic structure for taxonomy, which is one of the features that ontology has.
CS3	UML class has properties, while ontology has two types of properties: object property and data type property
CS4	UML class has relations such as associations and dependencies, while these relations represented as roles or properties in ontology.
CS5	Class diagram includes class name, attributes and operation, while in ontology includes concepts, relationships and instances
CS6	Class itself will be transformed into concept in the ontology
CS7	The attributes of the class will be transformed into properties of that concept in ontology
CS8	For the generalization classes, the relationships SubClassOf will be preserved by the subclass concepts.
CS9	For the inheritance classes, the relationships SuperClassOf will be preserved by the superclass concepts.
CS10	Association transformed into ConnnectTo property, and it is a symmetric property.
CS11	Dependency transformed into DependOn property and its inverse property Depend.
CS12	Aggregation transformed into HasA property.
CS13	Composition transformed into PartOf property.

ISBN: 978-1-387-00704-2

Conclusion

Ontology has become popular in several fields of information technologies including software engineering. In software engineering, ontology is understood as a conceptual model representing a domain knowledge in a set of concepts within the domain, the properties of the concepts and interrelations of those concepts. It is acknowledged that ontologies are important sources of knowledge in the conceptualisation of certain domains as well as the background for software development. In future work, the proposed knowledge integration will be applied as data source for information retrieval technique in concept location to find the relevance location in source code to implement change request. The aim is to facilitate the developers to find the location of source code prior implementing change request.

References

Abebe, S. L., & Tonella, P. (2010). Natural language parsing of program element names for concept extraction. In *Program Comprehension (ICPC), 2010 IEEE 18th International Conference on* (pp. 156–159). IEEE.

Bohnet, J., Voigt, S., & Dollner, J. (2008). Locating and Understanding Features of Complex Software Systems by Synchronizing Time-, Collaboration- and Code-Focused Views on Execution Traces. *2008 16th IEEE International Conference on Program Comprehension*, 268–271. http://doi.org/10.1109/ICPC.2008.21

Meng, W., Rilling, J., Zhang, Y., Witte, R., Mudur, S., & Charland, P. (2006). A Context-Driven Software Comprehension Process Model. *2006 Second International IEEE Workshop on Software Evolvability (SE'06)*, 50–57. http://doi.org/10.1109/SOFTWARE-EVOLVABILITY.2006.1

Petrenko, M., Rajlich, V., & Vanciu, R. (2008). Partial domain comprehension in software evolution and maintenance. *IEEE International Conference on Program Comprehension*, 13–22. http://doi.org/10.1109/ICPC.2008.14

Wilson, L. A. (2010). Using ontology fragments in concept location. *IEEE International Conference on Software Maintenance, ICSM*. http://doi.org/10.1109/ICSM.2010.5609555

ISBN: 978-1-387-00704-2

Article 3

Review on Program Slicing Techniques towards Program Comprehension Application

Rozita Kadar, Naemah Abdul Wahab, Jamal Othman
Faculty of Computer and Mathematical Sciences,
Universiti Teknologi MARA Pulau Pinang Branch, Malaysia

Abstract
Presently, the software system has grown in size. One of the main challenges faced by programmers is to keep up with thousand or million lines of source code that needs to be read and understood. The source code is an essential resource for programmers to become familiar with the software system. Program comprehension is important in software engineering activities before performing maintenance tasks. One of the techniques that can assist the programmers in comprehending software system is known as program slicing. Program slicing is the process of extracting parts of source code programs by tracing the programs' control and data flow related to some data item. In this paper, we conduct the literature review on program slicing in order to explore the direction of this method by focusing on various slicing techniques to provide a novel idea in program comprehension application.

Keywords: *Program Slicing, Program Comprehension, Software Maintenance, Source Code*

Introduction

Nowadays, most of the software developers have improve their way in developing simple source code representation to reduce the complexity of the system. This paradigm becomes widely applied in the enhancement of large-scale application where, the size of software system become huge and often exceeds a hundred or million lines of code. The main idea behind the usage of source code fragment is due to the extensive reuse of the existing system into a new system. We look into the role of program slicing technique in this paper to support the program comprehension activities prior to performing the maintenance tasks.

Program comprehension is one of the major problem in software maintenance phase (Maletic & Kagdi, 2008; Sasirekha

ISBN: 978-1-387-00704-2

&Hemalatha, 2011). The study of program comprehension is important in order to understand the problem domain. In recent time, software system grows in size causing additional program comprehension activities, as programmers have to face the complexity during maintenance phase. As a result of this problem, cost and time become a major constraints of this activity (Koushik & Selvarani, 2012; Roongruangsuwan & Daengdej, 2010). Norman and Vasilecas in (Lahtinen, Järvinen, & Melakoski-Vistbacka, 2007; Normantas & Vasilecas, 2013) stated that 41.8% of the total effort spent on maintenance phase.

Although, much research has been done directed to the problem of program comprehension but the studying of program comprehension remains incomplete and it should be continued in order to produce the best strategies to improve it (Maletic & Kagdi, 2008). Most researchers still have yet to discuss in great length on methods to facilitate software engineers in understanding a program.

One way to assist programmers to improve their program comprehension activity is by applying program analysis using the slicing technique. Program slicing provides mechanism to analyze and understand the program behavior for further restructuring and refinement (Koushik & Selvarani, 2012). It plays an important role in program comprehension, since it allows programmers to focus on the relevant portions of program (Barros, da Cruz, Henriques, & Pinto, 2011; Zhang, Zheng, Huang, & Qi, 2011). Moreover, previous works found that program slicing has unique importance in addressing the issues of cost and time, and can be helpful in producing effective cost and time (Koushik & Selvarani, 2012; Saleem, Hussain, Ismail, & Mohsin, 2009). Program slicing is one of the techniques in program analysis that evaluates the program by acquiring smaller fragments of code, therefore, this application will increases program understanding. The technique is to find all statements in a program that directly or indirectly influence the value of certain variable at some point in a program. The next section discusses in details on the process of program slicing technique.

ISBN: 978-1-387-00704-2

The organizations of the paper are as follows: the next section introduces the concepts of program slicing followed by the third section where, we review the previous work by comparing the techniques in this area. Finally, the last section will be the conclusion of the paper.

The Concepts of Program Slicing

The goal of program slicing technique is to eliminate some part of program statements that are unimportant, leaving only the program codes that are significance for the programmer to evaluate. There are various aspects to be considered in slicing technique that are listed in (Sasirekha & Hemalatha, 2011). In order to identify the relevant parts of programs, user must specify the *slicing criterion*, which indicates the program characteristics concerned by the programmer.

The discovery of slicing technique came from the work of Weiser(Weiser, 1982), which proposes a program understanding aid. The paper (Weiser, 1982) defined this technique as a process of breaking up any subset of the program and at the same time maintains the original program. The slicing process required the slicing criterion, a pair $c = (s, V)$, where s denotes a statement at a certain point in the program while V is represents a subset of the program's variables. The slicing variable is dependent on the variables specified in the criteria or all variables. The slicing point is the point of interest that can be placed either before or after a particular statement.

The basic idea of slicing technique is derived from two approaches, which are static slicing and dynamic slicing. A static slicing may contain statements that have no influence on the value of the variables of the interest for the particular execution whilst a dynamic slicing takes the input supplied to the program during its execution. In other words, it preserves the effect of the program for a fixed input. For example, Figure 1(a) illustrates the original program while in Figure 1(b), it shows the example of static slicing with respect to slicing criterion, $c = (8, a)$. The slicing criterion, $c = (8, a)$ means the "8" is the number of the line statement and "a" is the set of variables to be observed at

ISBN: 978-1-387-00704-2

statement "8". As compared to Figure 1(c) which depicts the result of dynamic slicing with respect to slicing criterion $c = (a=-2, 8, a)$. Dynamic slicing criterion, $c = (a=-2, 8, a)$, emphasizes on the input value "-2" to the observed variable "a". The result in Figure 1(c) shows that the slicing program getting smaller compared to the result in Figure 1(b). The result proves that dynamic slicing can give more contribution as compared to static slicing in the aspect of program size.

```
1.  sum=0;              1.  sum=0;           1.
2.  cin>>a;             2.  cin>>a;          2.  cin>>a;
3.  cin>>b;             3.                   3.
4.  if (a>0)            4.  if (a>0)         4.
5.  sum = sum+a;        5.  sum      =       5.
6.  if (b>0)                sum+a;           6.
7.  sum = sum+b;        6.                   7.
8.  cout<<a;            7.                   8.  cout<<a;
9.  cout<<b;            8.  cout<<a;         9.
10. cout<<sum;          9.                   10.
                        10.

      (a)                                               (c)
                              (b)
```

Figure 1 : (a) Example of source code program (b)Static slicing with respect to slicing criterion, c=(8, a), (c) Dynamic slicing with regard to slicing criterion, c=(a= -2,8,a)

The slicing method is classified into two directions, which are forward and backward. The forward direction requires tracing of the data and control dependences in forward direction. Usually, the result of this direction is used for modification activity in maintenance tasks. Forward is suitable for improving program comprehension because it is considered as the top-down approach in program comprehension strategies. The backward slicing direction is suitable for locating and tracing bugs. The output of this slicing direction is in the form of slices statements of a program, which has some effect on the slicing criterion.

Instead of viewing program slices statements in textual-base, program-slicing technique can be improved through visualization approach. The technique of program slicing can be enhanced by transforming a program slices into graphical-based. Essentially,

ISBN: 978-1-387-00704-2

program slicing technique is extracting parts of computer program by analyzing data and control flow dependence related to some data. Program Dependence Graph (PDG) is one of the graphical representations that can be used to represent data and to symbolize the control dependence of a program. In PDG, the vertices represent program statements; and the edges correspond to data and control dependences between them. These indicate a partial ordering on the statements of the program. For example, Figure 2 illustrates the PDG of the example program from Figure 1. Furthermore, this figure shows the vertices that represent the slices of program during static program slicing execution process took place.

Another factor to be considered of slicing technique is the application of slicing. Although in this paper we focus on program comprehension but slicing technique is also applicable in various areas of software engineering activities such as debugging, re-engineering, testing, model checking, verification, program segmentation and many more. In the next section, we explore the techniques of program slicing and the application of the technique in the field of software engineering.

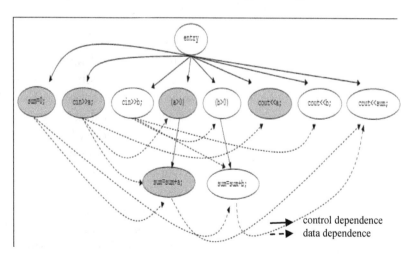

Figure 2:The PDG of the example program from Figure 1(a) and the grey vertices represent the slices of statement from Figure 1(b)

ISBN: 978-1-387-00704-2

Program Slicing Techniques and its Application

Understanding an application is important in a successful evolution of software system and program slicing is able to help programmers in comprehension phase for program maintenance purposes. This section will discuss various program slicing techniques that have been proposed in literature including static, dynamic, simultaneous, quasi and conditioned slicing as well as its application.

A static slicing is constructed by deleting those parts of the program that are irrelevant to the values stored in the chosen set of variables at the chosen point. The point of interest usually is identified by annotating the program with line numbers, which identify every primitive statement and each branch node. By exploring and understanding the slice of source code, it allows us to find the bugs faster than the original. The dynamic slicing takes the input supplied to the program during implementation and the slice contains only the statement that caused the failure during the specific execution of interest. Dynamic slicing uses dynamic analysis to identify all and only the statements that affect the variables of interest on the particular anomalous execution trace(Korel & Rilling, 1998).

The simultaneous technique combines the use of a set of test cases with program slicing. The method is called simultaneous dynamic program slicing because it extends and simultaneously applies to a set of test cases the dynamic slicing technique(Korel & Laski, 1990)which produces executable slices that are correct on a single input. Quasi-static slicing is a hybrid of static and dynamic slicing. Static slicing examines during compile time, using no information about the input variables of the program. On the other hand, dynamic slicing analyses the code by giving input to the program. It is constructed at run time with respect to a particular input. A conditioned slicing consists of a subset of program statements, which preserves the behavior of the original program relating to a slicing criterion for any set of program executions. The set of initial states of the program that characterize these executions is specified in terms of a first order

ISBN: 978-1-387-00704-2

logic formula on the input. Conditioned slicing allows a better decomposition of the program giving human readers the possibility to evaluate the code fragments concerning different perspectives.

The idea behind all approaches to program slicing is to produce the simplest program possible that maintains the meaning of the original program in connection with this slicing criterion. The conditioned criterion is the most general of these, subsuming both static and dynamic criteria as the special cases. The conditioned criterion consists of a set of variables, a program point of interest and a condition. There are some drawbacks between static and dynamic slicing methods. Static slicing needs more space, more resources and will perform every possible execution of the program. Conversely, dynamic slicing needs less space and is specific to a program execution. Dynamic slices are smaller than static slice(Binkley et al., 2005). For complete program understanding, one execution of the program is not enough. Hence, the Quasi static slicing method was first introduced by Venkatesh(Roongruangsuwan & Daengdej, 2010). In Quasi slicing, the value of some variables are fixed and the program is analyzed while the value of other variables vary. The behaviour of the original program is not changed with respect to the slicing criterion. Slicing criteria includes the set of variables of interest and initial conditions, therefore, quasi slicing is called as Conditioned slicing(Binkley et al., 2005). This is an efficient method for program comprehension.

Existing Works on Program Slicing Technique
This section explains the existing works on program slicing in supporting program comprehension. The discussion is based on selected papers focusing on the strengths and weaknesses of the work as well as the approaches, slicing criterion and the output representation.

The first work proposed by Servant & Jones (2013) uses the history slicing method to discover the historical change events to the source code. The proposed work is useful for understanding

ISBN: 978-1-387-00704-2

source code growth, however, it consumes much time when applying the proposed work. The output representative is in a set of lines of interest contains all their snap-shots in all the past revisions in which they were modified. The work provides a tool namely Chronos. Santelices et al. (2013) uses the quantitative slicing approach focusing on novice users to quantify the relevance of each statement in a slice. This method help user focus their attention on the part of slices that matter the most. The study is able to assess the potential impact of changing location for a given score to quantifies the lines but the method is ambiguous and just by estimation. The output representation is in a form of slices and source code snippets. They also develop a tool called SensA.

Jain & Poonia (2013) combined the static and dynamic slicing method to reduce the time taken in slicing process. The output representation is in slices and source code snippets. The tool is not available in this work. Maruyama et al. (2012) applied the program slicing technique to discover the historical change events to the operation of source code by replaying recorded past code changes. The output is in a set of lines of interest contains all their snap-shots in all the past revisions in which they were modified. Their study are useful for understanding source code growth, nevertheless, the implementation of their slicing task is time-consuming. On the other hand, the study proposed by Zhang et al. (2011) perform the dynamic slicing according to the calling relationship of the program. The work proposed the method called Structured Dynamic Program Slicing (SPS) that use the register or memory address in certain instruction of the program as slicing criterion. The work extracts a part of code, which influenced by users, and organizes the result using the call graph of the program. The summary of the works are shown in Table 1.

ISBN: 978-1-387-00704-2

Table 1 Summary of Existing Works on Program Slicing Technique

Authors	Method of Slicing	Direction	Technique of Slicing	Tool	Slicing Criterion
(Servant & Jones, 2013)	History Slicing	Backward	Static	Chronos	Set of lines of interest
(Santelices et al., 2013)	Quantitative Slicing	Hybrid	Hybrid	SensA	The score or probabilities of the set of interested lines
(Jain & Poonia, 2013)	Mixed S-D Slicing	Hybrid	Hybrid	N/A	Variables
(Maruyama et al., 2012)	History Slicing	Hybrid	Static	Operation Slice Replayer	Operations change of interest
(Zhang et al., 2011)	SPS - Structured Dynamic Program Slicing	Forward	Dynamic	SPS	The register or memory address in certain instruction of the program

Conclusion

Program slicing has been applied to a range of maintenance tasks. This paper attempts to provide the insight behind computing a program slice and reflects on several types of program slicing techniques that have been written. This study also aims to recommend excellent sources for further information on program slicing. Finally, we offers a direction for future work on program slicing research. We plan to apply this technique taking into consideration the use of domain knowledge in object-oriented programs. Program slicing of such programs is more complicated due to global and local variables, reference parameters, procedure call/return, and recursion. By extracting, the elements in OOP source code and represent it into a form of knowledge representation, this method will be able to enhance a successful evolution of program slicing.

References

Barros, J. B., da Cruz, D., Henriques, P. R., & Pinto, J. S. (2011). *Assertion-based slicing and slice graphs. Formal Aspects of Computing* (Vol. 24). http://doi.org/10.1007/s00165-011-0196-1

ISBN: 978-1-387-00704-2

Binkley, D., Danicic, S., Gyimóthy, T., Harman, M., Kiss, A., & Korel, B. (2005). Minimal slicing and the relationships between forms of slicing. In *Source Code Analysis and Manipulation, 2005. Fifth IEEE International Workshop on* (pp. 45–54). IEEE.

Jain, M. S., & Poonia, M. S. (2013). A New approach of program slicing: Mixed SD (static & dynamic) slicing. *International Journal of Advanced Research in Computer and Communication Engineering Vol, 2.*

Korel, B., & Laski, J. (1990). Dynamic slicing of computer programs. *Journal of Systems and Software, 13*(3), 187–195.

Korel, B., & Rilling, J. (1998). Dynamic program slicing methods. *Information and Software Technology, 40*(11), 647–659.

Koushik, S., & Selvarani, R. (2012). Review on Cost Effective Software Engineering Using Program Slicing Techniques. In *Proceedings of the International Conference on Information Systems Design and Intelligent Applications 2012 (INDIA 2012) held in Visakhapatnam, India, January 2012* (pp. 631–637). Springer.

Lahtinen, E., Järvinen, H.-M., & Melakoski-Vistbacka, S. (2007). Targeting program visualizations. *ACM SIGCSE Bulletin, 39*(3), 256. http://doi.org/10.1145/1269900.1268858

Maletic, J. I., & Kagdi, H. (2008). Expressiveness and effectiveness of program comprehension: Thoughts on future research directions. *2008 Frontiers of Software Maintenance*, 31–37. http://doi.org/10.1109/FOSM.2008.4659246

Maruyama, K., Kitsu, E., Omori, T., & Hayashi, S. (2012). Slicing and replaying code change history. *Proceedings of the 27th IEEE/ACM International Conference on Automated Software Engineering - ASE 2012*, 246. http://doi.org/10.1145/2351676.2351713

Normantas, K., & Vasilecas, O. (2013). A Systematic Review of Methods for Business Knowledge Extraction from Existing Software Systems, *1*(1), 29–51.

Roongruangsuwan, S., & Daengdej, J. (2010). A test case prioritization method with practical weight factors. *J. Software Eng, 4*, 193–214.

Saleem, M., Hussain, R., Ismail, V., & Mohsin, S. (2009). Cost effective software engineering using program slicing techniques. In *Proceedings of the 2nd International Conference on Interaction Sciences: Information Technology, Culture and Human* (pp. 768–772). ACM.

Santelices, R., Zhang, Y., Jiang, S., Cai, H., & Zhang, Y. (2013). Quantitative program slicing: Separating statements by relevance. *2013 35th International Conference on Software Engineering (ICSE)*, 1269–1272. http://doi.org/10.1109/ICSE.2013.6606695

Sasirekha, N., & Hemalatha, M. (2011). Program Slicing Techniques and its Applications. *International Journal of Software Engineering & Applications, 2*(3), 50–64.

Servant, F., & Jones, J. a. (2013). Chronos: Visualizing slices of source-code history. *2013 First IEEE Working Conference on Software Visualization (VISSOFT)*, 1–4. http://doi.org/10.1109/VISSOFT.2013.6650547

ISBN: 978-1-387-00704-2

Weiser, M. (1982). Programmers use slices when debugging. *Communications of the ACM, 25*(7), 446–452.

Zhang, R., Zheng, Y., Huang, S., & Qi, Z. (2011). Structured Dynamic Program Slicing. *2011 International Conference on Computer and Management (CAMAN)*, 1–4. http://doi.org/10.1109/CAMAN.2011.5778759

ISBN: 978-1-387-00704-2

Article 4

Selection of the Best Thermal Massage Treatment for Diabetes by using Fuzzy Analytical Hierarchy Process

Norpah Mahat, Syafiah Ahmad,
Faculty of Computer & Mathematical Sciences,
Universiti Teknologi MARA Perlis Branch, Malaysia

Abstract

Diabetes is a condition in which the human blood glucose (sugar) level is abnormally high due to the lack of insulin produced by the pancreas. As diabetes has been claimed to be a disease that is incurable, researchers have come out with numerous alternatives in making it curable and one of them is thermal massage treatment. This treatment refers to the application of chiropractic where it focuses on realigning the spine where diabetes is claimed to be related to the misalignment of thoracic 7 (T7). The objective of this study is to identify and select the best and most effective thermal massage treatment session(s) required for both T1D and T2D patients of different high glucose level in the blood to be reduced to the normal glucose level by using thermal massager. This study is conducted for the diabetic patients who receive treatments from Ceragem Healthcare Centre on how to optimise their thermal massage treatments to normalise their glucose level. Fuzzy Analytical Hierarchy Process (AHP) is utilised in this type of selection problem mainly due to the reliable results produced for the imprecise and uncertain preferences of the users in which able to be expressed as a fuzzy set (triangular fuzzy number). The findings indicated that the most significant criteria for effective thermal massage is determined by the "number of treatment session (per day)" where the best thermal massage treatment is derived from the normalised fuzzy weight of both criteria and sub-criteria.

Keywords: *Fuzzy Analytical Hierarchy Process, Diabetes, Thermal massage*

Introduction

Diabetes is defined as a condition in which the human blood glucose (sugar) level is abnormally high (Department of Human Services and Institute, 2013). Insulin; a hormone produced by the pancreas regulates human blood glucose level to maintain the normal level. In the case for Diabetes patient, the individual's blood glucose level is relatively high due to the failure of pancreas to produce insulin.

ISBN: 978-1-387-00704-2

There are five types of diabetes which are; type 1 diabetes (T1D), type 2 diabetes (T2D), gestational diabetes, diabetes insipidus and pre-diabetes (Department of Human Services and Institute, 2013). However, this research will mainly focus on two types of diabetes which are T1D and T2D. T1D is also known as insulin dependent diabetes (Department of Human Services and Institute, 2013), where insulin is no longer produced by the pancreas due to the destruction of insulin β-cells (Bruni et al., 2014). T2D or non-insulin dependent diabetes (Department of Human Services and Institute, 2013) is a state where the insulin produced by the pancreas is in a small amount, in which inadequate to lower elevated blood glucose level.

Treatment for diabetes is focused on complications prevention because both T1D and T2D are incurable as claimed by the World Health Organisation and Department of Human Service and Institute in 2014 and 2013 respectively. Thus, researchers around the world provided a number of alternative treatments for both types of diabetes in order to find the cure. Chiropractic technique; a technique in which focuses on curing the misalignment of spines in diabetes treatment is deemed to be one of the effective alternative treatments in addressing diabetes (Echeveste (2008), Sudano& Robinson (2011)). Essentially, the logic behind chiropractic technique is rooted in the nerve located in T7. This nerve acts as an information (impulse) transporter from the pancreas to the brain and vice versa. When there is a misalignment in T7, the nerve will be blocked from sending the information from pancreas to the brain in which hinder the insulin hormone to be produced by the pancreas.

Ceragem, a Korean company has applied chiropractic in its thermal bed massager, Ceragem Master V3 where the machine massages human spines and aligns any misalignments of the spines. This treatment had showed progressively positive result in reducing high blood glucose level of diabetic patients to the normal blood glucose level. In Malaysia, the Ceragem offers free trial treatments for their customers who seek treatments at their

ISBN: 978-1-387-00704-2

healthcare centres. Thus, this offer is an alternative for diabetes patients to reduce their cost of treatments.

The aim of this study is to identify and select the best and most effective thermal massage treatment session(s) required for both T1D and T2D patients of different high glucose level in blood to be reduced to the normal level in blood by using thermal massager.

Methodology
Past researches have shown that Fuzzy AHP is widely used for selection process such as selection of the diet meal while maintaining blood sugar level (Gaikwad et al., 2015). A model for diabetes treatment for T2D patients was introduced by Tadic et al. (2010) where they used fuzzy to develop the model.

Thus, Fuzzy AHP had been chosen to carry out the selection process where the data required for the study are derived from the opinions of the Directors of Ceragem on their decisions in selecting the best thermal massage treatment for diabetic patients, type T1D and T2D only. There are six criteria and twenty-two sub-criteria in which required to be studied in detailed for the selection process.

Fuzzy AHP required eight steps to be completed before the selection of the best thermal massage treatment for diabetes can be made. The eight steps are as follow:

Step 1: The hierarchy of the criteria and sub-criteria are constructed by decision maker as shown in Table 1.

ISBN: 978-1-387-00704-2

Table 1: The hierarchy of criteria and sub-criteria

Selection of the best thermal massage treatment for diabetes					
Duration (minutes)	Temperature (°C)	Massage technique	Number of treatment session (per day)	Number of days for treatment session (per week)	Total number of treatment session
1-20	41-50	Automatic	1	1	1-100
21-30	51-60	Mode 1	2	3	101-200
40		Mode 4	>2	7	201-300
		Automatic&Mode 1			>300
		Automatic&Mode 4			
		Mode1&Mode4			
		Automatic,Mode1 ,Mode4			

Step 2: The comparison of the criteria or alternatives are made by decision maker by using triangular fuzzy numbers(TFN) of linguistic terms. Pair-wise contribution matrices of criteria and sub-criteria are formed by using TFN for each decision maker.

Step 3: Eq. 1 $(\tilde{d}_{ij})$ is calculated when there is more than one decision maker after each decision maker's precedence $(\tilde{d}_{ij}^k)$ is averaged, where $\tilde{d}_{ij}^k$ is the kth preference of decision maker for i^{th} criterion via TFN.

$$\tilde{d}_{ij} = \frac{\sum_{k=1}^{K} \tilde{d}_{ij}^k}{K}$$

(1)

Step 4: Pair wise contribution matric is adjusted after precedence is averaged.

ISBN: 978-1-387-00704-2

Step 5: The calculation of every criterion of geometric mean of fuzzy comparison values as cited in Ayhan, (2013), the triangular values are still represented by $\tilde{r}_i$.

$$\tilde{r}_i = \left(\prod_{j=1}^{n} \tilde{d}_{ij} \right)^{1/n} , i = 1, 2, ..., n$$

(2)

Step 6: By using Eq. (3), the fuzzy weight for every criterion is calculated after the next three sub steps are implemented.

Step 6a: Vector summation is calculated for each $\tilde{r}_i$.

Step 6b: The TFN is replaced in order to arrange it in increasing order after the (-1) power of summation vector is found.

Step 6c: Each $\tilde{r}_i$ is multiplied with the reverse vector to find the criterion i's fuzzy weight $(\tilde{w}_i)$.

$$\tilde{w}_i = \tilde{r}_i \oplus \left(\tilde{r}_1 \oplus \tilde{r}_2 \oplus ... \oplus \tilde{r}_n \right)^{-1}$$
$$= \left(lw_i, mw_i, uw_i \right)$$

(3)

Step 7: The centre of area method as cited by Ayhan (2013) is applied to defuzzified $\tilde{w}_i$ because they are still TFN. This calculation is conducted by applying Eq. 3.6.

$$M_i = \frac{lw_i + mw_i + uw_i}{3}$$

(4)

Step 8: In Eq. (5), M_i is normalised although it is already a non-fuzzy number.

ISBN: 978-1-387-00704-2

$$N_i = \frac{M_i}{\sum_{i=1}^{n} M_i}$$

(5)

In order to normalise the weight of criteria and alternatives, all the eight steps are required to be performed. The result for multiplication of each weight of alternative with respective criteria is the score for each alternative. The highest score of alternative will be suggested to decision maker.

Results and Discussions

After performing all the steps of Fuzzy AHP, the criteria and sub-criteria had been ranked successfully. Table 2 shows the normalised relative weight and the ranks of the criteria.

Table 2: Normalised relative weight and the ranks of the criteria

Criteria	N_i	Ranks
Number of treatment session (per day)	0.317	1
Number of days for treatment session in a week	0.271	2
Total number of treatment session	0.235	3
Massage technique	0.106	4
Temperature	0.050	5
Duration	0.021	6

Based on the table above, a criterion of number of treatment session (per day) was at the first rank, followed by the number of days for treatment session in a week and the total number of treatment session. Consequently, the fourth, fifth and last ranks are massage technique, temperature and duration respectively. The ranks shown were based on the calculation of normalised relative weight, referring to the opinion from the Directors of Ceragem.

This postulates that the diabetic customers,type T1D and T2D, are advised to prioritise on the number of treatment sessions (per

ISBN: 978-1-387-00704-2

day), the number of days for treatment session in a week and the total number of treatment sessions in this order to reduce high blood glucose level to normal blood glucose level.

The sub-criteria were then ranked as shown in the Table 3 to take the highest prioritised criterion for the global importance weighting of the sub-criteria.

Table 3: The ranks of the global importance weightings

Sub-criteria	N_i	Ranks
3 times or more	0.251	1
7 days	0.214	2
301 times or more	0.159	3
201-300 times	0.053	4
2 times	0.048	5
Automatic mode, Mode 1 & Mode 4	0.046	6
51-60 (°C)	0.044	7
3 days	0.04	8
Mode 1 & Mode 4	0.023	9
1 time	0.018	10
1 day	0.017	11
40 minutes	0.016	12
Automatic mode & Mode 1	0.016	13
101-200 times	0.016	14
Automatic mode & Mode 4	0.011	15
1-100 times	0.007	16
41-50 (°C)	0.006	17
21-30 minutes	0.004	18
Mode 1	0.004	19
Automatic mode	0.003	20
Mode 4	0.003	21
1-20 minutes	0.001	22

Referring to the quantitative values in the table for the rank of global importance weightings of all criteria above, it is displayed that "3 times or more for number of treatment session (per day)"

ISBN: 978-1-387-00704-2

has the highest priority with the value of 0.251. "7 days" and "300 times or more" were at the second and third ranks with the values of 0.214 and 0.159 respectively. On the other hand, the sub-criteria for "massage technique", "temperature" and "duration" which were "Automatic Mode, Mode 1 & Mode 4", "51-60 °C" and "40 minutes" ranked sixth, seventh and twelfth with the values of global importance weight of 0.046, 0.044 and 0.016 respectively.

These values showed that the thermal massage for diabetes treatment,type T1D and T2D, is best to be done three times or more in a day and the effective thermal massage to treat diabetic customer is by undergoing the treatment every day until the total number of massage treatments exceeds three hundred times or more. In a nutshell, the best treatment for diabetic customer to reduce high blood glucose level to normal blood glucose level by using thermal massage is to receive the treatment three times or more every day until the total number of the treatment reaches three hundred times or more. Besides, the massage technique from the combination of automatic mode, mode 1 and mode 4 with the temperature of 51°C to 60°C and duration of 40 minutes per treatment session are deemed to be the most effective.

Conclusion
In this study, Fuzzy AHP method is used to select the best thermal massage treatment for diabetic customer at Ceragem Healthcare Centres in order to reduce high blood glucose level to normal blood glucose level. The selection of the best thermal massage treatment for diabetic customer is an uncertainty process due to the different level of high blood glucose and types of diabetes. This problem can be solved by using fuzzy number and linguistic variables to achieve higher accuracy and consistency results and outcomes.

In conclusion, based on the calculations of the normalised weight by using Fuzzy AHP method, the most important criteria in thermal massage treatment for diabetes,type T1D and T2D, is the "number of treatment session (s) (per day)" while its sub-criteria

ISBN: 978-1-387-00704-2

is "3 times or more". This indicates that it is the most important for the diabetic customer to receive thermal massage treatment three times or more in a day. Besides, the best thermal massage treatment for diabetic customer to reduce high blood glucose level to normal blood glucose level is by having three times or more treatment a day until the total number of treatment exceeds three hundred times. The treatment is also encouraged to be from the combination of Automatic Mode, Mode 1 and Mode 4 for 40 minutes per treatment session with temperature of 51°C to 60°C.

Acknowledgments
The authors would like to express our gratitude to Marketing Director of Ceragem Malaysia SdnBhd, Director of Ceragem branch Sungai Petani and Director of Ceragem branch AlorSetar for their opinions and willingness to share information on thermal massage treatment for diabetes.

References
Ayhan, M. B. (2013). A Fuzzy AHP approach for supplier selection problem: A case study in a gearmotor company. *International Journal of Managing Value and Supply Chains, 4*(3), 11-23.

Bruni, A., Gala-Lopez, B., Pepper, A. R., Abualhassan, N. S., & James Shapiro, A. M. (2014). Islet cell transplantation for the treatment of type 1 diabetes: Recent advances and future challenges. *Diabetes, Metabolic Syndrome and Obesity: Targets and Therapy, 7*, 211-223.

Department of Human Services,& Institute. (2013). *Diabetes.* Retrieved November 1, 2016 from https://www.betterhealth.vic.gov.au/health/conditionsandtreatments/diabetes

Echeveste, A. (2008). Chiropractic care in a nine year old female with vertebral subluxations, diabetes & hypothyroidism.*Journal of Vertebral Subluxation Research (JVSR)*, 1-5.

Gaikwad, S. M., Mualy, Dr. P., &Joshi,R. R. (2015). Analytical Hierarchy Process to recommend an ice cream to t a diabetic patient based on sugar content in it. *Procedia Computer Science, 50, 64-72.*

Sudano, N., & Robinson-LeBlanc, D. (2011). Improved A1 C levels in a patient with insulin- dependent type I diabetes undergoing chiropractic care : A case report. *J. Pediatric, Maternal & Family Health*, (4), 120-124.

Tadic, D., Popovic, P. &Dukic, A. (2010).A Fuzzy approach to evaluation and management of therapeutic procedure in diabetes mellitus treatment.*Yugoslav Journal of Operations Research, 20(1), 99-116.*

ISBN: 978-1-387-00704-2

World Health Organization (2016).*Global report on diabetes.* Retrieved October 30, 2016 from http://www.who.int/diabetes/publications/grd-2016/en/

ISBN: 978-1-387-00704-2

Article 5

Matching Final Year Project Topics with Students using Stable Marriage Model

Naimah Mohd Hussin (PhD), Ammar Azlan,
Faculty of Computer & Mathematical Sciences,
Universiti Teknologi MARA Perlis Branch, Malaysia

Abstract

Every semester, a new batch of final year students needs to find a topic and a supervisor to complete their final year project requirement. The problem with the current approach is that it is based on first come first serve. So, the pairing between student and supervisor is not the optimal ones, i.e. some students may not get their preferred topic or supervisor. Plus, it is also time consuming for both students and supervisors. The researcher is motivated to solve this long overdue problem by applying a stable marriage model that is introduced by Gale and Shapley hence the name Gale-Shapley Algorithm. To determine the functionality of this approach, a system prototype has been constructed and a random dataset is used. The result, 60% of the students get their first choice topics while the remaining students get their second or third choice. This is a remarkable outcome considering the time and effort saved compared to the current process. Therefore, stable marriage model is applicable in solving student-topic pairing.

Keywords *Gale-Shapley Algorithm, Stable Marriage Model, matching, optimization, pairing, final year project*

Introduction

Final year students are required to undergo a course, Information System Project Formulation, where they need to do a proposal of a final year project in any area related to their program. This project will be supervised by a lecturer from their department. Some lecturers may supervise more than one student, depending on their schedule and expertise. The lecturers involved in supervising final year projects and the total students they can supervise are determined at the departmental level. The project title however will be provided by the lecturers or proposed by the students.

ISBN: 978-1-387-00704-2

Therefore, the first step in this final year project development is for the students to find a supervisor with a project title that suits the students' interest. As simple as it may sound, there are many students who had made the wrong choice in finding either project title or supervisor that is suitable for them. This mistake is propagated throughout the semester. As a result, they might not perform well in their final presentation. Some are lucky to get away with a low grade. Unfortunately, for those who are not so lucky, they got a failed grade and had to repeat the course all over again.

This matching problem might occur from the students' lack of knowledge about the project title being proposed by their supervisor. On the other hand, the supervisors do not know the students well enough to determine whether the title is suitable for them or not. Therefore, it would be practical to have a platform which acts as the 'middle-man' to find the best match between students and project titles.

The algorithm that is used in performing this matching is Gale-Shapley's algorithm. This algorithm has been implemented in many areas such as to assign medical students to hospitals based on the preferences of students over hospitals and vice versa. It is implemented in many countries with different names. To name a few, it is known as NRMP in the US (Gusfeld and Irving, 1989), CaRMS in Canada and SPA in Scotland (Irving, 1998). Another application is reported by Teo et al (2001), which assigns students to secondary schools in Singapore. Since all of the problems are solved by using this algorithm, then it is a good hypothesis that the problem of matching students and project titles will be solved too.

Finding a suitable supervisor and project title is essential for final year students in order to perform their best in their final year project. It would also be best if this matching could be done automatically with high resemblance to manual selection.

ISBN: 978-1-387-00704-2

Unfortunately, until today, the matching between students and supervisors is still done manually. It is done where students would meet and ask supervisors about the project title. Students can choose the supervisor or the topic that they find interesting. The flaw in this system is that, the choosing is only done by students. Supervisors basically just accept the students based on first come first serve basis.

As a result, the quality of students' final year project will be fixed at the same level if no improvement is being done on this matching problem. The current matching approach is also time-consuming for both students and supervisors. These problems are believed can be solved by implementing Gale-Shapley algorithm.

This research studies the Gale-Shapley algorithm and determines if the algorithm can be implemented in matching problem with respect to project titles and students' interest in their final year project. This research focuses on the matching process and the quality of the solution produced.

Literature Review

Final Year Project in UiTM Perlis

Final year project is a project which every final year students have to carry out for two semesters. Currently no application has been implemented to manage the project. This includes from the beginning phase of the final year project, which is finding the suitable supervisor, to the last phase which is preserving the finished project. This project will concentrate on the first phase which is finding the best match between final year students and the project titles.

The perfect match between students and project titles is essential in order to optimize the performance of both parties. Students will produce better project if the project they are working on is suited with their interest and ability. On the other hand, supervisors would give a better guide to the students if the area of project is within their expertise.

ISBN: 978-1-387-00704-2

Stable Marriage Model

Stable matching problems were first studied by Gale and Shapley (1962). In a stable marriage problem there are two finite sets of participants: the set of men (M) and the set of women (W). In the Gale-Shapley model, the preference lists of the participants are required to be completed, and no one is to be declared as unacceptable. A matching is just a one-to-one mapping between the two sexes such that a man *m* is mapped to a woman *w* if and only if *w* is mapped to *m*, and *m* and *w* are acceptable to each other" (Teo et al, 2001).

The stable marriage model consists of two sides of conditions to be fulfilled which are the male side and the female side. The matching process will go through a number of recurrences until the most optimal match is found. There are also conditional and nested conditional statements exist within the recurrences. The first conditional statement matches a man with a free woman. The second one matches a man with an engaged woman if she prefers the man over his fiancé. This decision is done with a nested conditional statement within the second conditional statement. This whole process is shown in Figure 1.

The structure of this model has proven that there is close similarity between stable marriage problem and final year project problem. With a few modifications on the algorithm, it is possible to implement stable marriage model in finding the best match between students and topics in the final year project. In final year project case, the male and female part is represented by students and topics respectively.

```
functionstableMatching
{
    Initialize all m∈M and w∈W to free
while∃free man m who still has a woman w
to propose to
    {
        w = m's highest ranked such woman
    if w is free
            (m, w) become engaged
    else some pair (m', w) already exists
```

ISBN: 978-1-387-00704-2

```
if w prefers m to m'
            (m, w) become engaged
            m' becomes free
else
            (m', w) remain engaged
    }
}
```

Figure 1: Gale-Shapley Stable Marriage algorithm

Application of Stable Marriage Model

Gale-Shapley Stable Marriage Problem algorithm is a well known approach in solving matching problem. Many researchers have done studies where the algorithm is applied to other areas. Dean et al (2006) said that before becoming a doctor, a medical school graduate in the United States is required to complete a residency program at a hospital. The medical field has turned to a centralized marketplace, called the National Residency Matching Program (NRMP) since 1950s to help this marketplace. The program basically works by final-year medical students and hospitals each submit preferences over possible matches. Then, an algorithm determines which match is the most desirable. The system is considered as successful if the generated matches are stable. Computing a stable matching is a classic problem in economics and computer science. It can be solved in polynomial time by the deferred acceptance algorithm of Gale and Shapley.

Furthermore, there is also a case where the stable marriage problem is put into practice in hospital-residents problem. According to Unsworth and Prosser (2005), both the stable marriage problem and hospital-residents problem are stable marriage problems. They consist of two sets of objects that need to be matched to each other. In stable marriage problem, men need to be paired to women meanwhile in hospital-residents problem, residents need to be assigned to hospitals. Each set of objects expresses a weighted preference in the form of a preference list for the objects in the opposite set. The problem is then to find a matching of one set to the other set which is stable.

ISBN: 978-1-387-00704-2

This shows that stable marriage problem is a very flexible algorithm and has been used in solving problems in many areas. All the researches and implementation of stable marriage problem in other fields have proven to come up with satisfying results. It is believed that it can also be implemented in final year project and more importantly, it will produce good results. This could be further induced by a statement in an article entitled Geometric Stable Roommates as follows: *"The Stable Marriage problem is a true multidisciplinary problem: it is well-studied in economics, computer science, and combinatory. The problem and its numerous extensions continue to receive considerable attention, both from the theoretical point of view and for real-world applications"* (Arkin et al, 2009).

Construction

The system is implemented as a web-based application since it is necessary for the system to be accessible by all final year project students and supervisors. The process flow for the system is as shown in Figure 3.1 and is self-explanatory.

1. Login (as administrator, student or supervisor)
2. Registration (student and supervisor)
3. If (supervisor)
   a. Register topic(s)
   b. For each topic, rank students who have chosen the topic
   c. If (algorithm executed)
      i. Retrieve matching results
4. If (student)
   a. Rank topic(s) Note: 1 as the most preferable topic
   b. If (algorithm executed)
      i. Retrieve matching results
5. If (administrator)
   a. Register all supervisors and students
   b. If (supervisors and students have completed ranking)
      i. Run algorithm to find matching

ISBN: 978-1-387-00704-2

	ii. Display matching results
6. End	

Figure 2: Process Flow

Resultsand Findings

Table 1 shows the dataset used in the testing. Students are represented by their last two digits of their student number. Each column indicates how each student rank the topics. For example, the entry in the first column and the first row (shown in bold) indicates student whose student number ends with 26 ranks topic with ID number 14 as the first rank.

Table 1: Dataset – Students' ranking

		Student									
		26	32	36	38	64	76	84	86	94	68
Rank	1	**14**	10	3	14	3	11	4	3	5	3
	2	2	13	9	9	9	6	6	6	9	2
	3	12	12	10	12	4	9	7	8	12	13
	4	7	6	12	6	11	4	10	11	13	10
	5	15	7	6	13	13	10	13	14	6	7
	6	10	9	13	8	6	2	8	1	7	5
	7	6	8	5	2	15	1	15	5	10	15
	8	9	14	15	4	5	7	2	9	14	11
	9	11	15	4	3	8	12	3	12	15	12
	10	13	1	8	10	12	13	9	13	2	9

The dataset for supervisors' preferences is also done in similar way. For example, in column 1, supervisor for topic 1 has ranked student with student number ends with 86 as the first rank. Referring to Table 1, it is clear that not all topics have the same number of students to be ranked. The more number of students for that topic shows that the topic is preferable among students. In this case, topic 9 and 13 are the most preferable topics because all students rank them. Topic 1 is the least preferable topic because only three students rank it.

ISBN: 978-1-387-00704-2

Table 2: Dataset – Supervisors' ranking

Topic															
Rank	1	2	3	4	5	6	7	8	9	10	11	12	13	14	15
1	86	38	38	38	64	76	68	38	32	84	76	26	84	38	64
2	76	94	36	84	86	94	32	84	84	32	86	86	32	86	68
3	32	84	64	36	68	86	84	36	86	38	64	76	26	32	32
4		26	86	64	94	64	26	86	64	76	26	36	86	26	84
5		76	84	76	36	26	76	64	26	94	68	32	94	94	26
6		68	68			32	94	32	94	68		38	38		36
7						38			36	36		64	36		94
8						84			38	26		94	76		32
9						36			68			68	68		
10									76				64		

The matching result of these two preferences is shown by listing all the topics and the matching students. Besides generating the matched list between students and topics, it also shows the rank of the topics that students get (See Figure 3)

ISBN: 978-1-387-00704-2

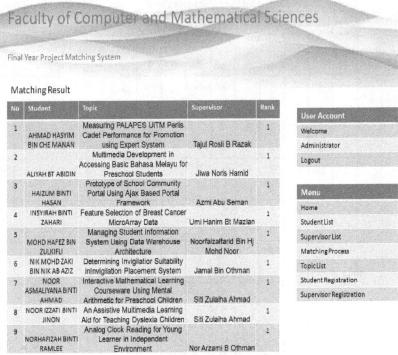

Figure 3: Matching result

Figure 4shows the pie chart that compares the number of students with the ranks of topic they get. The darkest section in the pie chart represents the number of students who get their first ranked topics. It can be concluded that the system satisfies more than half the students (60%).

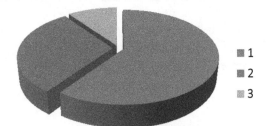

Figure 4: Percentage of students for each rank

ISBN: 978-1-387-00704-2

Conclusion and Recommendation

In this research, it is proven that stable marriage model can solve the problem in pairing students with final year topics. The system is able to find a match that satisfies 60% of first choice preference.

The actual system is recommended to be used by the Computer Science Department to manage their final year projects. However, the system needs to be improved in terms of its interface and user-friendliness. Secondly, user of the system will be more pleased if the system could be extended to enable the user to either accept or reject the title generated by the system. It will extend the timeline of the system but as with the current course registration used by UiTM, there is add and drop period where users can still alter the courses they have preregistered.

References

Dean, B.C., Goemans, M.X., Immorlica, N., (2006). *"The Unsplittable Stable Marriage Problem"*. In International Federation for Information Processing, Volume 209, Fourth IFIP International Conference on Theoretical Computer Science-TCS 2006, eds. Navarro, G., Bertossi, L., Kohayakwa, Y., (Boston: Springer), pp. 65–75.

Arkin, E. M., Bae, S.W., Efrat, A., Okamoto, K., Mitchell, J. S. B., &Polishchuk, V. (2009).*Geometric Stable Roomates*. In Information Processing Letters, Volume 109 Issue 4, January, 2009. pp 219-224.

Gale, D., & Shapley, L. S., (1962).*College admissions and the stability of marriage*. American Mathematical Monthly, Vol. 69, p. 9–15.

Gusfeld, D., & Irving, R. W. (1989).*The stable marriage problem: structure and algorithms*. MIT Press, Cambridge, MA, USA.

Irving, R. W. (1998). *Matching medical students to pairs of hospitals: a new variation on a well-known theme*. In Proceedings of ESA'98: the Sixth Annual European Symposium on Algorithms, Vol. 1461, p. 381-392.

Teo, C. P., Sethuraman, J., & Tan, W. P. (2001). *Gale-Shapley Stable Marriage Problem Revisited: Strategic Issues and Applications*. In Management Science © 2001 INFORMS Vol. 47, No. 9, September 2001 pp. 1252–1267

Unsworth, C., Prosser, P. (2005) *An n-ary Constraint for the Stable Marriage Problem*, The Fifth Workshop on Modelling and Solving Problems with Constraints, held at the 19th International Joint Conference on Artificial Intelligence (IJCAI 2005)

ISBN: 978-1-387-00704-2

Article 6

Comparison of Clustering Algorithms on Air Quality Substances in Peninsular Malaysia

Sitti Sufiah Atirah Rosly, Balkiah Moktar, Muhamad Hasbullah MohdRazali
Faculty of Computer & Mathematical Sciences,
Universiti Teknologi MARA Perlis Branch, Malaysia

Abstract
Air quality is one of the most popular environmental problems in this globalization era. Air pollution is the poisonous air that comes from car emissions, smog, open burning, chemicals from factories and other particles and gases. This harmful air can give adverse effects to human health and the environment. In order to provide information which areas are better for the residents in Malaysia, cluster analysis is used to determine the areas that can be clustering together based on their air quality through several air quality substances. Monthly data from 37 monitoring stations in Peninsular Malaysia from the year 2013 to 2015 were used in this study. K-Means (KM) clustering algorithm, Expectation Maximization (EM) clustering algorithm and Density Based (DB) clustering algorithm have been chosen as the techniques to analyze the cluster analysis by utilizing the Waikato Environment for Knowledge Analysis (WEKA) tools. Results show that K-means clustering algorithm is the best method among other algorithms due to its simplicity and time taken to build the model. The output of K-means clustering algorithm shows that it can cluster the area into two clusters, namely as cluster 0 and cluster 1. Clusters 0 consist of 16 monitoring stations and cluster 1 consists of 36 monitoring stations in Peninsular Malaysia.

Keywords: Air Quality, Clustering Algorithm, WEKA, k-mean, density based, expectation maximization

Introduction

Nowadays, a severe environmental problem such as air pollution has attracted much attention in many developed countries. People who are exposed to unhealthy air quality can suffer from short-term throat, eye and nose irritation. Moreover, a citizen who has lung and heart disease, children and senior citizen will be at dangerous risks because of air pollution. When the air is polluted, the population that is exposed to this air will experience increasingly adverse health effects. Different areas have their

ISBN: 978-1-387-00704-2

own air pollutant index which some of these areas will experience same environmental problems

Cluster analysis divides data into groups that are meaningful and useful. In other words, cluster analysis is the main method of data description in assorted sectors like image analysis, data mining, pattern recognition, machine learning, and bioinformatics. Cluster analysis is also recognized as an important method for classifying data and discovering clusters of a dataset based on similarities in the same cluster and dissimilarities between different clusters.

The aim of this study was to determine the areas that can be cluster together based on several air pollution substances. Three clustering algorithm namely as Expectation Maximization (EM), Density Based (DB) and *k*-mean were applied on the training dataset.

Related Works
i. Air Quality Analysis
Air is one of the most important elements for the existence of life on this world. However, an environmental problem such as air pollution could give negative impacts on human health and environment. Atmospheric pollution affects all societies; no matter the level of socioeconomic development they have where finally a large impact on human health (Cortina–Januchs et al., 2015). Generally, the level of air pollutions at industry and urban areas are increasing because of pollutant emission from factories, residential areas, and transportation into the atmosphere. Bishoi et al. (2009) stated that air pollution is a well-known environmental issue linked with ur-ban areas around the world. Saddek et al. (2014) shows that Fuzzy Inference System (FIS) can be a useful method for health effect identification and development of early warning systems to curb the nature of risk disease according to the Air Quality Index (AQI). Recent study by Ehsanzadeh et al. (2015), proved that Classification and Regression Tree algorithm (CART) method can be used to make decision and solve problem of air quality management better. Their main objective in this study is to imitate hourly air quality

ISBN: 978-1-387-00704-2

index through CART method using air pollutants and meteorological variables. They obtained the data of measured variables that are based on hourly slots throughout the year of 2007 and 2008 at the Gholhak monitoring station.

ii. Clustering Algorithms

A study conducted by Ghosh and Dubey (2013) found that Fuzzy C-Means clustering produces close results to K-Means clustering but it still needs more calculation time than K-Means clustering. Similarly to another study conducted by Bora and Gupta (2014) reported that K-Mean performance is better than Fuzzy C-Mean performance regarding computational time. They also conclude that K-Means algorithm is suitable for exclusive clustering task; meanwhile, Fuzzy C-Means is suitable for overlapping clustering task.

Whilst, Cibeci and Yildiz (2015) conducted a study to compare the competence of K-Means and Fuzzy C-Means algorithms on synthetically created datasets consisting of differently shaped clusters scattering with regular and non-regular patterns in two-dimensional space. As a nutshell, they conclude that there is no any algorithm, which is the best for all cases. Therefore, in order to determine for a suitable algorithm, the datasets should be carefully analysed for shapes and scatter of clusters.

In addition, a study conducted by Saithan and Mekparyup (2012), used cluster analysis as an approach to classify numerous variables that are present in the air and to determine the pattern of ozone in Thailand. The data of air quality are from year the 2006 to 2010 and has been obtained from two monitoring stations, which are General Education Centre, Mueang District, Chonburi and Map Ta Phut Health Office, MueangDistrict, Rayong. The result of this study clarifies that four clusters from variables in the air which are air quality variables as cluster 1, pressure as cluster 2, wind speed, temperature and sun radiation as cluster 3 and last cluster are wind direction, relative humidity, and rain. They also demonstrate that there are three different clusters based on the time of the day.

ISBN: 978-1-387-00704-2

Methodology

i.   Data Collection

The data for this study obtained from Department of Environment collected from 37 monitoring sites in Peninsular Malaysia during 2013 to 2015 summarized in Figure 1. Five types of air quality substances namely carbon monoxide (*CO*), ozone (*O3*), sulphur dioxide (*SO2*), nitrogen dioxide (*NO2*) and suspended particulate matter of less than 10 microns in size (*PM10*) which believed contributed to the pollutants were used in this study.

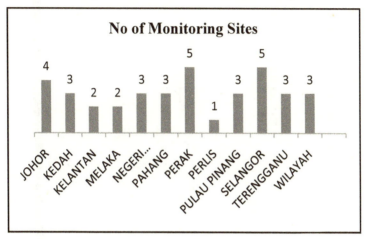

Figure 1: Total Monitoring Site

ii.   Expectation Maximization (EM) Clustering Algorithm

Steps:

1. Initialization:

   Randomly select initial parameters of k distributions.
2. Iteration:

   E-step:

   i.   Compute the $P(Ci|x)$ for all objects x by using the current parameters of the distributions.

   ii. Re-label all objects according to the computed probabilities.

   M-step:

ISBN: 978-1-387-00704-2

      i.   Re-estimate the parameters of the distribution to maximize the likelihood of the objects assuming their current labelling.

3. Stopping Criteria:

At convergence-when the change in log-likelihood after each iteration becomes small.

4. Repeat:

Repeat the step 2 until the stopping condition occurs.

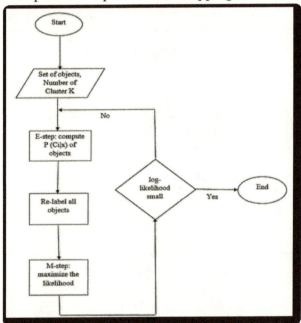

Figure 2: Flowchart for EM Algorithm Process

iii. Density Based (DB)Clustering Algorithm

In density-based clustering algorithms, dense areas of objects in the data space are considered as clusters, which are separated by low-density area (noise). Therefore, density-based is an impressive basic clustering algorithm for data streams (Karrar and Mutasim, 2016).

ISBN: 978-1-387-00704-2

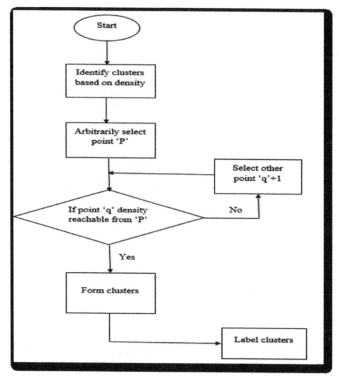

Figure 3: Flowchart for Density-Based Algorithm Process

iv. K-means (KM) Clustering Algorithm

Step 1: Decide the number of clusters k

Assume that there are two variables of dataset. Each variable will have n data points $x_i, i = 1,2,...,n$ that have to be divided into parts in k clusters. The number of clusters should fit the data. An inaccurate selection of the number of clusters will invalidate the entire process.

Step 2: Initialize the center of the clusters

Initialize the data points that have been clustered and calculate the mean of that cluster to choose k starting points, which are used as initial estimates of the cluster centroids. They are taken as the initial starting values $\mu_1, \mu_2, ..., \mu_k \in \mathbb{R}^n$ randomly.

ISBN: 978-1-387-00704-2

Step 3: Attribute the closest cluster to each data point

Consider each point in the dataset and assign it to the cluster, which its centroid is nearest to it. Assign each point by calculating the distance between data point and initial cluster centroid by using square Euclidean distance measure. Based on square Euclidean distance, each data point is assigned to one of the clusters, which are based on minimum distance. For square Euclidean distance is calculated as:

$$d_{ik} = \sum_{j=1}^{n} (x_{ij} - x_{kj})^2,$$

(1)

Where d_{ik} is the distance between variables x_{ij} and x_{kj} and j is the number of variables which are $j = 1, 2, ..., n$

Step 4: Recalculate cluster centers by finding mean of data points belonging to the same cluster

When each point in dataset has been assigned to its cluster, recalculate the new positions of the cluster centroids. Assign new position of the cluster centroids based on minimum Euclidean distance and update them to the same cluster.

Step 5: Repeat steps 3 and 4 until all the data points are convergence

The steps of 3 and 4 needed to be repeated until the cluster centroids no longer move and not change.

ISBN: 978-1-387-00704-2

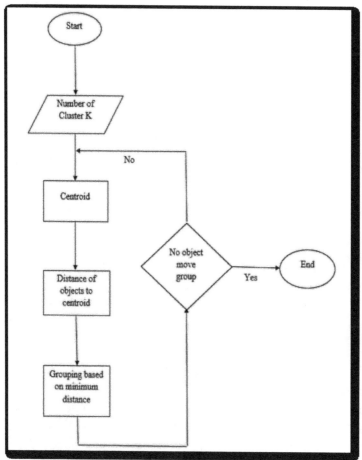

Figure 4: Flowchart for K-Means Algorithm Process

v. Knowledge Flow using WEKA

The data pre-processing and data mining was performed using the WEKA Data Mining tool. Figure 5 shows the data mining process to perform the cluster analysis. The process is started by loading the dataset using *CSV Loader*. The dataset was then split by default into 66% of training and 34% of test using *Train Test Split Maker*. Three cluster algorithm mentions previously were then applied. The performance for each algorithm were evaluate using *Clusterer Performance Evaluator* and the result will be view using *Text Viewer*

ISBN: 978-1-387-00704-2

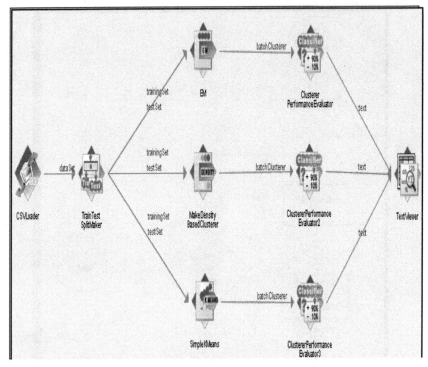

Figure5: Building Cluster using WEKA

Results

The summary of the analysis was presented in table 1. The output was summarized based on the model and evaluation of the test split. *K-means* and DB algorithm is much better than EM algorithm in time to build the model. Using log- likelihood value, DB Clusters have a negative value that does not show its perfection in results.

Every algorithm has their own importance and we use them on the behaviour of the data, but based on this study we found that *k*-means clustering algorithm is the simplest algorithm as compared to other algorithms due to its simplicity and shortest time to build the model. Figure 6 to 8 visualized the cluster formed by the algorithm. For the purposes of illustration, only two attributes were chosen, which is ozone (*O3*) versus nitrogen dioxide (*NO2*).

ISBN: 978-1-387-00704-2

Table 1: Comparisons of algorithm

Algorithm	No of cluster	Log likelihood	Clustered instances					Time to build model
			0	1	2	3	4	
EM	5	2.2593	102 (23 %)	90 (20 %)	100 (22 %)	114 (25 %)	47 (10 %)	12.29 second
DB	2	-0.1331	309 (68 %)	144 (32 %)				0.02 second
k-means	2		304 (67 %)	149 (33 %)				0.02 second

Figure 6. Selected Cluster Visualization using EM (O3 vs N02)

ISBN: 978-1-387-00704-2

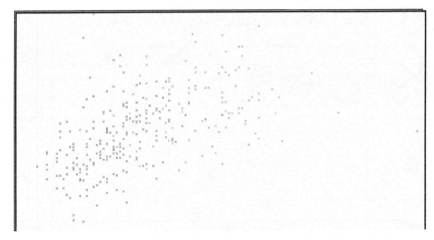

Figure 7:. Selected Cluster Visualization using DB (O3 vs NO2)

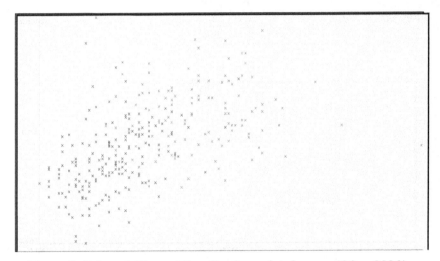

Figure 8: Selected Cluster Visualization using *k-mean* (O3 vs NO2)

Conclusion

As a conclusion, cluster analysis is able to cluster the area based on substances in air quality index. There are several algorithms for cluster analysis that can be applied to the dataset of air quality index. In this study, K-Means clustering algorithm, Expectation Maximization (EM) clustering algorithm and Density-based clustering algorithm have been applied in the dataset of air quality index using WEKA tools for cluster the area based on air quality's substances.

ISBN: 978-1-387-00704-2

The results of this study showed that the area that can be clustered together based on air quality through their fives substances. The output of K-means clustering algorithm shows that it can cluster the area into two clusters, which are cluster 0 and cluster 1. Cluster 0 has clustered 16 sites of the monitoring station and cluster 1 has clustered 36 sites of monitoring station in Peninsular Malaysia. From the WEKA's result, it can conclude that K-means clustering algorithm is the best method among other algorithms due to its simplicity and time took to build the model.

Acknowledgements

The authors would like to express our gratitude to Department of Environment for the data courtesy.

References

Bishoi, B., Prakash, A., & Jain, V. K. (2009).A comparative study of air quality index based on factor analysis and US-EPA methods for an urban environment. *Aerosol and Air Quality Research, 9*(1), 1-17.

Saddek, B., Chahra, B., Wafa, B. C., &Souad, B. (2014). Air quality index and public health: modelling using Fuzzy Inference System. *American Journal of Environmental Engineering and Science,1*(4), 85-89.

Ehsanzadeh, A., Nejadkoorki, F., Talebi, A., &Bahrami, S. (2015). Simulating hourly air quality index using the classification and regression tree (CART).*International Conference on Architecture, Urbanism, Civil Engineering, Art, Environment. Future Horizons & Retrospect ICAUCAE 2015* (pp. 1-8). Tehran, Iran: Institute of Art and Architecture (SID).

Ghosh, S., & Dubey, K. S. (2013).Comparative analysis of K-Means and Fuzzy C-Means algorithms.*International Journal of Advanced Computer Science and Applications, 4*(4), 35-39.

Bora, D. J., & Gupta, A. K. (2014).A comparative study between Fuzzy Clustering Algorithm and Hard Clustering Algorithm. *International Journal of Computer Trends and Technology (IJCTT), 10*(2), 108-113.

Cibeci, Z., &Yildiz, F. (2015).Comparison of K-Means and Fuzzy C-Means algorithms on different cluster structures.*Journal of Agricultural Informatic, 6*(3), 13-23.

Saithan, K., &Mekparyup, J. (2012). Clustering of air quality and meteorological variables associated with high ground ozone concentration in the industrial areas, at the east of Thailand. *International Journal of Pure and Applied Mathematics, 81*(3), 505-515.

ISBN: 978-1-387-00704-2

Karrar, A. E., &Mutasim, M. (2016). Comparing EM clustering algorithm with density based clustering algorithm using weka tool. *International Journal of Science and Research (IJSR), 5*(7), 1199-1201.

ISBN: 978-1-387-00704-2

Article 7

Forecasting the Financial Times Stock Exchange Bursa Malaysia Kuala Lumpur Composite Index Using Geometric Brownian Motion

Teoh Yeong Kin, Suzanawati Abu Hasan, Nashni Hamdan
Faculty of Computer and Mathematical Sciences,
UniversitiTeknologi MARA Cawangan Perlis Branch, Malaysia

Abstract
In Malaysia, Financial Times Stock Exchange (FTSE) of Bursa Malaysia Kuala Lumpur Composite Index (FBMKLCI) provides charts, companies' profile and other market data to help the local and foreign investors to make decisions involving their investments. Until now, there have been a lot of investors who faced losses due to making wrong investments at wrong times. The objective of this study is to forecast FBMKLCI for a one-month period using different periods of data. Besides, this study finds the suitable length of period when the forecasted values are the most accurate for FBMKLCI. Geometric Brownian motion (GBM) of stochastic calculus is used to predict the future indices. The results showed that the forecasted FBMKLCI needed 1 to 20 weeks of input data to come out with the best values. The forecasted FBMKLCI will only be accurate within 4 weeks; after that the values will diverge. Since the average value of MAPE for eight different forecasted values is 1.54%, GBM can be used to predict the future FBMKLCI.

Keywords: FTSE, FBMKLCI, geometric Brownian motion, MAPE

Introduction

The 21st century is a challenging new era for the world of investment market. The growth of the international market has opened opportunities for investors to involve in the stock market, share prices and bonds. Due to the expansion of open market, the demands for accurate future market prices are high in order to achieve higher profits within a reasonable risk.

Nikkei 225 (NKY), Hong Kong Hang Seng Index (HKHSI), NASDAQ Composite Index (NASDAQCI), Dow Jones Industrial Average (INDU) and EURO STOXX 50 Price EUR are among the main world indices. World stock indices can be searched using Bloomberg website (BLOOMBERG L. P, 2012).

ISBN: 978-1-387-00704-2

The future of stock prices are uncertain and unpredictable but there must be a model that can be derived from past data (Sengupta, 2004). In this study, we focused on geometric Brownian motion (GBM) method of stochastic calculus to forecast the future indices. The model was tested by using the data from FBMKLCI in order to evaluate the accuracy of forecasted indices compared to the actual indices. GBM is commonly used for modeling in finance (Vose Software, 2007). GBM is used to forecast the future market prices and numerous researches have been done with several modifications such as by Ladde and Wu (2009) and Gajda and Wylomanska (2012).

The remainder of this paper is set out as follows: Section (2) explains the data and research method used to test the GBM model and forecast the future indices. Section (3) presents the findings of the paper, and section (4) concludes and presents areas for future research.

Data and Research Method

i.   Procedure of forecasting the world indices
The procedure involved in the analysis of FBMKLCI is described generally through the flowchart in Figure 1.

ISBN: 978-1-387-00704-2

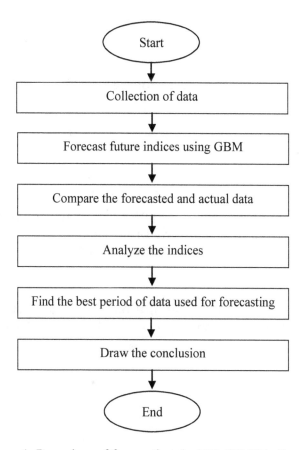

Figure 1: Procedure of forecasting the FBMKLCI indices

ii.   Data collection

Data from FBMKLCI was obtained from Bursa Malaysia official website (Bursa Malaysia,   2013). The data was standardized and the closing prices of the counters were collected daily   for   a 24-week period from 1 August 2012 to 31 January 2013. The 20-week data from   1 August 2012 to 31 December 2012 was used to forecast the next 4 weeks. The forecast   indices   were compared with the actual indices in the month of January 2013.

ISBN: 978-1-387-00704-2

iii. Steps in research method

Step 1: Application of GBM

Equation 1 below is used to forecast the future indices in this study:

$$S(t) = S(0)\, e^{\left(\mu - \frac{1}{2}\sigma^2\right)t + \sigma[X(t) - X(0)]} \tag{1}$$

where, the stochastic process $S(t)$ is the index value at time t and $X(t)$ is the random value at   time t. The index value at time t, $S(t)$ is followed by a geometric Brownian motion if it satisfies the stochastic differential equation to forecast the future index value at specific time, t.

According to Willmott (2007), if S_i is the asset value on the ith day, then the return from day i to $i + 1$ is given by equation 2 below:

$$R_i = \frac{S_{i+1} - S_i}{S_i} \tag{2}$$

The drift of the index, μ is shown in the following equation 3:

$$\mu = \overline{R} = \frac{1}{M} \sum_{i=1}^{M} R_i \tag{3}$$

where, M is the number of data sample. The volatility of the index, σ can be calculated   using   the   standard   deviation formula. In this study, the log volatility is used because the indices data obtained were limited to closing values. The log volatility formula is shown in equation 4 below:

$$\sigma = \sqrt{\frac{1}{(m-1)\partial t} \sum_{i=1}^{M} \left[log\, S(t_i) - log\, S(t_{i-1}) \right]^2} \tag{4}$$

ISBN: 978-1-387-00704-2

Step 2: Comparison between forecasted value and actual value

MAPE method is used to compare the forecasted value and the actual value for each period. The error can be calculated using the following equation 5:

$$\varepsilon = \frac{1}{n} \sum_{d=1}^{n} \frac{\left| X_A - X_P \right|}{X_A}$$

(5)

where, n is the number of days, X_A is an actual value of indices and X_p is a predicted value of indices. Table 1 below shows the scale judgement of forecast accuracy (Lawrence et al., 2000).

Table 1: A scale of judgement of forecast accuracy

MAPE	Judgement of Forecast Accuracy
$\varepsilon < 10\%$	Highly accurate
$10\% \leq \varepsilon < 20\%$	Good
$20\% \leq \varepsilon < 50\%$	Reasonable
$\varepsilon \geq 51\%$	Inaccurate

Step 3: Analysis of indices

The value of MAPE was analyzed based on the scale of judgement as shown in Table 1.

Step 4: Determination of best period of data

Each period input data was compared and the most accurate forecasted data was determined. The accurate length of each period was determined by the smallest value of MAPE.

Step 5: Making conclusion

The conclusion was drawn based on the objective of the study.

ISBN: 978-1-387-00704-2

Results and Discussion

In this study, Forecast 1 to Forecast 8 represented the forecasted indices using 1 to 20 months of input data to produce 1 to 4 weeks of output data. Table 2 shows the different length of input data used by each forecast.

Table 2: Different length of input data used by each forecast.

No.	Length of input data
Forecast 1	20 weeks
Forecast 2	16 weeks
Forecast 3	12 weeks
Forecast 4	8 weeks
Forecast 5	4 weeks
Forecast 6	3 weeks
Forecast 7	2 weeks
Forecast 8	1 week

Table 3 below shows the MAPE values of FBMKLCI for four different lengths of output data and for all 8 different forecasted values.

Table 3: Comparison of MAPE for FBMKLCI

No.	MAPE 4 weeks of output data	MAPE 3 weeks of output data	MAPE 2 weeks of output data	MAPE 1 week of output data
Forecast 1	1.01%	0.70%	0.57%	0.83%
Forecast 2	1.01%	0.77%	0.64%	0.94%
Forecast 3	1.04%	0.84%	0.71%	1.05%
Forecast 4	1.17%	1.00%	0.88%	1.33%
Forecast 5	1.66%	1.43%	1.25%	1.93%
Forecast 6	1.97%	1.68%	1.43%	2.23%
Forecast 7	2.43%	2.08%	1.72%	2.69%
Forecast 8	3.48%	2.89%	2.30%	3.64%

ISBN: 978-1-387-00704-2

From the result, three conclusions can be drawn. First, comparison of all Forecast 1 to Forecast 8 shows that Forecast 1 has the lowest MAPE values. Therefore, we can conclude that the more data we used, the higher accuracy of forecasted values was observed. Second, comparison of MAPE values from 1 week to 4 weeks of output data shows that 2 weeks of the output data has the lowest MAPE values and we can conclude that the forecasted value is most accurate within 2 weeks. Third, the lowest MAPE value is 0.57%. It shows that 20 weeks of input data and 2 weeks of output data produced the lowest MAPE value. For general conclusion, the longer the period of data used, the higher the accuracy of the forecasted value for the next 2 weeks.

Conclusion and Recommendations

This study used geometric Brownian motion model to predict the future FBMKLCI. The findings were encouraging as results show that the MAPE values for FBMKLCI are small, which is less than 10% as shown in Table 3. This observation is very useful to understand the importance of GBM in prediction. MAPE plays a significant role in analyzing the forecasted and actual data. It helps identify the length of input data needed in forecasting. It also provides information on the accuracy of forecasted values.

Future research involving data from other major countries may yield different results. Larger data would improve the accuracy of the indices. It would be interesting to compare the accuracy of GBM model with other models such as residual income model (RIM) in predicting the future indices.

References

Bloomberg, L. P. (2012). *World stock index.* Retrieved from
   http://www.bloomberg.com/markets/stocks/world-indexes/
Bursa Malaysia. (2013). *Indices.* Retrieved from
   http://www.bursamalaysia.com/market/securities/equities/indices/
Gajda, J., & Wylomanska, A. (2012). Geometric Brownian motion with tempered stable waiting times. *Journal of Statistical Physics, 148*(2), 742-752.
Ladde, G., & Wu, L. (2009). Development of modified geometric Brownian motion models by using stock price data and basic statistics. *Nonlinear Analysis, 71*(12), e1203-e1208.

ISBN: 978-1-387-00704-2

Lawrence, M., O'Connor, M., &Edmunson, B. (2000). A field study of scale forecasting accuracy and processes. *European Journal of Operational Research, 122*, 151-160.

Sengupta, C. (2004). *Financial modelling using Excel and VBA*. New Jersey, United States: John Wiley & Sons.

Vose Software. (2007). *Geometric Brownian motion model.* Retrieved from: http://www.vosesoftware.com/ModelRiskHelp/index.htm#Time_series/Geometric_Brownian_Motion_models.htm.

Willmott, P. (2007). *Paul Willmott introduces quantitative finance*, Second Edition, Chichester: John Wiley & Sons.

ISBN: 978-1-387-00704-2

Article 8

A Linear Programming Approach to Optimize Natural Rubber Production

Sarimah Baharudin, Noraini Noordin
Faculty of Computer and Mathematical Sciences,
Universiti Teknologi MARA Perlis Branch, Malaysia

Abstract
This article describes the design of a linear programming model to optimize production of natural rubber in Malaysia. Uptrend in natural rubber production which occurred after 2015 did not last long. Area for rubber cultivation was not only affected by efforts to convert rubber estates into real estate developments but also by factors such as increase in farmers' interest to cultivate oil palm, unstable rubber price, lengthy duration of low rubber price, insufficient number of rubber tappers, long waiting time before tapping rubber trees, changing land conditions for crops, and buyout offers for rubber wood from furniture-manufacturing factories. Results from two different software, namely Excel Solver and QM for Windows were compared. No significant difference in value was observed to take place, thus the development of linear programming model was considered to be successful.

Keywords:attractive corners, constraint, feasible region, linear programming, optimization

Introduction

Malaysia is ranked fifth as a world producer of rubber. When the new economic policies were introduced in 1971, the industry generated RM1.74 billion in the export values. In the year 2013, the values of export had increased to RM33.7 billion. Natural rubber (NR) will continue to function as a strategic crop due to the interest of industry to manufacture rubber-based products. The use of rubber material is expected to continue growing rapidly within the country and also globallybased on projection of Malaysia's economic structure by TN50 (Malaysian Rubber Board, 2011). Rubber product industry in Malaysia includes latex product, tyre, tyre-related products and shoes. As a result of an increase in domestic downstream rubber, domestic consumption of rubber has increased from 419,000 tons in 2000 to 434,000 tons in 2013, 87% of which are latex products. The

ISBN: 978-1-387-00704-2

first sets of outputs of latex productsincluded gloves, condom, catheters and rubber thread (Eng, 2001).

Uptrend in rubber production began in 2015. Production of natural rubber increased by 36.8%, namely from 14,367 tons (May 2015) to 53,383 tons (June 2015). This volume increased further by 41.4% to 124.6 kilogram per hectare. However, only approximately 1.45 % change was observed in the volume change at the end of 2014 to early 2015 (Department of Statistics Malaysia, 2016). Interestingly, the average monthly price for latex was observed to have increased by 10.9% to 496.52 cent per kilogram in June 2015 (Natural Rubber Statistics, 2016). This increasing trend did not last. Natural rubber production dropped by 4% to 45,279 tons from June 2016 to July 2016 (Department of Statistics Malaysia, 2016). The drop in natural rubber production was affected by the loss of rubber estates which were transformed into real estate developments or oil palm plantations.

The area for rubber cultivation wasalso seen shrinking due to factors such as more farmers' interest to cultivate oil palm, rubber prices were unstable and have been in the low for a long period, insufficient number of rubber tappers, long waiting time before tapping rubber trees, changing land conditions for crops, and buyout offersfor rubber wood from furniture-manufacturing factories (Federal Land Development Authority, 2014). Hence, the constraints affecting planting areas of natural rubber should be maximized in order to optimize the natural rubber production.

Use of Models for Optimizing Crop Production
The discussion in this section is divided according to two themes: i) use of models for optimizing crop production and ii) use of POM-QM for Windows.

iii. Use of Models for Optimizing Crop Production
Table 1 displays several research works at optimizing production of crops such as natural rubber, sugar cane, and watermelon included the use of goal programming, Artificial Neural Network (ANN), linear programming and forecasting.

ISBN: 978-1-387-00704-2

Table 1: Previous works at optimization of crop production

Author (year)	Findings
Hassan et al. (2013)	Goal programming approach method was used to maximize rubber production and planted areas of rubber. Goal programming deals with the multiple objectives decision-making problems. In this research, two objectives were developed to optimize the rubber planted areas and its production. A decision variable that was considered was the rubber planted area in hectares. The findings indicated that rubber production can be increased by increasing the planting area.
Obe and Shangodoyin(2010)	ANN model was developed in this study to forecast sugar cane production in Nigeria. The performance of the ANN model was measured using the Mean Squared Error (MSE), Normalized Mean Squared Error (NMSE), correlation coefficient (r), Akaike's Information Criterion (AIC) and Minimum Description Length (MDL). Results obtained showed that 85.70 % accuracy was obtained by ANN at predicting sugar cane production output.
Urrutia et al. (2002)	The research was conducted in Candaba, Pampanga. Linear programming model was developed to maximize the profit of small-scale farmers in the production of watermelon and melon. Constraints considered were budgets for seeds, plant operating expenses, delivery requirements or demands in the market and the area of planting field. Results showed maximum revenue of PHP 701,340 was obtained by planting 7,284 seeds of watermelon and 2,584 seeds of melon.

The suitable method for this case study is linear programming because there are similarities with previous works and it focuses only on a single linear objective function.

iv. Use of POM-QM for Windows
Linear programming calculations in this case study have used Excel Solver. QM for Windows has been chosen here to validate the answers obtained. According to Weiss (2011), POM-QM for Windows provides mathematical analysis for Operations Management, Quantitative methods, or Management Science. It

ISBN: 978-1-387-00704-2

also features calculation methods for PERT/CPM, Linear Programming, Decision Analysis, Transportation problem, Statistical functions, Game Theory, Goal Programming, etc. Excel Solver uses a series of rules and computations to optimize a solution and the rules can be adjusted by the user. On the contrary, QM is designed specifically for equations. It will return optimum values for correctly defined equations.

Methodology

According to Fah (2011), data analysis is the process of compiling the data collected and the data is then divided into units that are simpler to facilitate in interpretation. In this study, data collected is categorized according to Malaysia's natural rubber consumption and production of natural rubber per area. The data is stored and solved using Excel solver and Quantitative Method (QM) software. A 10-year time series data from 2006 to 2015 was obtained from Malaysian Rubber Board. The objective function of the linear programming used to maximize the production of natural rubber is given below:

$$\text{Maximize: } Z = \sum_{i=1}^{n} c_i X_i = c_1 X_1 + c_2 X_2$$

where:

X_1 = Malaysia's natural rubber consumption

X_2 = production of natural rubber per area

c_1 = the profit of using X_1

c_2 = the profit of using X_2

subject to:

$a_{j,i} X_1 \leq b_j$

$a_{j,i} X_2 \leq b_j$

$X_1, X_2 \geq 0$ (Non-negativity conditions)

where:

$a_{j,i}$ = the amount of resource j used for each unit of activity

b_j = total amount of resource j

ISBN: 978-1-387-00704-2

Results and Discussion

Table 2 presents optimum production results from Excel Spreadsheets. In particular, the optimal production of natural rubber per area was found to be6,122,290,544.25 tons.

Table 2: Optimization in Excel

	A	B	C	D	E	F	G
1							
2		Consumption (Tons)	Production per area (Tons/Hectare)	Left Hand Side		Right Hand Side	Slack
3	Objective function	8770	6000	6122290544.25			
4	2006	383,324	1.01586	1036565.01	<=	1,283,632	247,066.99
5	2007	450,246	0.96115	980739.93	<=	1,199,553	218,813.07
6	2008	468,894	0.85994	877467.09	<=	1,072,365	194,897.91
7	2009	468,669	0.83348	850467.79	<=	857,019	6,551.21
8	2010	457,919	0.92048	939241.00	<=	939,241	0.00
9	2011	401,923	0.96998	989749.90	<=	996,210	6,460.10
10	2012	441,398	0.88629	904354.15	<=	922,798	18,443.85
11	2013	434,192	0.78166	797591.60	<=	826,421	28,829.40
12	2014	448,484	0.62743	640218.13	<=	668,613	28,394.87
13	2015	474,773	0.66948	683125.18	<=	722,122	38,996.82
14							
15	Solution Values	0	1020382				

This type of problem can also be solved graphically in the QM software since there are only two variables involved. A graph was drawn with the x-axis and the y-axis representing Malaysia's natural rubber consumption and production of natural rubber per area, respectively. The two constraint lines were plotted by finding the x and y-intercepts for both constraint equations. In particular, Figure 1 displays the constraints specified for this case study as displayed in QM for Windows.

ISBN: 978-1-387-00704-2

Constraint Display

- Max 6000X1+800X2
- 1015.861X1+3611.287X2<=1283632
- 961.149X1+3268.27X2<=1199553
- 859.935X1+2579.723X2<=1072365
- 833.481X1+2689.278X2<=857019
- 920.482X1+1775.369X2<=939241
- 969.982X1+1477.684X2<=996210
- 886.292X1+1937.634X2<=922798
- 781.656X1+2133.58X2<=826421
- 627.434X1+2417.518X2<=668613
- 669.481X1+2755.034X2<=722122
- none

Corner Points		
X1	X2	Z
0	0	0.
1020.38	0	6,122,277.
0	262.11	209,688.
1008.697	6.057086	6,057,028.
845.2786	56.70495	5,117,036.

Figure 1: Constraint Display

The two constraint lines were plotted by finding the x and y-intercepts for both constraint equations.Area on the valid side for all constraint lines is called the feasible region.Since the objective of the study aimedto optimize the natural rubber production to maximize the profit, Z, a line parallel to the objective function lines was drawn and it touched the last point in the feasible solution, as shown in Figure 2. By definition, the most attractive corner is the last point in the feasible solution region touched by a line that is parallel to the objective function lines (Reeb and Leavengood, 1998). This point when identified will give the amounts of natural rubber production that can maximize profit.

ISBN: 978-1-387-00704-2

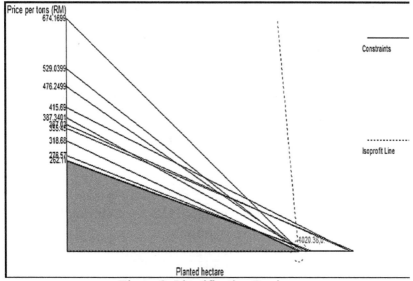

Figure 2: Identification Region

Figure 3 shows the optimum result obtained from production optimization by using QM for Windows. As can be seen, optimal production of natural rubber per area has been given by points $X_1 = 0$ and $X_2 = 1020382$, similar to that found using Excel Solver.

Variable	Status	Value
X1	NONBasic	0
X2	Basic	1020382.0
slack 1	Basic	247067.0
slack 2	Basic	218813.1
slack 3	Basic	194897.9
slack 4	Basic	6551.212
slack 5	NONBasic	0
slack 6	Basic	6460.097
slack 7	Basic	18443.84
slack 8	Basic	28829.37
slack 9	Basic	28394.85
slack 10	Basic	38996.79
Optimal Value (Z)		6122291000

Figure 3: Optimal Solution in QM for Windows

ISBN: 978-1-387-00704-2

Reliable results must be able to replicate the real life system, in this case the natural rubber production (Murugan et al., 2013). As stated earlier on, results in Excel may be subject to errors but QM for Windows will return optimum values for correctly defined equations. A summary of results obtained from using Excel and QM for Windows is given in Table 3. The profits which were closely similar in value (6,122,290,000 tons) were generated by attractive corners assigned to $X_1 = 0$ and $X_2 = 1020382$.

Table 3: Results from Excel and QM for Windows

Variables	Solution by using POM-QM for Windows	Solution by using Excel
X_1	0	0
X_2	1,020,382	1,020,382
Profit	6,122,291,000	6,122,290,544

Conclusion
The result of the proposed model is similar to that generated by QM for Windows software. Thus, this case study has successfully developed a linear programming model which can optimize natural rubber production in Malaysia. Many other constraints may affect production of natural rubber such as conditions of the rubber trees, numbers of workers, climate, import and export of natural rubber, and development of industrial technologies. It is recommended that these factors be taken into consideration in future works in this area.

Acknowledgements
The researchers wish to acknowledge Malaysia Rubber Board for allowing the use of data for this case study.

References
Department of Statistics Malaysia. (2016). Retrieved December 22, 2016, from https://www.dosm.gov.my/
Department of Statistics, Malaysia | Data and Statistics.(2011). Retrieved December 22, 2016, from https://knoema.com/atlas/sources/Department-of-Statistics-Malaysia.

ISBN: 978-1-387-00704-2

Eng, L. O. (2001). Recent advances in the Malaysia's glove industry in meeting today's healthcare challenges. Latex 2001 Conference Munich Germany, 4-5.

Fah, L. C. V. (2011). Refleksipembelajarantentangteknikmenganalisis data dalampelaksanaanpenyelidikantindakanbertajuk "penggunaan combo set dalammembantu murid tahuntigamenjawabsoalan long division". JurnalPenyelidikanTindakan IPG KBL, 5, 15.

Federal Land Development Authority. (2014). Retrieved June 16, 2017, from http://www.usahawan.com/umum/felda-dan-penanaman-getah.html/

Hassan, N., Hamzah, H. H. M., & Zain, S. M. M. (2013). A goal programming approach for rubber production in Malaysia. American-Eurasian Journal of Sustainable Agriculture, 7(2), 53, 50-53.

Reeb, J., &Leavengood, S. (1998). Using the graphical method to solve linear programs.Perfomance Excellence in the Wood Products Industry, 1-24.

Malaysian Rubber Board - Towards Sustaining the Viability of the Malaysian Rubber Industry. (2011). Retrieved December 22, 2016, from http://www.lgm.gov.my/

Murugan, S., Choo, J. K., &Sihombing, H. (2013).Linear programming for palm oil industry. International Journal of Humanities and Management Sciences (IJHMS), 1(3), 184-187.

Natural Rubber Statistics (2016, March 11). Retrieved December 20, 2016, from http://www.lgm.gov.my/

Obe, O. O. and Shangodoyin, D., K. (2010). Artificial Neural Network based model for forecasting sugar cane production. Journal of Computer Science, 6(4), 439-445.

Urrutia, J. D., Gayo, W. S., &Malvar, R. J. (2014).Optimization of the productions of watermelon and melon in Candaba, Pampanga. The Countryside Development Research Journal, 2(32), 25-31.

Weiss, H.J. (2011). POM for Windows, Pearson Education Inc.

ISBN: 978-1-387-00704-2

Article 9

Applying Fuzzy Analytical Hierarchy Process to Evaluate and Select the Best Car between Domestic and Imported Cars in Malaysia

Wan Nurshazelin Wan Shahidan, NazatulNaziraSu'if
Faculty of Computer and Mathematical Sciences,
University of Technology Mara Perlis Branch, Malaysia

Abstract
Malaysian are more selective in purchasing cars. Due to that, more than one criterion becomes effective on making decision on purchasing an automobile. This study does not only attempt to select the best car between domestic and imported cars in Malaysia market but at the same time also tries to compare the important criteria that purchaser need to consider and to rank the sub-criteria in order to purchase a car in Malaysia. The data for the study has been collected from four respondents through the use of structured questionnaires. The methodology of this study is by using Fuzzy Analytical Hierarchy (FAHP) Method. In addition by stating the steps of Fuzzy AHP clearly and numerically, this study can be a guide of the methodology to be implemented to other multiple criteria decision making problems.

Keywords: fuzzy analytic hierarchy process, multi criteria decision making, car selection, decision analysis, fuzzy logic

Introduction

Car industry has an important role in the lives of people. In today's competitive world, chances of survival of an institution are related to continually providing its customers satisfaction and to attain their loyalty and support. Diversity in car production persuades the buyer and customer to make a selection of human life. Among various products, buying cars is more sensitive because it deals with health and safety issues of the buyer. For the average Malaysian consumer, with this arising cost of living, the purchasing power has decrease in term of what one can afford to buy.

Malaysians are more selective in purchasing car either domestic or imported cars. Consumer behaviour is fairly complex as car

ISBN: 978-1-387-00704-2

purchase decision involves high level of social, psychological and financial involvement (Shenda, 2014). Purchasing a new car is regarded as a decision making problem and a reflection of customer's preference. Buying expensive goods, hazardous, rarely, and very self-expressive items such as automobiles, its need involvement from customer due to the noteworthy contrasts between brands.So, before someone purchases a brand new car, they must consider taking a look at their finance and options.However, Malaysians demand toward branded cars is high and some even forget to look at the important criteria before purchasing domestic or imported cars.

In Malaysia, selecting the best car among domestic and imported brand cars is one of the most complicated decisions to make among the purchaser. It is due to involvement of multi-criteria decision making in order to purchase car either domestic brands or imported car brands. In this case, if they decide too hastily, it can be hazardous and delaying too long might mean missed opportunities. In the end, it is crucial for people to make up their mind. Tan and Govindan (2014) stated that Malaysian buyers make their own choice and judgments based on their own preferences and personal requirements to purchase a car. This problem, can be a multi criteria decision making (MCDM) problem.

MCDM is a way of dealing with complex problems by breaking the problems into smaller pieces. In recent years, several MCDM techniques and approaches have been suggested in choosing the optimal probable options.Martin et al. (2013) stated that MCDM method spicks the best choices where numerous criteria appeared, as well as expected to be acquired by breaking down the diverse extent of the criteria, weights for the criteria and after that pick the ideal ones utilizing any multi criteria decision making procedures.There are many methods to solve MCDM that have been developed to support the buyers in their unique and personal decision process, especially in selecting the best car case. Methods that have been develop by past researchers such as FAHP, Technique for Order Preference by Similarity to Ideal

ISBN: 978-1-387-00704-2

Solution (TOPSIS), TOPSIS Fuzzy logic, and Fuzzy Analytic Network Process (FANP) are also used in order to select the best car. The FAHP is used due to this method helps the decision makers to select a better alternative from all by satisfying the minimal score to rank each decision alternative based on how well each alternative meets them. (Tiryaki and Ahlatcioglu, 2008).Other than that, FAHP also provides a simple and very flexible model for a given problem and provides an easy applicable decision making methodology that assist the decision maker to precisely decide the judgments. More than that, FAHP relies on the judgments if experts from different backgrounds.

Therefore, the main focus or the problem can be evaluated easily from different aspects. This study is mapped as the literature is reviewed according to the different criteria and methods used for selection of the best car in the second part. Part 2 explains the Fuzzy AHP method in detail which is utilized to solve the best car selection in Malaysia elaborated as a case study in the fourth part. Part 4 presents the conclusion and directs for further steps of this study with the references following.

Fuzzy Analytical Hierarchy Process (FAHP)
FAHP is one of the methods to MCDM in selecting the best car. FAHP is the fuzzy extension of AHP and was developed to solve the hierarchical fuzzy problems. FAHP is one of the most convenient methodologies to evaluate transportation issues. First of all, any selection or decision issue consists of various criteria. Frequently these criteria have sub-criteria as well. In this case, the criteria that have to be taken into consideration are quite many. Either objective or subjective considerations or either quantitative or qualitative information can be evaluated with FAHP technique. In this case, three criteria which are safety, performance and economic assumptions and ten sub-criteria which are price, fuel consumption, air bags, ABS brake, alarm systems, breaking ability, engine power, maximum speed, noise, and comfort will be evaluated in this study in order to select the best car in Malaysia market. The main frame for selection of the

ISBN: 978-1-387-00704-2

best car model is summarised in a hierarchy structure as shown in Figure 1.

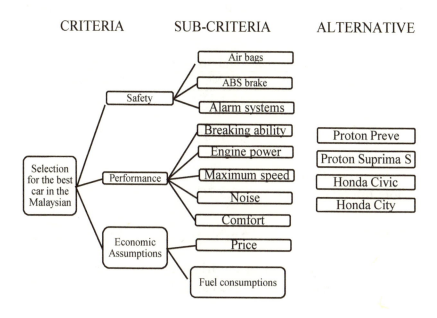

Figure 1: Hierarchical structure of selecting the best car

The main objective of this study is to compare and select the best car in between domestic and imported car in Malaysian market. Meanwhile, the specific objectives for this study are to determine what important criteria that purchasers need to consider when purchasing car. Besides that, this case study also to ranking the sub-criteria in order to purchasing a car in Malaysia and to determine the best model of car with respect to each sub-criterion.

Questionnaires were designed on criteria of car selection to be asked to four experts who are knowledgeable on automobiles industry in Malaysia. They need to give details on domestic brand (Proton) and imported brand (Honda). Data were analysed using Microsoft Excel 2007. There are eight steps involved in this method. The steps of the procedure are as follow:

ISBN: 978-1-387-00704-2

Step 1: The Triangular Fuzzy Numbers (TFNs) used in pair wise comparison have been refer to Tolga et al. (2005), the one that seems to corresponds better to the preference scale of crisp AHP is as summarized in Table 1.

Table 1: Linguistic scales and fuzzy scales for importance

Linguistic scale	TFNs	Reciprocal TFNs
Equally important (EI)	(1,1,1)	(1,1,1)
Very Unimportant (VU)	(2/3,1,3/2)	(2/3,1,3/2)
Less Important (LI)	(3/2,2,5/2)	(2/5,1/2,2/3)
More Important (MI)	(5/2,3,7/2)	(2/7,1/3,2/5)
Very Important (VI)	(7/2,4,9/2)	(2/9,1/4,2/7)

Step 2: The development of the triangular fuzzy scale for pair-wise comparison matrices are used as follows.

Table 2: The pair-wise comparison matrix of the expert's evaluation

	$\widetilde{A}_1^k$	$\widetilde{A}_2^k$	$\widetilde{A}_3^k$	$\widetilde{A}_n^k$
$\widetilde{A}_1^k$	(1,1,1)	$\widetilde{e}_{12}^k$	$\widetilde{e}_{13}^k$	$\widetilde{e}_{1n}^k$
$\widetilde{A}_2^k$	$\widetilde{e}_{21}^k$	(1,1,1)	$\widetilde{e}_{23}^k$	$\widetilde{e}_{2n}^k$
$\widetilde{A}_3^k$	$\widetilde{e}_{31}^k$	$\widetilde{e}_{32}^k$	(1,1,1)	$\widetilde{e}_{3n}^k$
$\widetilde{A}_n^k$	$\widetilde{e}_{n1}^k$	$\widetilde{e}_{n2}^k$	$\widetilde{e}_{n3}^k$	(1,1,1)

Where $\widetilde{A}_n^k$ = criteria, sub-criteria and alternatives, and $\widetilde{e}_{ij}^k$ indicates the kth expert's preference of ith criterion over j^{th} criterion, via fuzzy triangular numbers.

The operation on TFNs can be calculated in addition, multiplication, and inverse. Suppose M_1 and M_2 are Triangular Fuzzy Scale where $M_1 = (l_1, m_1, u_1)$ and $M_2 = (l_2, m_2, u_2)$, the basic operations are given by Equations (1) to Equation (3).

ISBN: 978-1-387-00704-2

Addition: $\tilde{M}_1 \oplus \tilde{M}_2 = (l_1 + l_2, m_1 + m_2, u_1 + u_2)$ (1)

Multiplication: $\tilde{M}_1 \otimes \tilde{M}_2 = (l_1.l_2, m_1.m_2, u_1.u_2)$ (2)

Inverse: $\tilde{M}_1^{-1} = \left(\dfrac{1}{u_1}, \dfrac{1}{m_1}, \dfrac{1}{l_1}\right)$ (3)

Step 3: After collecting the fuzzy judgement matrices from all experts, the matrices can be aggregated by using fuzzy geometric mean method of Buckley (1985).

$$\tilde{r}_i = \left(\prod_{j=1}^{n} \tilde{e}_{ij}\right)^{\frac{1}{n}} \quad , \quad i = 1,2,\ldots,n \text{ where } \tilde{e}_{ij} = \dfrac{\sum_{k=1}^{K} \tilde{e}_{ij}^{k}}{K} ,$$

Where, $K=4$ (4)

Step 4:

Then, the reverse power of vector summation $(vs)^{-1}$ was computed. Next, replace the triangular fuzzy number to arrange it in an increasing order.

$$(vs)^{-1} = \left(\sum_{i=1}^{n} l\tilde{r}_{A_n}, \sum_{i=1}^{n} m\tilde{r}_{A_n}, \sum_{i=1}^{n} u\tilde{r}_{A_n}\right)^{-1}$$

(5)

Step 5: Based on increasing order of $(vs)^{-1}$, the fuzzy weight $(\tilde{w}_i)$ determined by multiply each $(\tilde{r}_i)$ with $(vs)^{-1}$ obtained from step 4.

$$\tilde{w}_i = (l\tilde{r}_{A_i}, m\tilde{r}_{A_i}, u\tilde{r}_{A_i}) \otimes (u_{vs}, m_{vs}, l_{vs})^{-1} \quad , \quad \text{where } i = 1,2,3,\ldots,n \quad (6)$$

Step 6: Since $\tilde{w}_i$ are still fuzzy triangular numbers, they need to be de-fuzzified by Centre of area method proposed by Chou and Chang (2008).

$$M_i = \dfrac{l\tilde{w}_{A_i} + m\tilde{w}_{A_i} + u\tilde{w}_{A_i}}{3} \quad , \text{where } i = 1,2,3,\ldots,n$$

(7)

Step 7: Since non fuzzy weight are not normalized, the weight need to be normalized $(\tilde{N}_i)$.

ISBN: 978-1-387-00704-2

$$\tilde{N}_i = \frac{M_i}{\sum\limits_{i=1}^{n} M_i} \quad \text{, where } i = 1, 2, 3, \ldots, n$$

$$(8)$$

Step 8: Next, the normalized weight will be formed in terms of priority alternative weight.

$$\text{weighted evaluation for alternative} = \sum_{i=1}^{t} \left(\text{weight}_i \times \text{evaluation rating}_{ik} \right)$$

$$(9)$$

Where $i = 1, 2, \ldots, t$

Once all priority weighted of alternative are obtained, there is a need to multiply the normalized weighted criteria with respect to selection of the best car model with priority weighted of alternative by using Eq. (9) to get result on the best alternatives. According to these results, the alternative with the highest score is suggested to the purchaser. In order to make the methodology clear and see its applicability, a real case study in order to select the best car is revealed in the next section.

Application in Selecting the Best Car in Malaysia

1. Determining Weight of Criteria With Respect to Selecting the Best Car

The relative weight of criteria is as illustrated in Table 3. The relative weight has to be normalized to allow them to be analogous to weights defined from the FAHP method.

Table 3: Non fuzzy weight and normalized fuzzy weight of the criteria with respect to selecting the best car

Criteria	Non fuzzy weight	Normalized weight
Safety	0.482	0.464
Economic assumptions	0.359	0.346
Performance	0.198	0.19

The normalized weight indicates that, 'Safety' is the important criteria in order to select the best car between domestic cars and

ISBN: 978-1-387-00704-2

imported cars for the first hierarchy of FAHP in this study. The study also denotes that the purchaser should focus not only in 'Safety', but they also need to give importance on criteria of 'Performance' and 'Economic Assumptions'.

2. Determining the Weight of the Sub-Criteria with Respect to Criteria and its Ranking

After determining the most important criteria in selecting between domestic car and imported car, the next objective is to select the most important sub-criteria as compared to criteria. The relation weight and normalized weight of sub criteria based on each criterion are as shown in Table 4 respectively.

Table 4: Non fuzzy weight and normalized fuzzy weight of the sub-criteria with respect to each criteria

Criteria	Sub criteria	Non fuzzy weight	Normalized weight	Ranking
Safety	Air bags	0.445	0.440	2
	ABS Brake	0.313	0.309	3
	Alarm system	0.253	0.250	7
Economic assumptions	Price	0.270	0.269	5
	Fuel consumption	0.734	0.731	1
Performance	Breaking ability	0.269	0.264	6
	Engine power	0.308	0.302	4
	Maximum speed	0.137	0.134	9
	Noise	0.169	0.166	8
	Comfort	0.137	0.134	9

Table 4 shows sub criteria of 'Air Bags' is important under 'Safety' criteria in order to select the best car. This is because, sub criteria of 'Air Bags' has a normalized weight value with 0.440 which is the highest as compared with others. It is means that purchaser need consider more to air bags of that car before willing to purchase. For criteria of 'Economic Assumptions', sub criteria of 'Fuel Consumptions' is more important that need to be considered. While under criteria 'Performance', purchaser need

ISBN: 978-1-387-00704-2

to consider 'Engine Power' of that car compared to other sub criteria. Hence, based on all ranking of sub-criteria, purchaser need consider more on 'Fuel Consumptions' of that car before willing to purchase it.

3. Determining the Weight of Alternative with Respect to each Sub-Criterion.

Table 5 shows the weight of alternative with respect to each sub criteria. 'Price' that has highest weight is means for the cheapest. It is because, questionnaires constructed are more to positive judgement from 4 experts respondent. Here, based on judgments, experts are more prefer to the cheapest price of that car. So based on table above, can concluded that under 'Proton Preve', price is cheaper compared to other car models. Therefore purchaser can consider more to 'Proton Preve' because of the cheapest price for domestic car. While for 'Proton Suprima S', it can be concluded that, if purchaser wants the good air bags (weight value 0.300), purchaser are preferred to buy the 'Proton Suprima S'. This car also consider good in fuel consumption (weight value 0. 0.229) and can speed in maximum level (weight value 0.336).

Table 5: Weight of alternatives with respect to each sub-criterion

Criteria	Sub criteria	Alternative			
		Domestic car		Imported car	
		Proton Preve	Proton Suprima S	Honda Civic	Honda City
Safety	Air bags	0.268	**0.300**	0.262	0.179
	ABS Brake	0.186	0.170	**0.450**	0.194
	Alarm system	**0.331**	0.281	0.171	0.216
Economic assumptions	Price	**0.342**	0.228	0.207	0.223
	Fuel consumption	0.152	**0.229**	**0.356**	**0.263**
Performance	Breaking ability	0.230	0.183	**0.430**	0.157
	Engine power	0.305	0.211	0.303	0.182
	Maximum speed	0.109	0.336	0.318	**0.237**
	Noise	0.217	0.292	0.275	0.216
	Comfort	**0.336**	0.179	0.364	0.122

ISBN: 978-1-387-00704-2

For imported car, under model 'Honda Civic', purchaser can purchase this model if want the car that safety in term of 'ABS Brake' (weight value of 0.450) is good besides also can save money in term of fuel consumptions. Besides that, this model also perform well in 'Breaking Ability' since the value of weight highest compared with other sub-criteria of performance under this model. It is means that, if purchasers want the breaking ability that performs well, they can buy model of 'Honda Civic'. .Meanwhile 'Honda City' is also good performing in 'Fuel Consumption' followed by 'Maximum Speed'. It is means that, purchaser also prefer to purchase this model if want to save in fuel consumption but at the same time can speed in maximum level.

4.   Determining the Priority Weights for each Alternative.

To achieve the main objective, the priority weight for each alternative was calculated. The combination of priority weights for sub-criteria, criteria and alternatives are to determine priority weights for selection of best car between domestic and imported brand cars in the Malaysian market. The summary of combination of priority weight is as shown in Table 6.

Table 6: Priority weights of alternatives with respects to each criteria and respect to select the best car

| Criteria | Alternative priority weight (criteria) | | | | Weight |
| | Domestic car | | Imported car | | |
	Proton Preve	Proton Suprima S	Honda Civic	Honda City	
Safety	0.258	0.255	0.297	0.189	0.464
Economic assumptions	0.248	0.229	0.342	0.180	0.346
Performance	0.203	0.229	0.316	0.252	0.190
Alternative priority weight (select car)	0.244	0.241	**0.316**	0.198	

Based on priority weight, it can be concluded that 'Honda Civic' is the best car in criteria of 'Safety' because; 'Honda Civic' has the highest priority weight with value of 0.297. While in

ISBN: 978-1-387-00704-2

'Performance' criteria, 'Honda Civic' shows the highest priority weight with the value of 0.342. Its means that 'Honda Civic' performed well as compared to other car models. Thus, it can be concluded that 'Honda Civic' is the preferred car for purchaser to select car with good performance. Meanwhile, 'Honda Civic' is better in 'Economic Assumptions' with its highest priority weight value which is 0.316.

Hence, by using all alternative priority weight for each criteria, priority weight of each model car chosen in order to select the best car model are obtained and also summarised in Table 6. This study concludes that alternative 'Honda Civic' is the best car model among domestic and imported cars in Malaysian market. The findings show that 'Honda Civic' has the highest priority weight with the value of 0.316. Followed by next car models namely 'Proton Preve' and 'Proton Suprima S' with their priority weight 0.244 and 0.241 respectively. Finally is 'Honda City' which has the lower priority weight with the value of 0.198. Therefore it can be concluded that 'Honda Civic' is the best car model in the three criteria compared to other car models.

Conclusions and Recommendations
From this study, it reveals that Fuzzy AHP method can be applied to select best car between domestic and imported brand cars in Malaysian market. All objectives had been successfully achieved. For future study, comparison between the study method with other methods of MCDM such as TOPSIS, Fuzzy Logic and Fuzzy Analytic Network Process can be proposed. The three methods can be applied for the same case in selecting the best car and the results need to be compared. The comparison of various methods in the selection process would be a great help in determining accuracy, appropriateness, suitability, fairness, practicality and efficiency of such study

References
Buckley, J. J. (1985). Fuzzy hierarchical analysis.Fuzzy Sets Systems, 17(1), 233247.

ISBN: 978-1-387-00704-2

Chou, S. W., & Chang, Y. C. (2008).The implementation factors that influence the ERP (Enterprise Resource Planning) benefits. Decision Support Systems, 46(1), 149-157.

Martin, A., Miranda, L. T., &Prasanna, V. V. (2013). A survey on multi criteria decision making methods and its applications. *American Journal of Information Systems*, 1(1), 31-43.

Shende, V. (2014).Analysis of Research in Consumer Behavior of Automobile Passenger Car Customer.*International Journal of Scientific and Research Publications*, 4(2), 1-8.

Tirayaki, F., &Ahlatcioglu, B. (2008).Fuzzy portfolio selection using fuzzy analytic hierarchy process. Information Sciences, 179 (2009), 53–69.

Tolga, E., Demircan, M. L. &Kahraman, C. (2005).Operating system selection using fuzzy replacement analysis and analytic hierarchy process.*International Journal Production Economics*, 97(1), 89-117.

ISBN: 978-1-387-00704-2

Article 10

Comparison between Clustering Algorithm for Rainfall Analysis in Kelantan

Wan Nurshazelin Wan Shahidan, SitiNurasikin Abdullah
Faculty of Computer and Mathematical Sciences,
University of Technology Mara Perlis Branch, Malaysia

Abstract

Analysis of rainfall behaviour has become important in many regions because it is related to many factors such as agricultural sector, water resource management, and flood disaster and landslide occurrence. The weather in Malaysia is characterised by two monsoon regimes called as Southwest Monsoon and Northeast Monsoon. Heavy rainfall will cause water level of river to reach its maximum level that may lead to flood disaster. Floods become more serious when people start losing the life of beloved ones and property. Although natural disasters are caused by nature and there is nothing that we can do to prevent them from happening, but yet being aware of its impact is a much required process that should be looked into thoroughly. The goal of this study is to analyse the rainfall analysis in Kota Bharu, Kelantan in order to overcome any bad consequences in future. Three types of clustering algorithm were used in this study, namely K-Means clustering, density based clustering and expectation maximization (EM) clustering algorithm. Comparisons between the clustering algorithms were conducted in this study to identify which clustering algorithm is the most suitable and simple for rainfall distribution. So, in this study clustering algorithm on rainfall distribution dataset is done using WEKA 3.8 software. The results found that K-Means clustering was the suitable and simple clustering algorithm based on time taken to build model.

Keywords: *clustering algorithm, K-mean clustering, density based clustering, expectation maximization clustering, rainfall analysis*

Introduction

Analysis of rainfall behaviour has become important in many regions because it is related to many factors such as agricultural sector, water resource management, and flood disaster and landslide occurrence. The weather in Malaysia is characterised by two monsoon regimes called as Southwest Monsoon and Northeast Monsoon. Southwest Monsoon occurs during late May to September while for Northeast Monsoon it occurs during

ISBN: 978-1-387-00704-2

November to March (Ismail, 2015).Contribution of heavy rainfall will lead to natural disaster such as flood.According to Toriman et al., (2014) flood is also defined as the domination of high water flow in river system. There are several factors that cause flood disaster to happen such as natural phenomenon which is La Nina, heavy rainfall, drainage system failure, rapid economic development, and illegal logging activity. La Nina is the natural phenomena that will affect rainfall pattern in Malaysia to change until flood disaster occurs. Flood disaster will give bad impact to human life, damage to property, destruction of crops, problem in health condition and loss of livestock.

In 2014, the massive flood hit Malaysia and more than 200,000 Malaysians were affected by the flood while 21 people were killed due to floods and the floods in 2014 was the worst in decades.Kelantan is one of the areas in Peninsular Malaysia that often vulnerable with a big flood and it also affected all local mains road and housing areas. Kelantan was the worst state in Malaysia that was destroyed and damaged during the occurrence of flood in 2014.Although natural disasters are caused by nature and there is nothing that we can do to prevent them from happening, but yet being aware of its impact is a much required process that should be looked into thoroughly. The main objective of this study is to find out which clustering algorithm will be the most suitable and simple for rainfall distribution and show the comparison of different clustering algorithm using WEKA 3.8 software. It is important to study the rainfall distribution since heavy rainfall will lead to natural disaster such as floods. Flood disaster may lead to property and life loss.

Data Mining Technique

Generally, data mining involves transformation of raw data into relevant patterns. Primarily, data mining is predominantly used for data pattern identification to achieve a firm understanding in data generating process as well as assisting useful predictions. In addition, there are two types of data mining namely direct and indirect data mining.In order to identify pattern and relationship in large data set, methods such as statistical model, mathematical

ISBN: 978-1-387-00704-2

algorithm and machine learning could be used (Phyu, 2009). Phyu also highlighted that besides collecting and managing data, data mining was also useful in analysing and predicting data.

Clustering Algorithm

Clustering, cluster analysis, segmentation analysis, taxonomy analysis or unsupervised classification is a method of creating similar groups of object, or cluster, in such a way that objects in one cluster are very similar and objects in different cluster are quite distinct (Jain et al,. 2010).The purposes of using clustering were because clustering had ability to deal with noisy data, had scalability to deal with large dataset and had ability to deal with different kind of attributes. Several clustering techniques could be applied such as k-means clustering, density based clustering and expectation–maximization (EM) algorithm.

Various Clustering Algorithm
i.   K-Means Clustering

K-means clustering is a partitioning method. The function partitions data into k mutually exclusive clusters, and returns the index of the cluster to which it has assigned each observation K-means clustering introduced by J.B. McQueen in 1967 (Dhakshinamoorthy and Kalaiselvan, 2013). K-means clustering is the most common clustering that groups data with similar characteristics.The basic step of k-means is simple. First, the number of cluster k which is assumed as the centroid or centre of the clusters should be determined. Any random number objects can be taken as the initial centroid. Then, the k-means will do the three steps below until convergence.

Step 1: Determine the centroid coordinate

Step 2: Determine the distance of each object to the centroids.

Step 3: Group the object based on the minimum distance.

ISBN: 978-1-387-00704-2

ii. Density Based Clustering

Density based clustering was proposed by Martin Ester, Hans-Peter Kriegel, Jorge Sander and Xiaowei Xu in 1996. It is a density-based clustering algorithm because it finds a number of clusters starting from the estimated density distribution of corresponding nodes (Sharma et al., 2012). Most of scientific literature cited about density based clustering and it is one of the most common clustering algorithms. According to Raviya and Dhinoja (2013) clusters for density based clustering are identified by looking at the density of points. The advantages of density based clustering are the shaped of clusters can find arbitrarily and can find the clusters completely surrounded by different clusters. It is robust to noise and do not need any priori k deterministic. Density based finds a number of clusters starting from the estimated density distribution of corresponding nodes. Density based clustering algorithm is an important part of clustering technique which is mainly used in scientific literature. Density is measured by the number of objects which are nearest the cluster.

iii. Expectation Maximization (EM) Clustering

Expectation maximization is a type of model based clustering method. Umale and Nilav (2014) declared that expectation maximization algorithm assigns objects to cluster according to parameters of probabilistic clusters or the current fuzzy clustering. The expectation maximization algorithm gains its name by Arthur Dempster, Nan Laird, and Donald Rubin in a classic 1977 paper. Besides that, expectation maximization algorithm is an iterative method in finding maximum likelihood or maximum a posteriori (MAP) estimates of parameters in statistical models. . Expectation maximization algorithm consists of two key stages. The two stages were showed below.

Stage 1: E (expectation) was the calculation of the cluster probabilities. In this stage, assume that we know the values of all the model parameters.

Stage 2: M (maximization) was the calculation of the model parameters. In this stage, the process was aimed to

ISBN: 978-1-387-00704-2

maximize the likelihood of the model given the available data.

These stages are repeated until the algorithm starts to converge.

Waikato Environment for Knowledge Analysis (WEKA)
Waikato Environment for Knowledge Analysis (WEKA) is one of the software or machine learning for data mining. WEKA is freely available for download and offers many powerful features. Besides that, WEKA provides the extensive support for the whole process of experimental data mining. WEKA implements algorithms for data pre-processing, classification, regression, clustering and association rules and also includes visualization tools. Jain et al., (2010) conclude that WEKA has made an outstanding contribution to the data mining.

Methodology
There were four processes in this study such as data collection, data pre-processing, data clustering and comparison results by clustering algorithm. The rainfall distribution data was analysed one by one in WEKA using the three clustering algorithm. This study uses the secondary rainfall distribution data from Kota Bharu, Kelantan Station. The rainfall distribution data is from January 2008 to December 2014. The data recorded is daily rainfall distribution for 365 or 366 days per year. The average rainfall distribution also consists in this study. There were three attributes from the data such as wind, radiation and humidity.After conducted k-means, density based and expectation maximization clustering algorithm thus, compared the result from the output in WEKA. The comparison based on the time taken to build the model, values of log likelihood and the number of clusters. The significant of this comparison is to see the suitable and simple clustering algorithm for rainfall distribution data.

Results Analysis
K-means clustering, density based clustering and expectation maximization clustering was conducted one by one in WEKA in

ISBN: 978-1-387-00704-2

order to find the results and made comparison table. The comparisons of clustering algorithm were based on the number of cluster, time taken to build model and the values of log likelihood.From WEKA we found results using the entire clustering algorithm as shown in Table 1.

Table 1: Result of Comparison of Three Clustering Algorithms

Clustering Algorithm	Number of Clusters	Clustered Instances				Time Taken to Build Model (Seconds)	Log Likelihood
		0	1	2	3		
K-means	2	26 %	74 %			0	-
Density Based	2	26 %	74 %			0.02	-6.4439
Expectation Maximization	4	39 %	21 %	26 %	13 %	0.23	-5.4829

Table 1 compares the results for three different types of clustering algorithm such as k-means, density based and expectation maximization. Density based clustering was better than the expectation maximization clustering because the time taken to build the model is 0.02 seconds which is less than expectation maximization clustering. The lower the time taken to build the model means that the model was simple. Density based clustering take less time to build a cluster but it does not better than the k-means clustering because density based clustering has high log likelihood value, if the value of log likelihood is high which is negative value than it does not make good cluster. Log likelihood measured the goodness of the clustering. K-means clustering has the lowest time taken to build the model which is 0 seconds and smaller number of clusters. As a conclusion, k-means clustering was the suitable and simple clustering algorithm in this study based on the time taken to build model. K-means clustering algorithm is the simplest clustering algorithm as compared to other clustering algorithms.

ISBN: 978-1-387-00704-2

Conclusion

This study wants to obtain the most suitable and simple clustering algorithm by using rainfall distribution data in Kota Bharu, Kelantan. The selection of appropriate clustering algorithm is really important in order to gain better analysis for rainfall distribution data. Besides, the main challenges while conducting this study is to use WEKA 3.8 software in order to come out with the best clustering and able to build the clustering model which it is an important issue that had been discuss by the researchers.Results shows that the model that had been developed and conduct in WEKA 3.8 software were able to identify the best and simple clustering algorithm based on rainfall distribution data from years 2008 until 2014. K-means clustering give the lowest time taken to build this model in WEKA 3.8 software. It is simply means that k-means clustering is simple clustering algorithm.This study recommends continuous study in future to make comparison with the other clustering algorithm or make some adjustment for clustering algorithm in order get the best clusters. Besides, this study also recommends a study in future to apply using other open sources software that provides for data mining. Furthermore, this study can be used as the reference for future studies.

References

Dhakshinamoorthy, P., &Kalaiselvan, T. (2013).Crime pattern detection using data mining.*International Journal of Advanced Research in Computer Science and Applications, 1*(1), 46-51.

Ismail, N. A. (2015). A Study on social influences during annual flood occurance in Kota Bharu, Kelantan: the positive sides of disaster. *Advances in Environmental Biology, 9*(27), 456-460.

Jain, S., Aalam, M. A., &Doja, M. N. (2010). K-means clustering using weka interface. *Computing for Nation Development.*

Phyu, T. N. (2009). Survey of classification techniques in data mining.*InternationaLMUlticonference of Engineers and Computer Scientists,*18–20.

Raviya, K. H., &Dhinoja, K. (2013).An empirical comparison of k-means and DBSCAN clustering algorithm.*Indian Journal of Research, 2*(4), 153-155.

Sharma, M., Bajpai, A., &Litoriya, R. (2012).Comparison the various clustering algorithms of weka tools.*International Journal of Emerging Technology and Advanced Engineering, 2*(5), 73-80.

ISBN: 978-1-387-00704-2

The Star. (2014). *Floods in Kelantan, Terengganu Worsen.* Retrieved 14 June
    2017
    fromhttp://www.thestar.com.my/news/nation/2014/12/23/floods-
    kelantan-terengganu/

Toriman, M. E., Abdullahi, M. G., D/iya, S. G., &Gasim, M. B. (2014). Floods
    in Malaysia historical reviews, causes, effects and mitigations
    approach. *International Journal of Interdisciplinary Research and
    Innovations, 2*(4), 59-65.

Umale, B., &Nilav, M. (2014).Overview of k-means and expectation
    maximization algorithm for document clustering.*International
    Journal of Computer Applications,* 5-8.

ISBN: 978-1-387-00704-2

Article 11

Volume of Hill Estimation for Engineering Earth Work

Nordianah Jusoh
Department of Computer & Mathematical Sciences
Universiti Teknologi MARA Melaka Branch, Malaysia

Noorzalianee Ghazali
Department of Surveying Science and Geomatic
Universiti Teknologi MARA Perlis Branch, Malaysia

Siti Hafawati Jamaluddin, Siti Nor Nadrah Muhamad, Wan Juliyana Wan Ibrahim
Department of Computer & Mathematical Sciences
Universiti Teknologi MARA Perlis Branch, Malaysia

Jamaludin Md. Ali
Department of Computer & Mathematical Sciences
University of Science, Malaysia

Wan Mohd Zulkifle Wan Yaacob
Department of Arts & Design
Universiti Teknologi MARA Melaka Branch, Malaysia

Abstract

This study centralizes on the development of volume estimation calculation platform for earth engineering work. Estimation and comparison were done by using Foresight Civil Design and Survey (CDS) and Mathematica 7.0 software. Currently, Land Surveying companies are using Foresight Civil Design and Survey (CDS) software for its speed and automation. There are two methods used in Mathematica 7.0, which are Rational Quadratic Bezier Curve and Rational Cubic Bezier Curve. From this research, Rational Cubic Bezier Curve show its total hill measurement (volume) is nearer to value using Foresight Civil Design and Survey (CDS) software. Therefore, the Rational Cubic Bezier Curve is an alternative method to estimate the volume of the hill. The discrepancy between Rational Cubic Bezier Curve and Foresight Civil Design and Survey (CDS) mainly caused by curve tolerance has been generalized in Rational Cubic Bezier Curve.

Keywords: *volume estimation, Rational Quadratic Bezier Curve, Rational Cubic Bezier Curve*

ISBN: 978-1-387-00704-2

Introduction

Volume calculation is crucial for cut and fill work. For civil engineering, volume calculations are important in order to identify the need of filling up the area with the cut volume (Yunos, 1996). Along with technology advancement, land survey companies have been using professional software to calculate soil volume. This research uses Foresight Civil Design and Survey (CDS) and Mathematica 7.0 software. Mathematica 7.0 has been used to estimate hill volume by using Rational Quadratic Bezier Curve and Rational Cubic Bezier Curve. The results were later compared to volume estimation by CDS software.

Bezier Curve is commonly used in computer graphic and geometry modelling. This algorithm uses 3D point's geometry parameters to generate a curve (Kenneth, 2000). Rational Bezier Curve is a Bezier Curve in 3D with rational polynomial or ratio of two polynomials.

This study uses both Rational Quadratic Bezier Curve and Rational Cubic Bezier Curve. Aiming to provide alternative software for cut and fill project for a small land survey company, this study utilizes Mathematica 7.0 to estimate hill's volume. Consecutively, this research focuses on control value, h_i derivations and analysis for a smooth surface, estimates hill volume and analytical comparison for volume estimation between CDS and Mathematica 7.0.There are numerous researches for land surface volume calculation inclusive of soil, hill, mountain, coal mine among others.

Chun-Shung Chen and Hung-Cheng Lin (1990) in "Estimating Pit-Excavation Volume Using Cubic Spline Volume Formula" has extended cubic spline polynomial and develop a new formula to estimate coal mine excavation. Various size rectangles have been constructed by connecting two lines from ground profile point's selections. Irregular grid areas were later used to estimate coal mine excavation volume. Newly develop volume estimation formula in this research is accurate because it produces a smooth curve from cubic spline polynomial.

ISBN: 978-1-387-00704-2

Pyramid Frustum Formula for Computing Volumes at Roadway Transition Areas" (Said, 1991) used Average-End-Area (AEA) and Pyramid Frustum (PF) formula to calculate cut and fill volume in road transition design. In AEA, volume was obtained by a multipliedaverage of the end areas by the distance between cross sections. In PF, the volume is calculated by multiplied base area by height and is divided by three. This research indicates a large error in AEA compared to PF. Therefore, PF is more suitable for road transition design volume calculations.

Methodology

This research uses simulation coordinate (x_i, y_i, z_i) data with $i = 1,..., 10$ as a control point. x_i, y_i are Easting and Northing, with z_i as a height. Assuming the base and top of the hill have an equal width, there will only be two Northing (y_1 and y_2). Control points $i = 1$-5 are coordinated for front surface and $i = 6$-10 are back surface. Curve for both surfaces are similar (Figure 1).

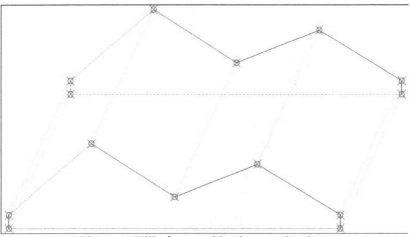

Figure 1: Hills front and back control points

This study uses both Rational Quadratic Bezier Curve and Rational Cubic Bezier Curve. Hill volume was determined by these steps:

ISBN: 978-1-387-00704-2

Develop new equations with a constant Mean Sea Level (MSL) datum using Rational Quadratic Bezier Curve, equation (2) and Rational Cubic Bezier Curve, equation (4)

$$R_i(x) = r_i(x) - 7.5$$

(1)

where $r_i(x)$ is a Rational Quadratic Bezier Curve or Rational Cubic Bezier Curve and 7.5 is an arbitrary value for Mean Sea Level.

$$r_i(t) = \frac{(1-t^2)z_i + 2(1-t)tw_i h_i + t^2 z_{i+1}}{(1-t)^2 + 2(1-t)tw_i + t^2}$$

(2)

where,

$$t = \frac{(x - x_i)}{(x_{i+1} - x_i)}$$

(3)

with control point r_i, $i = 1,\ldots,5$.

$$r_i(t) = \frac{(1-t^2)z_i + 2(1-t)^2 tw_i h_i + 2(1-t)t^2 w_{i+1} h_{i+1} + t^2 z_{i+1}}{(1-t)^2 + 2(1-t)^2 tw_i + 2(1-t)t^2 w_{i+1} + t^2}$$

(4)

where,

$$t = \frac{(x - x_i)}{(x_{i+1} - x_i)}$$

(5)

with control point r_i, $i = 1,\ldots,5$.

ISBN: 978-1-387-00704-2

i) Calculate areas for each surface (A_1, A_2, A_3 & A_4)

$$A_i = \int_{x_{i-1}}^{x_i} R_i(x)dx$$

(6)

where i = 1, 2, 3 and 4.

ii) Calculate volume for each surface (V_1, V_2, V_3 & V_4)

$$V_i = A_i[y_2 - y_1]$$

(7)

where i = 1, 2, 3 and 4 and $y_2 - y_1$ is hill's width.

iii) Calculate hill's volume, V

$$V = V_1 + V_{21} + V_3 + V_4$$

(8)

Both results were then compared to CDS result in order to evaluate the efficiency of the equations in calculating hill's volume.

Results and Discussion
The result from this research is obtained from Rational Quadratic Bezier Curve and Rational Cubic Bezier Curve. Both Bezier Curves were based on control value, h_i ,weightage, w , Iterative Formula, h_{i+1}, hill's curvature based on weight, w and hill's volume.

ISBN: 978-1-387-00704-2

The relationship between control value, h_i and weightage, w.

Control point, h_i, in this section is represented by h_1, the first control point. Table 1 are three arbitrary coordinates used in the simulations. Table 2 shows result for control point, h_i byRational Quadratic Bezier Curve with a different weightage, w. Figure 2 illustrates first and second curves from Rational Quadratic Bezier Curve. Rational Cubic Bezier Curve however, indicate a correlation between h_i and z_i. It was demonstrated by an Iterative Formula, $h_{i+1} = z_{i+1}$.

$$r_1 = \frac{\left[(1-t_1)^2 z_1\right) + \left(2(1-t_1)t_1 w h_1\right) + \left(t_1^2 z_2\right)\right]}{\left((1-t_1)^2\right) + \left(2(1-t)_1 t_1 w\right) + \left(t_1^2\right)}$$

(9)

$$r_2 = \frac{\left[(1-t_2)^2 z_2\right) + \left(2(1-t_2)t_2 w h_1\right) + \left(t_2^2 z_3\right)\right]}{\left((1-t_2)^2\right) + \left(2(1-t_2)t_2 w\right) + \left(t_2^2\right)}$$

(10)

Table 1: Coordinates (1-3)

i	x_i	y_i	z_i
1	3000.349	172.972	8.5
2	3667.444	172.972	18.5
3	4334.539	172.972	12.5

Table 2 : Value for h_1 by different w

w	h_1
0.8	31.293
0.9	19.185
1.0	29.440

ISBN: 978-1-387-00704-2

Iterative Formula, h_{i+1}

Figure 2, 3 and 4 are the curves generated from Rational Quadratic Bezier Curve represented by first and second curves as (r_1 & r_2), second and third curves as (r_2 & r_3) and third and fourth curves as (r_3 & r_4). Figure 2 with r_1 and r_2, when

$$r_1'[x_2 = 3667.444] = r_2'[x_2 = 3667.444] \text{ and } x = x_2, \text{ therefore}$$

$$h_2 = \frac{h_1(x_3 - x_2) + (x_1 - x_3)z_2}{x_1 - x_2}.$$

In Figure 3, both curves r_2 and r_3, when

$$r_2'[x_3 = 4334.539] = r_3'[x_3 = 4334.539] \text{ with } x = x_3, \text{ it produced}$$

$$h_3 = \frac{h_2(x_4 - x_3) + (x_2 - x_4)z_3}{x_2 - x_3}.$$

For Figure 4, r_3 and r_4 curves, when

$$r_3'[x_4 = 5001.634] = r_4'[x_4 = 5001.634] \text{ and } x = x_4, \text{ resulted with}$$

$$h_4 = \frac{h_3(x_5 - x_4) + (x_3 - x_5)z_4}{x_3 - x_4}.$$

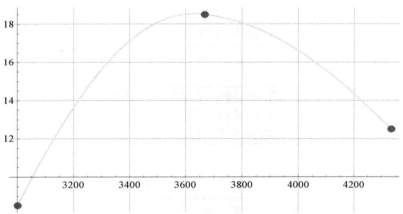

Figure 2: First and second curves by Rational Quadratic Bezier Curve

ISBN: 978-1-387-00704-2

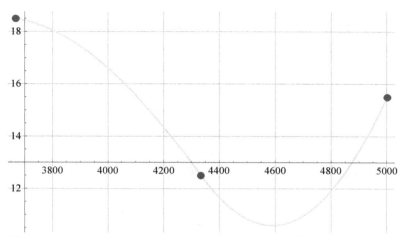

Figure 3: Second and third curves by Rational Quadratic Bezier Curve

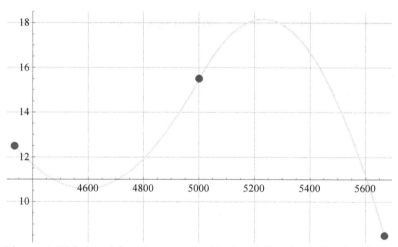

Figure 4: Third and fourth curves by Rational Quadratic Bezier Curve

In Rational Cubic Bezier Curve, the coordinate's differences have been set up to zero to represent C^1 continuity. For first and second curves $(r_1 \& r_2)$, when $r_1'[x_2 = 3667.444] = r_2'[x_2 = 3667.444]$ and $x = x_2$. For the second and third curves $(r_2 \& r_3)$, when

ISBN: 978-1-387-00704-2

$r_2' \left[x_3 = 4334.539 \right] = r_3' \left[x_3 = 4334.539 \right]$ and $x = x_3$. Finally, the third and fourth curves $\left(r_3 \, \& \, r_4 \right)$, when $r_3' \left[x_4 = 5001.634 \right] = r_4' \left[x_4 = 5001.634 \right]$ with $x = x_4$.

Overall results for both formula are $h_2 = z_2$, $h_3 = z_3$ and $h_4 = z_4$. Therefore, equation (11) and (12) define the Iterative Formula for Rational Quadratic Bezier Curve and Rational Cubic Bezier Curve.

$$h_{i+1} = \frac{\left(x_i - x_{i+2} \right) z_{i+1} - \left(x_{i+1} - x_{i+2} \right) h_i}{x_i - x_{i+1}}$$

(11)

$$h_{i+1} = z_{i+1}$$

(12)

Curve's transition proxy of Weightage, w value

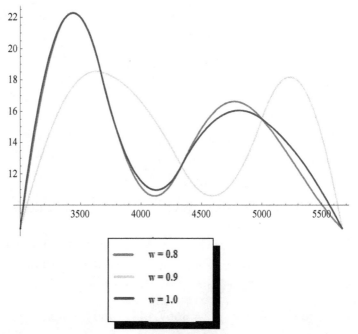

Figure 5: Rational Quadratic Bezier Curve with w variant

ISBN: 978-1-387-00704-2

Figure 5 demonstrates the effect of weightage, w variant to the hill's curve shape in Rational Quadratic Bezier Curve.

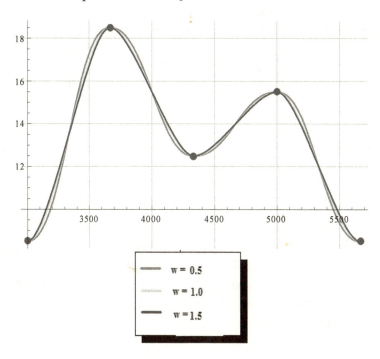

Figure 6: Rational Cubic Bezier Curve with w variant

Figure 6 displays the effect of weightage, w variant to the hill's curve shape in Rational Cubic Bezier Curve.

Hill's Volume

Table 3: Hill's volume estimation

Method				Volume ($unit^3$)
CDS				16677381.667
	Weightage, w	**Rational Bezier quadratic**	**Weightage, w**	**Rational Bezier cubic**
Mathematica				
	0.8	19192390.570	0.5	16677379.50
	0.9	19387790.787	1.0	16677379.50
	1.0	19568124.373	1.5	16677379.50

ISBN: 978-1-387-00704-2

In regards to hill's volume calculations in Table 3, Rational Cubic Bezier Curve formula is almost identical to hill's volume computed by CDS compared to Rational Quadratic Bezier Curve formula. This insignificant volume difference however, was the succession of Rational Cubic Bezier Curve tolerance. Hence Rational Cubic Bezier Curve is an adequate CDS alternate method to calculate hill's volume.

Conclusion

To conclude, it is safe to mention this research has delivered the objective. The h_i and weightage, w relationship only happened in Rational Quadratic Bezier Curve. For Rational Cubic Bezier Curve, the correlations mainly rely on z_i coordinates. The contrast in iterative formula for both Rational Quadratic Bezier Curve and Rational Cubic Bezier Curve formula were shown in equation (11) and (12) respectively. Both formulas however, have a different hill's curve for different weightage, w. Hill's volume usesRational Cubic Bezier Curve, in which is overall nearer to CDS hill's volume. The slight difference is caused only by curve tolerance. This finding in another way offer cost effective options for land survey companies to be able to monitor cut and fill work progress. Progressing forward, it is suggested that future research should include higher detail in hill's shape and surface to gain better volume calculation precisions.

Suggestion

To summarize, Rational Cubic Bezier Curve method is able to resolve software and cost constraint to calculate cut and fill volume among land survey companies in Malaysia. However, the real contribution only can be verified by future research using scattered, inconsistent ground truth coordinates.

ISBN: 978-1-387-00704-2

References

Ahmad, A. & Ali, J.M. (2006).Mencirikanlengkungankubiknisbahalternatif.*MATEMATIKA.* *22(1)*, pp. 77-89.

Chun, S.C. & Hung, C.L. (1991).Estimating pit-excavation volume using cubic spline volume formula.*Journal of Surveying Engineering, ASCE.* *117(2)*, 51-67.

James, W.E. & Marion, W.C. (1989). Cut and fill calculations by Modified Average-End-Area method. *Journal of Transportation Engineering, ASCE.116(5)*, pp.683-690.

Karim, S.A. (2008). *Fungsi ball teritlaknisbahuntuklengkunginterpolasicembungdanberekanada.*Master thesis, UniversitiSains Malaysia.

Kenneth, I.J. (2000). *On-Line Geometric Modeling Notes: Quadratic Bezier Curve Visualization and Graphic Research Group.*

Mohamed, A.H. (2000). *AsasUkurKejuruteraan*, 1[st]edn. Malaysia: UniversitiTeknologi Malaysia.

Mohamed, S.A. (2006). *Lengkungdanpermukaan Bezier nisbah.*Master thesis, UniversitiSains Malaysia.

Rasid, A. & Habib, Z. (2011).*Gear tooth designing with cubic Bezier transition curve.*Retrieved from http://www.cslhr.nu.edu.pk/GCCS/Summer2010/papers/AishaCurve.pdf.

Rasid, K.A., Ahmad, A. &Ariff, S.M. (1993).*IlmuUkuruntukJurutera*, 2[nd]edn. Malaysia: UniversitiTeknologi Malaysia.

Said, M.E. (1991). Pyramid frustum formula for computing volumes at roadway transition areas. *Journal of Surveying Engineering, ASCE.* *117(2)*, pp. 98-101.

Wahab, A.F. (2008) *Permodelangeometrimenggunakan set kabur.* Ph.D thesis, UniversitiSains Malaysia.

Yunos, M.Z. & Amin, Z.M. (1996).*UkurKejuruteraanLanjutan:MasalahdanPenyelesaian.* Malaysia: UniversitiTeknologi Malaysia.

ISBN: 978-1-387-00704-2

Article 12

Particle Swarm Optimization: Optimizing Transportation Cost Problem

SitiHafawati Jamaluddin, Norwaziah Mahmud, NurSyuhadaMuhammatPazil, NurulHidayah Ab Raji,and NurulainGhazali.
Faculty of Computer & Mathematical Sciences
UniversitiTeknologi MARA Perlis Branch, Malaysia

NordianahJusoh
Faculty of Computer & Mathematical Sciences
UniversitiTeknologi MARA Melaka Branch, Malaysia

Abstract

Transportation is literally defined as an act, process or instance of transporting or being transported. Many business organizations are relying on transportation in running their business. In these years, the transportation cost has increase from time to time and become a problem to the organization to maintain the cost and profit. To overcome this problem, the optimization of cost is applied in order to make sure the business is in the right financial condition by finding the minimum cost of transporting a single commodity from a given number of sources to a given number of destinations. In this study the modified Particle Swarm Optimization is used to solve the Transportation Cost Problem (TCP) in finding the optimal solution of the amount of product transported with the minimum cost. The model of nonlinear cost function had been used throughout this study. As a result, the minimum cost of transportation is 340.69 with the amount of product transported 17, 15, 32, 16, and 20 following the arc A(x)={(1,5), (2,4), (2,6), (3,4), (3,5)} respectively.

Keywords: Transportation Cost Problem, Particle Swarm Optimization, Optimization.

Introduction

In this era of ever-increasing competitive market, the companies of businesses become highly competitive to produce high level of service at the lowest possible cost. A stable operational cost need to be maintained by the organization to survive in the market for a long term. Operational cost is aimed on monitoring some important parts in the organization. It is importance in minimizing the cost, stabilize the company performance, achieve company's objectives and maintain company's revenue. The cost

ISBN: 978-1-387-00704-2

minimization is often applied by an organization as a cost stabilization approach. Cost optimization is about to find the most effective cost or high achievable performance under the given constraints, by increasing desired factors and decreasing undesired ones (Free Dictionary).

The optimization of cost should be applied in any business in order to make sure the business is in a right financial condition. Recently, the transportation cost is a crucial problem. Transportation cost includes the expenses involved in moving product or assets to different places which are often passed on consumer (Business Dictionary). Based on the article in SinarHarian online which was published on 4 September 2013 by WartawanSinarHarian, it stated that, the charge of transportation will increase by 4 to 5 percent due to the increasing in petrol charge.

Nowadays, the global market competition among business is unpredictable and to achieve the business goals, it requires high involvement in transportation. The transportation cost must be at the lowest state so that the business can get more benefit.The objective of this study is to obtain the optimal solution of the amount of product transported of the nonlinear cost function by using Particle Swarm Optimization (PSO).

The research is a continuance from the previous study on a genetic ant colony approach for concave cost transportation problem carried out by Altiparmak and Karaoglan in 2007. This study will use the model proposed by them and will be implemented using PSO method. The model introduced transportation model which consist of three constraints which are the nonlinear cost function, the capacity constraint and the guarantees of all demands are met. The model is based on the transportation cost problem with three demand nodes, three supply nodes and five routes, A(x) which are A(x)={(1,5), (2,4), (2,6), (3,4), (3,5)}.

ISBN: 978-1-387-00704-2

Related Work in Minimizing Transportation Cost

The problem of transportation cost problem is crucial over century. Previous study showed that the cost problem is a large scale problems and time consuming (Altiparmak and Karaoglan, 2007).The study implemented the Ant Colony (AC) and Genetic Algorithm (GA) method to solve the Concave Cost Transportation Problem (CCTP). They introduced a new algorithm with the combination of hybrid GA and AC which is h_GACO. The effectiveness of the h_GACO is then compared using five different approaches. The result showed that h_GACO performs a good approach with respect to the solution quality and suggested the ACO can be used in other optimization that deals with problems of scheduling, vehicle routing and others. The combination of PSO and GA is implemented in the next study on minimizing an adapted vendor managed inventory and transport problem with fuzzy demand (Sadeghi et al., 2014).

This study is carried out to find the optimal retailer's order quantities so that the inventory and transportation cost can be decreased while satisfying several constraints. Because of the NP-hardness of the problem, an algorithm based on Particle Swarm Optimization (PSO) is proposed to find a near optimum solution, where the centroid defuzzification method is employed for defuzzification. Since there is no benchmark available in the literature, another meta-heuristic, namely genetic algorithm (GA), is presented in order to verify the solution obtained by PSO. Besides, to make PSO faster in finding a solution, it is improved by a local search. The parameters of both algorithms are standardized using the Taguchi method to have better quality solutions.

Particle Swarm Optimization (PSO)

Previous studies have used and implemented PSO extensively especially in solving optimization problem and is also proven to be very effective in solving Vehicle Routing Problem (VRP) in terms of finding the most suitable optimum cost ((Xuedan& Wang, 2009 and Chun, 2007).They also said that PSO is a well-known method due to its simplicity and effectiveness in wide

ISBN: 978-1-387-00704-2

range of application with low in computational cost. In general, PSO is defined as an optimization method imitating from social behavior of bird flocking and fish schooling (Hu &Eberhart, 2002).This method was adopted to a group of birds aimlessly looking for food in an area but they do not know how far the food is in each iteration (Kulkarni et al., 2015). Therefore, the effective way is to follow the bird which is nearest to the food. PSO was rooted from that scenario and used it to describe the optimization problems.

Some studies also focused on Vehicle Routing Problems (VRP) where the objective is to find the most suitable path to cut cost and save time. The problem of transportation routing and time give important impact on the controlling of inventory costs, transportation costs and economic efficiency (Xuedan& Wang, 2009). The study focused on solving the problem faced by dispatching vehicle with regards that each customer is served exactly once in each delivery in a fixed route and the total demand of all customers must not exceed the capacity of the delivery vehicle.

This study used the improved discrete PSO algorithm with mutation operation (in which all the particles are reinitialized when the swarm is decayed). The result is then compares from the improved discrete algorithm and concluded that modified discrete PSO is an efficient method to solve the discrete combination optimization such as VRP. In other study, the VRP is solved using predicting PSO with Time Windows (TW) (Chun, 2007). In this paper, the predicting PSO algorithm which modified by three new solution strategies has been proposed to adjust the continuous properties of basics PSO to be more suitable to be applied in Vehicle Routing Problem with Time Windows (VRPTW) presentations. The findings illustrate that the suggested algorithm achieve other experimental algorithm and the predicting PSO algorithm not only can adjust the variance between current status and memorial best status, but also can forecast the best position at the next status based on memory.

ISBN: 978-1-387-00704-2

In conclusion, there has been extensive research on the TCP which is mostly carried out to achieve the same objective which is to find optimal solution or minimize the cost or routes. Mostly, the method used to solve the TCP and VRP is Ant Colony (AC), Genetic Algorithm (GA) and several combination of PSO with other method to solve the problems and the result obtained is optimized and suitable for the problems.

Research Methodology

The model of concave cost transportation problem which originally proposed by Altiparmak and Karaogalan in 2007 is represented as follows:

$$\text{Minimize} \quad f(x) = \sum_{i=1}^{m}\sum_{i=1}^{n} c_{ij}\sqrt{x_{ij}}$$

$$(3.1)$$

$$\text{Subject to:} \quad \sum_{i=0}^{n} x_{ij} < a_i, \qquad \forall i \in N,$$

$$(3.2)$$

$$\sum_{i=0}^{m} x_{ij} \geq b_j, \qquad \forall j \in M,$$

$$(3.3)$$

$$x_{ij} \geq 0, \text{integer}, \qquad (i,j) \in A,$$

$$(3.4)$$

where,

A   :   Set of all arcs,

M   :   Set of all demand nodes (customers, warehouse, etc),

N   :   Set of all supply nodes (facilities distribution, centers, etc),

a_{ij} :   The capacity of suppliers $i, i \in N,$

b_j :   The demand of the customer $j, j \in M,$

x_{ij} :   The amount of product transported (i.e flow),

c_{ij} :   The per unit variable cost corresponding to (i,j).

The cost function in Eq. (3.1) is considered as nonlinear cost function. The amount of the product to be transported from

ISBN: 978-1-387-00704-2

supply node, i to each demand node, j must be determined so that all constraints is satisfied and the transportation cost can be minimized.

PSO Algorithm

The PSO algorithm begins by generating the initial particles, and allocating each of initial velocity. Since in this study is using CNOP, there are some modifications in PSO's original algorithm which involve the process of initialization and computation of *pbest* and *gbest* (Hu &Eberhart, 2002). For the process of initialization, all particles are constantly adjusted until they fulfill all constraints while when computing the *pbest* and *gbest* values, only those conditions in feasible space are calculated.

The Modified PSO Algorithm

Six steps on performing the modified PSO algorithm are defined as follows:

Step 1 : Initialize the particle.
The particle and velocity initialization is usually performed randomly in space and the initial velocities are often distributed randomly (Ho et. al, 2008).

Step 2 : Evaluating the initial particle to get personal best and global best. For each particle, the initialized positions are set as their personal best positions
$P_i = [\, p_{i1} \,,\, p_{i2} \,,...,\, p_{iN} \,]^T$, where $i = 1,..., m$. Then, all particles should be evaluated according to the project duration using the proposed serial scheme to determine the global best, *gBest*.

Step 3 : Velocity updating.
Based on the previous velocities and the distances of the current positions from personal best and global best, all particles' new velocities are calculated using Eq. (3.5) below.

$$v_i(t+1) = wv_i(t) + c_1 r_1 [x_i(t) - x_i(t)] + c_2 r_2 [g(t) - x_i(t)]$$

(3.5)

where,

i : the particle index,

$v_i(t)$: the particle's velocity at time t,

$v_i(t+1)$: the velocity of particle i at iteration $t+1$ (ne

$x_i(t)$: the current particles (solution),

ISBN: 978-1-387-00704-2

121

r_1 and r_2	:	random number within the range $[0,1]$,
w	:	the inertial coefficient,
c_1 and c_2	:	acceleration coefficient,
$\hat{x_i}(t)$	:	the particle's individual best solution at time t
$g(t)$	:	the swarm's best solution at time t or gBest.

The value of inertial coefficient is between 0.8 and 1.2 while the value of acceleration coefficient is a random number uniformly distributed within the range $[0,2]$.

Step 4 : Particle updating.
Based on the updated velocity, the new position is calculated according to Eq. (3.6).

$$x_i(t+1) = x_i(t) + v_i(t+1)$$

(3.6)

Step 5 : *pBest* and *gBest* updating.
Each updated particle is transformed to the schedule using the revised serial scheme based on the current position. The new *pBest* and *gBest* are determined.

Step 6 : Stopping criteria.
The particle will terminate if it meet the maximum iteration. If the current iteration does not meet the termination signal, then it will repeat step 3.

Results and Discussions

Data Analysis

The data gained by generating the initial population of the model after determine the initial transportation tree by a Heuristic Approach based on the characteristics of concave cost network flow problems (Altiparmak and Karaoglan, 2007). Fig. 1 will illustrate the initial transportation tree.

ISBN: 978-1-387-00704-2

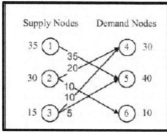

Figure 1: Transportation Tree (Basic Solution)
(Source: Altiparmak and Karaoglan, 2007)

Table 1: Data of Transportation Tree

Arc, A(x)	Source	Destination	Cost, (c_{ij})	Supply, (a_j)	Demand, (b_j)
p	1	5	35	35	40
q	2	4	20	30	30
r	2	6	10	30	10
s	3	4	10	15	30
t	3	5	5	15	40

Table 1 shows three demand nodes (1,2,3) and three supply nodes (4,5,6) involved. The total arc is five which are p, q, r, s, t and the set of arcs in the transportation tree is $A(x) = \{(1,5),(2,4),(2,6),(3,4),(3,5)\}$. Using the above data, all the values will be substituted into the model to check if the constraints are satisfied or not. The constraints is checked as stated in Eq. (3.2), (3.3) and (3.4) and assumed to be true.

The method of modified PSO is implemented in this study. In this study, the maximum iteration is set as 1000 iterations. The value of the particle will iterate 1000 times and the best value (minimum value) in all iterations will be assigned as *gBest*.

Optimizing Transportation Cost Problem using Modified PSO Algorithm
After running the algorithm, the result obtained is approximately lower than the actual cost. Table 2 shows the optimal solution of supply in order to have a minimum cost in TCP.

ISBN: 978-1-387-00704-2

Table 2: The Optimal Solution of TCP

Arc,A(x)	Source	Destination	New supply	New cost
p	1	5	17	144.31
q	2	4	15	77.46
r	2	6	32	56.57
s	3	4	16	40.00
t	3	5	20	22.36
			Total cost	**340.69**

Based on the result in Table 2, the new supply from the arc p, q and r is 17, 15 and 32 respectively. While for the arc s and t, the new supply after optimized is 16 and 20. With these optimal values, the new TCP is 340.69 which is lower than the actual cost, 429.47.

Conclusions

This study is useful to find the optimal solution for the amount of product transported and minimum cost of the problem. The result shows that the optimal solution for the amount of product transported from source to the desired destination is optimized where the new value is 17, 15, 32, 16 and 20 following the arc, $A(x)=\{(1,5), (2,4), (2,6), (3,4), (3,5)\}$ respectively with the total cost of 340.69.

References

Altiparmak, F., &Karaoglan, I. (2007).A genetic ant colony optimization approach for concave costtransportation problems.*2007 IEEE Congress onEvolutionary Computation (CEC 2007)*, 1685-1692.

Business Dictionary.com - Online Business Dictionary. Retrieved from www.businessdictionary.com/.

Chun, T. L. (2007). Using predicting particle swarm optimization to solve the vehicle routing problem with timewindows.*Proceedings of the 2008 IEEE IEEM*, 810-814.

Hu, X., &Eberhart, R. (2002). Solving constrained nonlinear optimization problems with Particle Swarm Optimization.

Kulkarni, N. K., Patekar, S., Bhoskar, T., Kulkarni O., Kakandir, G. M., &Nandedkar, V.M., (2015). Particle swarm optimization applications to mechanical engineering- a review. *Material Today: Proceedings 2*, 2631-2639.

The Free Dictionary: Dictionary, Encyclopedia and Thesaurus. Retrieved from www.thefreedictionary.com/.

Sadeghi, J., Sadeghi, S., Taghi, S., &Niaki, A. (2014). Optimizing a hybrid

ISBN: 978-1-387-00704-2

vendor managed inventory and transportation problem with fuzzy demand: An improved particle swarm optimization algorithm, *Information sciences, 272,* 126-144.

Xuedan, H.L., & Wang, L.Q. (2009). Routing optimization for dispatchingvehicles based on an improved discrete particle swarm optimization algorithm with mutation operation. *2009 Third International Conference on Genetic andEvolutionary Computing,* 624-627.

ISBN: 978-1-387-00704-2

SECTION II:

COMPUTER NETWORK
&
MATHEMATICAL
SCIENCES

Article 13

Physical Layer Jamming Attack Detection in MANET

Ahmad Yusri Dak, Farhah Rosidi
Faculty of Computer and Mathematical Science,
Universiti Teknologi MARA Perlis Branch, Malaysia

Noor Elaiza Abd Khalid
Faculty of Computer and Mathematical Science,
Universiti Teknologi MARA Shah Alam, Malaysia

Abstract

Mobile Ad Hoc Networks (MANETs) is gaining popularity in recent years due to being low-cost, flexible, and user-friendly. Users can easily create a spontaneous ad hoc network services for military use, emergency rescue purposes, or deploy it in rural areas, situations where mobile devices needs to communicate with each other. However, the nature of MANETs, such as open medium, dynamic mobility and lack of security, renders these networks susceptible to a range of attacks. In addition, its limitations such as hidden terminals signal interference and its open nature allows attackers to interrupt the network by denying access to users. One common technique used is jamming-based DoS(Denial-of-Service) attack, which is done by sending high frequency radio signals to disrupt communication between sender and receiver, leading to severe network damage. Most attacks exists at the physical layer, such as constant and random jammers. According to statistics recorded in 2017 by the MyCERT Response Team Malaysia, jamming attacks have increased up to 184% since 2007. To address these attacks, a study is conducted to find viable solutions to this issue. Two different scenarios were simulated and tested which involve random and constant jammers. Performance of simulated networks attacked by these jammers is evaluated using three performance metrics, Bit Error Rate (BER), Signal to Noise Ratio (SNR), and Throughput., Analyzed results concludes that these three performance metrics shows significant potential as detection mechanisms that offers insights and benchmarks for future research based on detecting jamming attacks.

Keywords: *MANET, Jamming, Physical, Constant, Random*

ISBN: 978-1-387-00704-2

Introduction

In recent times, advancement of technology in wireless networking has brought fundamental changes to human life, allowing users to freely connect to the network anytime and anywhere, thus becoming part of our daily life. Wireless Network is the most popular technology available among users. For instance, MANET is a wireless ad hoc network that does not need pre-existing communication infrastructure, easy to connect and user-friendly. Mobile devices can easily enter or exit the network without disrupting other mobile devices in that network(Dak, Elaiza, & Khalid, 2012). However, the popularity of wireless networking, specifically MANETs that uses the Wi-Fi network standard poses potential security issues as attackers can exploit and cause blockage to the network.

Limitations of MANETs like hidden terminals, signal interference and its open nature gives attackers opportunity to interrupt the network by denying access to users. These attackers may use several attack techniques such as Radio Frequency (RF) jamming by injecting powerful high frequency signals to interrupt and bring down network services. Jamming attack using radio frequency technique is generated at physical layer of the protocol stack and disrupts the transmission between sender and receiver leading to severe network damage. Attacks that occur at the physical layer are usually constant and random jammers.

Statistics recorded by the Malaysian Computer Emergency Response Team [MyCERT], as shown in Figure 1, show that jamming based DoS attacks are increasing every year. Statistics compiled in 2013 indicate 19 attacks, 29 incidents in 2014 and this number increased to 66 attacks in 2016. The decreasing number of attacks from 23 in 2012 to 19 in 2013 was due to user action as they strengthened their security by implementing better security protection. However, many organizations overlook the potential impact of jamming attacks against wireless networks especially 802.11n.

ISBN: 978-1-387-00704-2

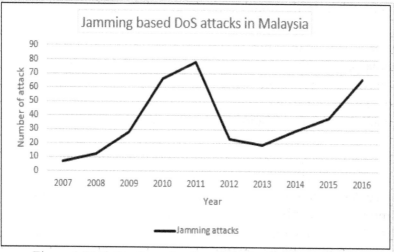

Figure 1 Statistics Jamming based DoS attack in Malaysia
(Source: MyCERT, 2017)

Due to critical issues of jamming attacks in MANETs, a study is proposed to cater to these issues and provide necessary solutions for future research. This research helped the society and other researchers for further understanding of constant and random jamming attacks.

Related Works

Xu, Trappe, Zhang and Wood, (2005)provides a complete description of the radio interference attacks and identifies the serious issue of the presence of the jamming attack. Four different jamming attack models were suggested that can be employed by an antagonist to disable a wireless network, and formulated their efficiency in terms of how they influence the capability of a wireless node to send and obtain packets from the destination node. The authors also talked about various measurements that forms the basis for discovering a jamming attack, and explained various scenarios where every measurement is not sufficient to reliably classify the existence of a jamming attack. The author realized that carrier sensing time and signal strength are unable to conclusively determine the presence of a jammer.

ISBN: 978-1-387-00704-2

Hamieh and Ben-Othman (2009) explains that military and other sensitive security procedures are still important applications for ad-hoc networks. One important challenge in planning these networks is their susceptibility to Denial-of-Service (DoS) attacks. In this paper, the author takes a specific class of DoS attacks known as Jamming. A new way to determine such an attack through formulation of error distribution was suggested.

Lu, Wang, Wang, Wang, Zhuo (2011) simulated and presented jamming attacks against time-critical traffic. The author presented a new metric, message invalidation ratio, to measure time-critical applications performance. The author indicated through real-time experiments and gambling-based simulator that there exists a phase modulation process for a time-critical application under jamming attacks.

Methodology
Two scenarios simulating physical layer jamming attacks were based on configuration from (Gonzalez, 2007) and (Babar, 2015). Each scenario is configured and simulated using MANET environment set up as described in Table 1.

Table 1 MANET's configuration

Parameters	Attributes
Protocol	None
Simulation Time	7200 seconds
Simulation Area	100 x 100 meters
Data Rate(bps)	11 Mbps
Packet Size(bits)	1024
Transmit Power(W)	0.05 Watt
RTS Threshold (bytes)	1024(bytes)
Modulation	BPSK
Packet Interarrival time(seconds)	Constant (1.0)
Performance Parameters	BER, SNR and Throughput,

ISBN: 978-1-387-00704-2

a) Scenario 1: MANET with Constant Jammer

Scenario 1 is designed to simulate a constant jamming attack as shown in Figure 2. It consists of a transmitter, a receiver, and a constant jammer with MANET environment. The attributes of transmitter and receiver for Scenario 1 is developed based on the model proposed by (Gonzalez, 2007) and (Babar, 2015).

This attack contains a transmitter sending valid traffic receiver without any MAC protocol and a single jammer that is constantly emitting high frequency non-valid packets at a constant bit rate (1024 bps), trying to jam transmission and increase the probability of errors received.

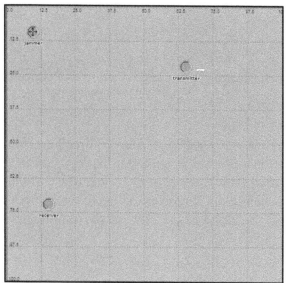

Figure 2 Network with constant jammer

b) Scenario 2: MANET with Random Jammer

Figure 3 shows the scenario for random jammer. It is a simulation with an activated random jammer. Random jammer was constructed to send data for period of time and sleep for another

ISBN: 978-1-387-00704-2

random period. Transmitter sends a valid data packet (1024 bps) to the receiver, turning on and off mode randomly.

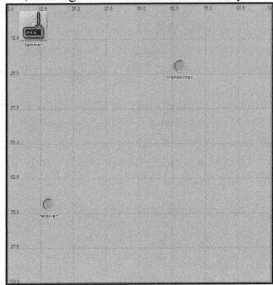

Figure 3 Network with random jammer

Results and Findings

Network performance test for scenario 1 and 2 are compared and analyzed. Network performance test that consists of BER, SNR and throughput data were chosen to identify constant jamming and random jamming. Comparative analyses for both jammers are necessary to determine effective identification metrics.

ISBN: 978-1-387-00704-2

a. BER test

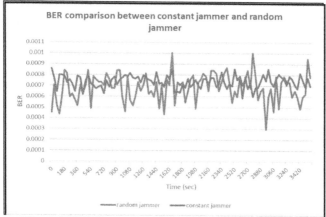

Figure 4 BER for constant jammer and random jammer

Figure 4 shows a graph for BER test that simulated constant and random jammer captured using OPNET version 13. Random jammer has the highest BER value up to 0.001% compared to constant jammer which is 0.0009%. This show that a random jammer is more effective in interrupting and corrupting bits transmission.

BER is chosen as the detection mechanism because the capability to identify physical layer jamming attack on the receiver side is based on its definition. It can define the number of bit errors received over a data stream in a communication channel that has been altered due to noise, interference, and distortion or bit synchronization errors.

ISBN: 978-1-387-00704-2

b. SNR test

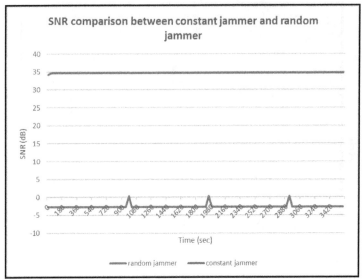

Figure 5 SNR test for constant jammer and random jammer

Figure 5 shows the graph of SNR simulation test conducted for constant jammer and random jammer. Average value captured for constant jammer is at 34.69dB, higher than random jammer which averages at -2.68118 dB for the same duration.

Constant jammer shows a constant signal capture rate over time. The higher detection rate of SNR in dB indicated a poor detection performance in RF that show more noise than signal. This result is in line with (Tan, Hu, & Portmann, 2012) that show the maximum and minimum range of result is set to distinguish between signal noise jamming and normal signal. If frequency detected is below or above the assigned limit, it is assumed to be a jammed signal; otherwise, the original signal is transmitted.

Graph for random jammer showed a high peak (0.28675 dB) and a lower peak signal (-2.68118 dB) indicatingthat the signal is affected by a random jammer during sleep and active time frame. Random jammer capture value below than 0 db is due to a tradeoff that occurs between jamming and sleeping mode. The

ISBN: 978-1-387-00704-2

ratio between sleeping and jamming time can be manipulated to adjust this trade-off between efficiency and effectiveness. The detection rate is average -2bB, showing a jamming attack can be considered effective if the SNR is less than one(Pintea & Pop, 2014).

c. Throughput Test

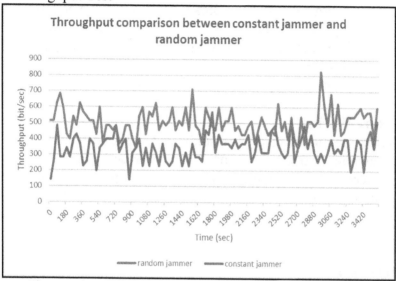

Figure 6 Throughput test for constant jammer and random jammer

Throughput is defined as the ratio of expected delivered data payload to the expected transmission time(Ekpenyong & Joseph Isabona, 2010). It is the percentage of undistorted data packets received without errors and what the user sees after overhead. Figure 6 showed the graph of throughput tested for constant jammer and random jammer. Random jammer has the highest throughput value at 80.6%, compared to constant jammer at 52.8%. This showed that random jammer allowed more bits to arrive at the receiver compared to constant jammer. Under random jammer attack, a node tries to gain more throughput by transmitting more packets. This becomes higher when large packets are transmitted. Node gains more throughputin comparison to other nodes, causing some packets to be dropped there. Therefore, throughput rate is more effective to detect

ISBN: 978-1-387-00704-2

random jammer compared to constant jammer. Thus, the result showed that random jammer allowed more throughput than constant jammer.

Conclusion

Constant and random jamming attacks at the physical layer disrupt and corrupt data transmission, which happens due to the nature of MANET. Results obtained from experiments done in this study show that these jamming attacks affects the transmission's BER, SNR and throughput. The evaluation of the three metrics mentioned also shows that random jammer causes more disruption compared to constant jammer.

Future Works

Further continuation of this study in the future would include researching two other jamming attacks: reactive and deceptive jammers. These jammers are more complex as they can manipulate the wireless protocols in the network. Thus, more work is needed to understand the characteristics of these jammers.

References

Dak, A. Y., Elaiza, N., & Khalid, A. (2012). A Novel Framework for Jamming Detection and Classification in Wireless Networks. In *8th International Conference on Computing and Networking Technology (INC, ICCIS and ICMIC)* (pp. 240–246).

Hamieh, a., & Ben-Othman, J. (2009). Detection of Jamming Attacks in Wireless Ad Hoc Networks Using Error Distribution. *2009 IEEE International Conference on Communications*, 1–6. http://doi.org/10.1109/ICC.2009.5198912

Tan, W. L., Hu, P., & Portmann, M. (2012). SNR-based Link Quality Estimation. In *Vehicular Technology Conference (VTC Spring), 2012 IEEE 75th.*

Xu, W., Trappe, W., Zhang, Y., & Wood, T. (2005). The feasibility of launching and detecting jamming attacks in wireless networks. *Proceedings of the 6th ACM International Symposium on Mobile Ad Hoc Networking and Computing MobiHoc 05*, 46. Retrieved from http://portal.acm.org/citation.cfm?doid=1062689.1062697

Lu, Z., Wang, W., Wang, C., & Wang, Zhuo Lu Wenye, C. (2011, April). From jammer to gambler: Modeling and detection of jamming attacks

ISBN: 978-1-387-00704-2

against   time-critical   traffic. http://doi.org/10.1109/INFCOM.2011.5934989

Babar, S. D. (2015). *Security Framework and Jamming Detection for Internet of Things*. Aalborg University, Denmark.

Dak, A. Y., Elaiza, N., & Khalid, A. (2012). A Novel Framework for Jamming Detection and Classification in Wireless Networks. In *8th International Conference on Computing and Networking Technology (INC, ICCIS and ICMIC)* (pp. 240–246).

Ekpenyong, M., & Joseph Isabona. (2010). Modeling Throughput Performance in 802 . 11 WLAN. *IJCSI International Journal of Computer Science Issues*, *7*(3).

Gonzalez, J. M. (2007). *Exploring Jamming Attack using OPNET 12.0*. University of Pittsburgh.

Hamieh, a., & Ben-Othman, J. (2009). Detection of Jamming Attacks in Wireless Ad Hoc Networks Using Error Distribution. *2009 IEEE International Conference on Communications*, 1–6. http://doi.org/10.1109/ICC.2009.5198912

Lu, Z., Wang, W., Wang, C., & Wang, Zhuo Lu Wenye, C. (2011, April). From jammer to gambler: Modeling and detection of jamming attacks against   time-critical   traffic. http://doi.org/10.1109/INFCOM.2011.5934989

Pintea, C., & Pop, P. C. (2014). Sensitive Ants for Denial Jamming Attack. *Advanced Intelligent Soft Computing Journal*, *239*, 1–4.

Tan, W. L., Hu, P., & Portmann, M. (2012). SNR-based Link Quality Estimation. In *Vehicular Technology Conference (VTC Spring), 2012 IEEE 75th*.

Team(MyCert), M. E. R. (2017). MyCERT Incident Statistics. Retrieved March 30, 2016, from https://www.mycert.org.my/statistics/2012.php

Xu, W., Trappe, W., Zhang, Y., & Wood, T. (2005). The feasibility of launching and detecting jamming attacks in wireless networks. *Proceedings of the 6th ACM International Symposium on Mobile Ad Hoc Networking and Computing MobiHoc 05*, 46. Retrieved from http://portal.acm.org/citation.cfm?doid=1062689.1062697

Gonzalez, J. M. (2007). *Exploring Jamming Attack using OPNET 12.0*. University of Pittsburgh.

Babar, S. D. (2015). *Security Framework and Jamming Detection for Internet of Things*. Aalborg University, Denmark.

Team(MyCert), M. E. R. (2017). MyCERT Incident Statistics. Retrieved March 30, 2016, from https://www.mycert.org.my/statistics/2017.php

ISBN: 978-1-387-00704-2

Article 14

Home Monitoring System(HMS) using Raspberry Pi Model B

Faten Fatehah Rosli, Ahmad Yusr iDak
Faculty of Computer and Mathematical Science,
Universiti Teknologi MARA Perlis Branch, Malaysia

Abstract
Nowadays, numbers of robbery crime keeps increasing as reported by Royale Malaysian Police(RMP) which usually occurs in daylight and also when the owner is not around. This scenario makes the people feel unsafe when leaving their properties since there is a limited monitoring system available. As the current surveillance system needs larger space, expensive and unreliable hence most people usually don't care with their belonging anymore. Besides, if the person does not have a proper security system, their belongings become the target of crime. Thus, HMS is proposed and developed to cater the security issues related to home security. It is designed with condition such as signal is recorded as the intruder move near a motion sensor. Motion sensor generated a TRUE input that detected a signal based on the moving object. Raspberry Pi model B is proposed as a server that responsible to send data directly to database thus the owner can view and easily identify the entity of the moving object when the data recorded via web application. Experimental results showed the ability of the motion sensor to detect movement increase when the distance of movement at the area of sensor decreases. Does, some recommendation had been made in order to improve the performance of the system detection.

Keywords: Monitoring, Sensor, Raspberry PI, Surveillance

Introduction

Nowadays, due to high living cost, migration of illegal immigrant and high employability security is a major concern especially involving luxurious properties. Reports, news, media social and television showed huge number of crimes for instance a breaking in either at home, shop, office and others even on during daylight as stated in Malaysian Insider (2015) and the research of Criminal Investigation Department who is Chief Datuk Mohd Adnan said that gangs targeted mostly on residential area after the owner

ISBN: 978-1-387-00704-2

leaves the house. According to statistics reported by PDRM, since 2009 property crime like house break-ins and theft makes up the bulk with about 80% of the crime rate Mohit et al (2010). However, many security systems that have the high capability to alert notify and record the event but cost is an issue and cannot be afford by an ordinary people. Some of the security system require high maintenance fees, bidder storage and can cause high electricity Nguyen et al (2015).

In addition, reported by Adriansyah and Dani (2014) that it may cause higher in maintenance cost due tothe implementation of this system. The methodology for the development of the proposed system based on setup, configures and testing purposes. Raspberry Pi configured to integrate with PIR sensor, camera module and database. The practice of this system is the motion detection sensor detects the movements of an object in real time and it will capture an image of that moving object so the user can check the image on web application. Thus, the user receives their security concern and enables them to evaluate the received image. There are two types that are generated by Raspberry Pi such as static image and small size video. Static image defines as a not moving image while video image define as a moving image such as video or animation. This project system focused on capturing static image.

Related Work

i.   Study by Kaltiokallio and Bocca (2011)
This project aimed to process the receiving signal strength indicator (RSSI). It also used Wireless Sensor Network to extract useful information upon receiving RSSI signal. This project differs to HMS since it uses motion sensor to detect and capture image of the moving object. However, this project has similarity with HMS in which both emphasis on motion detection to detect motion change cause by human. Lastly, this project indicates that

ISBN: 978-1-387-00704-2

changes in motion can be detected using RSSI rather than using motion sensor.

ii. Advanced Raspberry Pi Surveillance (ARS) System by Vamsikrishna et al (2015)

Vamsikrishna et al (2015)proposed a method by using SimpleCV as a simple computer vision library, ARS system captures surrounding and detects human presence. This presence of motion notifies the user. This notification process is completed by sending short message service. Apart from that, ARS system used MPEG-Streamer to allow user see the live streaming anywhere. This shows the limitation of the system when user can only see this live streaming video anywhere over internet only. However, this project has similarity to my project since both use current technology, which is Raspberry Pi.

Methodology

Methodology is a specific step taken during the project. Table 1shows the flow of methodology design process.

Table 1: Phase' Activity

PHASE	KEY ACTIVITIES	DELIVERABLE
INFORMATION GATHERING	Feasibility study Primary Study: - -Identify research area -Identify problem statement -Identify research objective -Identify research scope -Identify research significant	Findings: Review related articles and journals
PROJECT REQUIREMENT	Instrument design - Hardware requirement - Software requirement System design	System requirement: - Raspberry Pi - PIR Sensor -USB WIFI Dongle - PHP language - MySQL Database -PhpMyAdmin
DESIGN AND DEVELOPMENT	Develop solution as requirements.	Integrate the Raspberry Pi and the Home Monitoring System for the motion detection using PHP language.
TESTING AND EXPERIMENTATION	Testing on: - -Usability Test -Functionality Test -Network Test	-Raspberry Pi and PIR Sensor module was installed and configure. -Repeat if testing fails.
DOCUMENTATION	Writing report	Full set of report

ISBN: 978-1-387-00704-2

i.   Phase 1: Information Gathering
Information Gathering phase covers on literature review, which
has been briefly explained in Literature Review section. The
information is taken from journals, articles and websites that are
related for this project. Current issues related to home security
searched in order to develop a product that might contribute to
overcome the problem for example current CCTV required large
space to implement while R-PI need small space.

ii.   Phase 2: Project Requirement
Project requirement, which showed the equipment that used to
develop all of the designs needed in this project. These
requirements are dividing into two categories, which hardware
and software. Hardware requirement needed for this system such
as Raspberry Pi 3 Model B, PIR Sensor, USB WIFI Dongle and
male-to-male wire while software requirement includes Raspbian
OS, PhpMyAdmin and MySQL.

iii.   Phase 3: Design and Development
In the development phase, it involved the installation step of
Raspbian OS in Raspberry Pi 3 model B, the placement of every
electronic part on Raspberry Pi and its own coding which will
make the electronic part to work. The Raspbian OS was chosen
as the operating system for this project. There are many operating
systems that can be installed in Raspberry Pi, which includes
Archilinux, Pidora, Raspbmc and others. However, Raspbian is
the easiest API compared to others. This phase also focuses on
the step taken in the making of the R-PI. The schematic diagram
of the proposed system was sketched in order to explain how the
system works as shown in Figure 1. Then, work flow of program
design was presented and steps taken one very phase were
explained.

ISBN: 978-1-387-00704-2

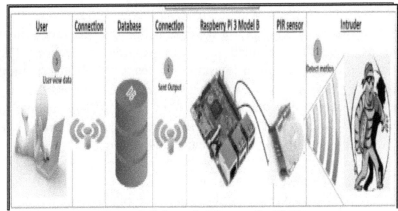

Figure 1: Schematic Diagram for HMS

HMS consists of Home Surveillance, Raspberry Pi, Motion Sensor, web application and script coding. However, the main part for the technique or algorithm used to solve this problem is the programming part. HMS being coded in PHP and Python language since the usage of Python language is simpler but has a long coding for overall system as shown in Figure 2.

```
          fromgpiozeroimportMotionSensor
          frompicameraimport PiCamera
camera = PiCamera
pir – MotionSensor(4)
while True
          pirwait_for_motion()
          camera start_preview()
          pirwait_for_no_motion()
          camera stop_preview()
```

Figure 2: Coding for HMS in Python Language

ISBN: 978-1-387-00704-2

iv. Phase 4: Testing and Experimentation

In testing phase, HMS was tested on several scenarios selected in order to evaluate the functionality and usability of the HMS. Network test consist of two experimentations that test based on time taken.

v. Phase 5: Documentation
Final phase involved the documentation of the result and write up to thesis completion. The thesis also compared with other research project to ensure this project is suitable based on current technology.

Results and Findings
Respondents involved in this study consist of 30 peoples with 15 females and 15 males that involved in pre-study and post survey. Respondents that have been selected consist of students, lecturers, government servants and housewives. A functionality and usability test were conducted by allowing several people to evaluate the proposed system.

i. Functionality test

Table 2 shows the results tested collected from experiment to measure the real time detection of PIR sensor with reflex to distance. Scenarios were configured based in three different distances for instance 4, 8 and 10 meters. Scenario 1 is conducted at 4 meters distance, with time of the movement is at 11.00 p.m. and the response time of the PIR sensor to detect the movement is also at 11.00 p.m. Then, scenario 2 is tested for 8 meters distance with the time of the movement is at 11.10 p.m. Finally, scenario 3 is conducted at 11.23p.m. to detect the movement at 10 meter distance. It showed that from the distance of 4 meters, 8 meters and 10 meters, the PIR sensor enable to detect the movement with less than 60 seconds. Therefore, with the far distance from PIR sensor, the effectiveness is become less effective. The outcome showed that a PIR motion sensor enable to detect the

ISBN: 978-1-387-00704-2

motion movement based on three different distances successfully but the effectives of the PIR sensor parallel with distance.

Table 2: PIR sensor vs distance

Distance (meter)	Time of Movement	Time of the PIR sensor to Detect Movement	Time taken to detect the movement (seconds)
4	11.00 p.m.	11.00 p.m.	03
8	11.10 p.m.	11.10 p.m.	15
10	11.22 p.m.	11.23 p.m.	60

Table 3 shows details of the result collected from Experiment 2 to measure the data store inside database when PIR detected a movement of intruder. Based on 4 meters distance, the time of the PIR sensor detected movement is at 11.00 p.m. and the time of the data stored in database is received at 11.00 p.m. which showed no delay in time. As for the 8 meters distance, the result showed that a PIR sensor detected a movement at 11.10 p.m. and the time of the data stored is at 11.11 p.m. Based on the results of the 8 meters distance showed that the delay time is 60 seconds. Lastly, based on the 10 meters away, the delay time of the PIR sensor to detect the movement and send the data to database is around 120 seconds which from 11.23 p.m. to 11.25 a.m. This showed that some delay occurs when distance is far away from PIR motion sensor but detection record still accepted by database.

Table 3 Database response time

Distance (meter)	Time the PIR sensor Detect Movement.	Time the data Stored in Database
4	11.00 p.m.	11.00 p.m.
8	11.10 p.m.	11.11 p.m.
10	11.23 p.m.	11.25 p.m.

ISBN: 978-1-387-00704-2

ii.   Usability Test

This section was performed to evaluate the effectiveness of the system. Post study was conducted with 30 respondents using usability test.

Figure 3 demonstrated a result based on HMS contribution to reduce crime theft especially on house break cases in the future. From the result presented showed that 75% of the respondent confident that HMS enable to reduce that crime since the characteristics of system which can alert the owner with real time notification. In contrast, only 25% of respondents are unsatisfied with HMS to show a reducing in house breaking case. This can be concluded that one third of respondent believes HMS as an alternative to reduced crime cases and can be implemented as home security system.

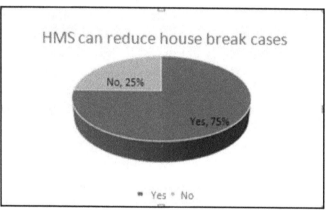

Figure 3 Breaking cases survey

Figure 4 showed the result collected from post study to analyze users' perception on implementing HMS. From the result presented showed that about 50% of respondents satisfied with the performance of HMS, 35% give a positive feedback and only 15% of total respondents request a better monitoring system.

ISBN: 978-1-387-00704-2

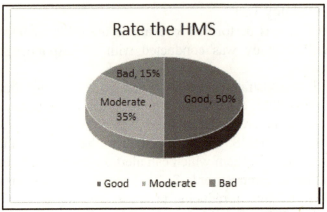

Figure 4 Users' perception against HMS

Discussions

This project is designed to ensure the owner of house can be check if there are house break activity occurs at their place and at the same time shows the method on sending data taken using Raspberry Pi 3 to the database. Home Monitoring System (HMS) was developed based on several phases presented detailed in previous section, which all the software needed such as Raspbian OS was installed in order to have a programming environment in the Raspberry Pi. Then, PIR sensor module was installed and tested using some program to ensure its functionality. Lastly, some software to develop web application and database was installed which allow the Raspberry Pi send the notification with attachment of the output from PIR sensor to the web and stored in database.

Conclusion

In conclusion, the development of the movement sensor with database through web application has been successfully developed according to its objectives and desired Specifications.

References

Kaltiokallio, O., & Bocca, M. (2011). Real-Time Intrusion Detection and Tracking in Indoor Environment Through Distributed RSSI Processing.

ISBN: 978-1-387-00704-2

17th IEEE International Conference on Embedded and Real-Time Computing Systems and Applications, 61–70. https://doi.org/10.1109/RTCSA.2011.38

Nguyen, H., Thi, T., Loan, K., Mao, B. D., & Huh, E. (2015). Low Cost Real-Time System Monitoring Using Raspberry Pi. *Ubiquitous and Future Networks (ICUFN), 2015 Seventh International Conference on*, 857–859. Retrieved from http://doi.org/10.1109/ICUFN.2015.7182665

Vamsikrishna, P., Hussain, S. R., Ramu, N., & Rao, P. M. (2015). Advanced Raspberry Pi Surveillance (ARS) System. In *2015 Global Conference on Communication Technologies (GCCT)* (pp. 860–862).

For Journals:

Mohit, M. A., Mohamed, H., & Elsawahli, H. (2010). Crime And Housing In Malaysia : Case Study Of Taman Melati Terrace Housing. *Asian Journal of Environment-Behaviour Studies, 1*(3), 26–36.

M ohit, M. A., Mohamed, H., & Elsawahli, H. (2010). Crime And Housing In Malaysia : Case Study of Taman Melati Terrace Housing. *Asian Journal of Environment-Behaviour Studies, 1*(3), 26–36.

Malaysian Insider. (2015). Selangor cops cripple house break-in gang - The Malaysian Insider. Retrieved December 2, 2015, from http://www.themalaysianinsider.com/citynews/greaterkl/article/selangor-cops-cripple-house-break-in-gang/selangor-cops-cripple-house-break-in-gang

Adriansyah, A., & Dani, A. W. (2014). Design of Small Smart Home System Based on Arduino. *Electrical Power, Electronics, Communications, Controls, and Informatics Seminar (EECCIS)*, 121–125. Retrieved from http://doi.org/10.1109/EECCIS.2014.7003731

ISBN: 978-1-387-00704-2

Article 15

Intrusion Detection System (IDS) : Investigating Snort Performance in Windows and Ubuntu due to Flooding Attack

Abidah Mat Taib, Nur Syahirah Shayuthi,
Faculty of Computer and Mathematical Sciences,
Universiti Teknologi MARA Perlis Branch, Malaysia

Abstract
Intrusion detection is an important technology that can help in managing threats and vulnerabilities in this changing environment. Computer technology is more and more ubiquitous, the penetration of computer in society is a welcome step towards modernization but society needs to be better equipped with challenges associated with technology. Thus, with the help of intrusion detection system (IDS) that can be used to monitor network for any attack and intrusion, it can reduce the security issues and help people to curb with the advance threat. This project aims to provide insight to small organization, employee and student to have a secure environment in their personal computer. The objectives of this project is to set up an isolate local area network (LAN) to imitate a real network environment using Graphical Network Simulator-3 (GNS3) and to create the scenario for analyzing Snort IDS performance in Windows and Ubuntu due to flooding attack. Basically, this project uses a router in GNS3 that can act as a real router. The IDS was implemented on the PC1 while PC2 acts as an attacker that send a flooding attack to PC 1. The timer was set for 2 minutes and the performance was analyzed based on drop packet and throughput. The result shows that the performance of Snort is better in Ubuntu compared to Windows in term of its drop packet and throughput.

Keywords: *Intrusion Detection System, Snort, GNS3, performance analysis, flooding attack*

Introduction

Internet is becoming very important in people's lives since it can be a medium for them to communicate with others easily at a lower cost. Furthermore, people usually use internet as a medium to share files, get entertainment, search for information and do other activities that give benefits to them (Muniandy, 2010).

ISBN: 978-1-387-00704-2

However, not all things connected to the internet give advantages to the users. People who are connected to the internet have their own intentions and make choices whether to do good or bad things.

There are many types of computer security risk that can cause damage to personal computers such as internet and network attacks, unauthorized access and use, hardware theft, software theft, information theft and system failure (Ahmad, 2012). So, it is important for all users to give attention about computer security. There are various ways to secure and defend the system from unauthorized use for example encryption, use of a firewall, anti-virus software and intrusion detection (Debra & Shinder, 2006). Intrusion detection system (IDS) can provide security services using many conventions or patterns and it can provide robust, highly flexible, portable and fully controlled protection against an entire field of threats (Jeganathan & Prakasam, 2014). Snort is an open source IDS that can be freely installed in various OS.Kuldeep, Tyagi and Richa (2014) have implemented Snort IDS in cloud environment to deal with pretense attacks.

Problems happen when people are not concerned about the security issues while using the internet and they do not know how to secure their own personal computers ("Computer Threats | Monster.com," 2017). In common, users either use Windows, Ubuntu or other operating systems (OS). As reported by 3schools (2013), most users prefer to use Windows OS with usage percentage of 77.3%, Linux OS with 5.5% and other operating system with 6.4%. Thus,knowing how Snort on Windows and Snort on Ubuntu operate is important. Hence, this project aimed to investigate and give understanding about installing and applying IDS in a local network and observing how a host detects an intrusion. The observation was focused on the performance of a computer running IDS on Windows and Linux operating system towards denial of service (DoS) attack.

ISBN: 978-1-387-00704-2

This paper aims to provide insights about the importance of detecting intrusion and how Snort can be used for that purpose. Thus, investigation of Snort implementation in Windows and Ubuntu was carried out where respective testing and experimentation had been set up on an isolated network using a GraphicalNetwork Simulator-3 (GNS3) (GNS3 2016). The remainder of this paper is organized as follows. Next section will be presenting the overview of DoS and IDSs and where they are used. It follows with explaining the methodology and experiment setup, result and analysis, and finally the conclusion.

Overview of DoS Attack

Flooding attack is a common DoS attack that is intended to bring a system or service down by flooding the system with a large amount of data (Manna & Amphawan, 2012). Protecting a network against distributed DoS attack is quite a challenge. Nevertheless, a possible effort can be taken by applying appropriate IDS rules to guard against flooding attack. It is one of the mechanisms that is likely capable of defending DoS attack at the early stage. Some well known flooding attacks are related to Transmission Control Protocol (TCP) and User Datagram Protocol (UDP) (Li, Li, & Zhao, 2009). The flood attack of TCP SYN or TCP ACK is a very common attack. TCP SYN flood is a type of DoS attack in which an attacker sends a progression of SYN requests to a target's system and tries to consume enough server resources to make the system unresponsive to genuine activity (Bogdanoski, Shuminoski, & Risteski, 2013).

The attack starts as an ordinary TCP connection in which the client and server exchange data in TCP packets. The attacker can craft a huge number of SYN packets with spoofed source IP addresses that represent TCP client keeps on sending SYN packets to the server, these SYN packets tell the server that a connection is requested. The server consequently reacts to each client with an ACK packet. The client is supposed to react with another ACK packet accepting the connection in order to set up the session. The server holds these sessions open, anticipating the

ISBN: 978-1-387-00704-2

last packet in the sequence. In this attack, no response ACK packets from the clients arrive at the server. This scenario makes the server fills up the accessible connection and denies any request of client access (Anand, 2012).

UDP utilizes a basic transmission model without implicit handshaking dialogues for providing dependability, requesting, or data integrity. Therefore, UDP gives an unreliable service and datagram may arrive out of order, show duplicate, or missing without notice. So, the user application (program) responsible of taking care UDP assumes that error checking is either necessary or performed, to avoid from the overhead of such handling at the network interface level. Furthermore, in UDP flood attack, it is similar to Internet Control Message Protocol (ICMP) flood attack, it sends a substantial number of UDP messages to the target in a short time, so that the target will be busy responding and transmitting the normal data packets (Kumar & Rai, 2012).

Overview of IDS
IDS is the process of monitoring the events occurring in a computer or networked system and analyzing events for signs of possible incidents which are violations or imminent threats of violation of computer security policies, acceptable use policies, or standard security practices (Kumar et al., 2013). IDS can be in the form of a software application that operates based on misused (signature-based) detection or anomaly detection (Buchanan, 2011). An IDS can be placed within the network to monitor network traffic, such as looking for known attacks or virus signature or it can be placed on hosts to detect an actual host intrusion. IDSs that monitor data packets on the network and try to determine an intrusion based on network traffic is known as network IDSs (NIDS). NIDS can run on a host or on network-based. Snort (Orebaugh, Biles & Babbin, 2005) is an open source NIDS that is freely available. Honeypots (Buchanan, 2011) also is an example of IDS that is used to attract an intruder and detect the intrusion at the early stage.

ISBN: 978-1-387-00704-2

This project focuses on Snort since it is widely used and can detect both signature- and anomaly-based detection. Snort runs as a background process and reads-in a set of rules and monitors the network traffic to produce event data and a log (Buchanan, 2011). In order to learn the application of host-based IDS, an experiment test bed was setup to investigate Snort performance in detecting DoS attack in Windows and Ubuntu. The respective experiment was conducted in an isolated network that was built using GNS3. The testing involved is described in the methodology.

Methodology
The first step was getting the appropriate hardware and software ready for the setting up of the experiment testbed. Then, installation of the required software on the respective hardware was done. Upon installation finished, an isolated network was created using a GNS3. GNS3 allows us to design complex network topologies. It can run simulations or configure devices ranging from simple workstation to powerful Cisco routers. It is based on Dynamips, Pemu/Qemu and Dynagen(GNS3, 2016). To make sure the network is correctly configured and ready for testing, network connectivity test was carried out. Subsequently, four scenarios of experiment were conducted that aimed to investigate performance of Snort running on Windows and Ubuntu in detecting SYN flood and UDP flood attacks. Time was set for 2 minutes for all experiment scenarios. Each experiment was repeated three times.

Experiment setup
This testbed setup involves two PCs. First PC was operated by Windows OS and installed with a GNS3 version 1.5.3. This PC also was installed with Virtual Box that also runs another guest OS, Ubuntu 12.04 that acted as an attacker. Another PC (a laptop) was installed with dual stacked OS: Windows 7.0 and Ubuntu 12.04. This PC acted as a victim. Figure 1 shows the experiment testbed. An isolate network was setup by configuring two routers that are connected to PC1 and PC2 respectively. They represent two different networks that are connected in the cloud.

ISBN: 978-1-387-00704-2

Snort 2.9.9.0 was installed as an IDS on the victim machine. TCP and UDP flooding attacks were launched using an open source attacking tool, Hping3 (Sectools.org). A packet analysis software, Wireshark (Sanders, 2007), was also set to run on both attacker and victim to monitor the behavior of the network.

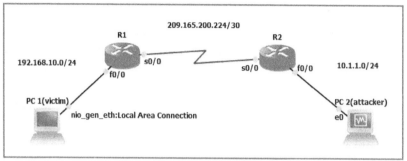

Figure 1: Experiment Test bed

Studying the performance involved creating a valid and reliable record of performance by means of systematic observations that can be analyzed with a view to facilitating change (Alhomoud, Munir, Disso, Awan, & Al-Dhelaan, 2011). The performance metric used in this project are throughput and packet input /output total that consist of the results for drop packet.

Throughput is a measure of how many number of units of data that a system can handle in a given measure of time (Wuu, Hung, & Chen, 2007). It is connected comprehensively to the system that running from different parts of PC and network system to associations. Related measures of system profitability incorporate the speed with which some particular workload can be finished, and reaction time, the measure of time between a solitary intuitive client demand and receipt of the reaction. The basic output in IDS include the timing statistics. In timing statistic, it includes the total second and packets as well as packet processing rates. This output is used to measure the throughput (Liao, Richard Lin, Lin, & Tung, 2012).

ISBN: 978-1-387-00704-2

Packet input/ output totals in IDS can be measured after setting up the packet size. Then, the performance of IDS can be measured after the dropped packet segment shows its percentage (Rani & Singh, 2012).

A work by Alhomoud, Munir, Disso, Awan and Al-Dhelaan (2011) has tested and analyzed the performance of Snort and Suricata. They implemented both IDS on three different platform which are ESXi virtual server, Linux 2.6 and FreeBSD. They created three different scenarios with a different packet size and speed to analyze the performance of IDS. The result stated is based on dropped packet in each platform. In contrast, this work concerns only on Snort performance in Windows and Ubuntu platform while detecting SYN flood and UDP flood attacks.

Results and Analysis
Wireshark was activated to capture activities in Windows and Ubuntu before and after the attack was launched. Thus, it can demonstrate whether the attack was successful or not. In the experiment, attacker launched flooding attack to the victim for 2 minutes. Before the attack, no activities were spotted in the Wireshark display. During the occurrence of attack, Wireshark screen shows flooding of packets from many sources targeting the victim. These are presented in Figure 2 and Figure 3.

ISBN: 978-1-387-00704-2

Figure 2: Wireshark during the attack in Windows

Figure 3:Wireshark during the attack in Ubuntu

i.Performance Analysis

Performance analysis of Snort IDS in Windows and Ubuntu are based on its dropped packet and throughput. During the attack, Snort was running until the set time is finished. Table 1 shows the overall results obtained from the experiments.

Table 1: Overall results

	Flooding attack	Windows			Ubuntu		
		Exp 1	Exp 2	Exp 3	Exp 1	Exp 2	Exp 3
Drop packet (%)	TCP	32.226	32.544	36.379	32.087	29.992	34.756
	UDP	35.06	34.934	34.524	27.075	27.332	29.534
Throughput (packet/min)	TCP	58146	59455	57968	106326	106445	106634
	UDP	65105	64821	67442	102432	102876	105066

For drop packet, either Snort on Windows or Snort on Ubuntu that has lower drop packet will be considered as better performance. While for throughput, Snort in which operating system that captured higher packet during the attack is considered as better performance. As can be noticed in Table 1, the value of drop packet in Ubuntu is smaller than in Windows. While for the observation on throughput, it can be seen clearly that the value of

ISBN: 978-1-387-00704-2

packet captured per minute for throughput in Ubuntu is higher than Windows.Figure 4and Figure 5 present the performance of Snort in term of its throughput on Windows and Ubuntu for TCP SYN flood and UDP flood respectively. Generally, if the packet captured per minute is higher, it means that the performance of snort is better in that platform. In order to confirm, further testing was implemented by conducting T test on both results.

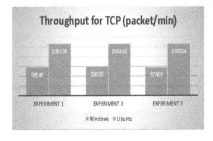

Figure 4:Throughput for TCP Flood

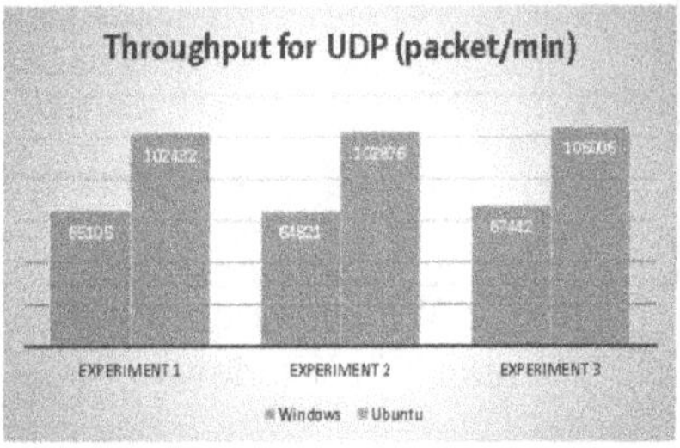

Figure 5:Throughput for UDP Flood

ii. T-TestResult

In order to determine whether the result is significant or not to the difference between the performance of Windows and Ubuntu in terms of dropped packet and throughput, independent T-test had been carried out.T-test is one of the analytical statistic to test the difference between the sample with variances of two unknown normal distributions. Basically, in this experiment the two sample that is used are Windows and Ubuntu whereas the two unknown normal distribution are dropped packet and throughput. Figure 6 shows the T-test results of drop packet for TCP SYN flooding attack.

ISBN: 978-1-387-00704-2

→ **T-Test**

[DataSet1]

Paired Samples Statistics

		Mean	N	Std. Deviation	Std. Error Mean
Pair 1	windows	33.71633	3	2.311412	1.334494
	ubuntu	32.27833	3	2.387756	1.378572

Paired Samples Correlations

		N	Correlation	Sig.
Pair 1	windows & ubuntu	3	.866	.333

Paired Samples Test

		Paired Differences							
					95% Confidence Interval of the Difference				
		Mean	Std. Deviation	Std. Error Mean	Lower	Upper	t	df	Sig. (2-tailed)
Pair 1	windows - ubuntu	1.438000	1.217091	.702688	-1.585422	4.461422	2.046	2	.177

Figure 6: Drop packet for TCP SYN flooding attack

The result shows that there is no significant different between the performance of Snort IDS on Ubuntu and Windows in term of drop packet due to SYN flooding attack, as the ($p > 0.05$). That means, the performance of Snort IDS in both Windows and Ubuntu is similar. On the other hand, the T-test result for drop packet in Windows and Ubuntu during UDP flooding attack shows that the ($p < 0.05$). This means, the different of performance of Snort IDS in Windows and Ubuntu in term of drop packet is significance. Thus, it can be concluded that Snort IDS on Ubuntu has better performance in terms of its drop packet when dealing with UDP flooding attack.

As for throughput in Windows and Ubuntu during the TCP flooding attack, the result of T-test indicates that the performance of Windows and Ubuntu in term of throughput is significance as the ($p < 0.05$). Therefore, it can be concluded that Snort IDS on Ubuntu has better performance in term of throughput while dealing with TCP flooding attack. The similar T-test result ($p < 0.05$) also was showed for throughput in Windows and Ubuntu

ISBN: 978-1-387-00704-2

during the UDP flooding. It indicates that there is a significancedifferent. Thus, it can be concluded that Snort IDS on Ubuntu has better performance in terms of throughput for UDP flooding attack.

Conclusion

This paper has described IDS and how it can be applied for attack detection. Although the Snort IDS only was installed in two OS: Ubuntu and Windows and tested against two types of flooding attack, readers can acquire some fruitful information related to installation and experiment setup. Users can gain some knowledge from description of the experiment in which the paper has demonstrated the tests and discussed the results accordingly. As discussed in the result, Snort on Ubuntu is most likely has better performance in term of drop packet and throughput compared to Windows. In future, more testing of attacks can be conducted to observe the performance of IDS.

References

3schools. (2013). OS Statistics. Retrieved June 10, 2017, from https://www.w3schools.com/browsers/browsers_os.asp

Ahmad, A. (2012). Type of Security Threats and It 's Prevention, *3*(2), 750–752.

Alhomoud, A., Munir, R., Disso, J. P., Awan, I., & Al-Dhelaan, A. (2011).Performance evaluation study of Intrusion Detection Systems.*Procedia Computer Science, 5,* 173–180. https://doi.org/10.1016/j.procs.2011.07.024

Anand, A. (2012). An Overview on Intrusion Detection System and Types of Attacks It Can Detect Considering Different Protocols. *International Journal of Advanced Research in Computer Science and Software Engineering, 2*(8), 94–98.

Bogdanoski, M., Shuminoski, T., & Risteski, A. (2013). Analysis of the SYN Flood DoS Attack. *I.J. Computer Network and Information Security, 8*(8), 1–11. https://doi.org/10.5815/ijcnis.2013.08.01

Buchanan, W. J. (2011). *Introduction to Security and Network Forensics*, USA :CRC Press.

Computer Threats | Monster.com. (2017). Retrieved June 16, 2017, from https://hiring.monster.com/hr/hr-best-practices/monster-training/security-center/avoid-computer-threats.aspx

Debra, B., &Shinder, L. (2006). 10 things you can do to protect your data.

ISBN: 978-1-387-00704-2

Retrieved June 16, 2017, from http://www.techrepublic.com/article/10-things-you-can-do-to-protect-your-data/

GNS3 | The Network Journal. (2016). Retrieved March 15, 2017, from https://cyruslab.net/tag/gns3/

Jeganathan, I. T. V. S., &Prakasam, A. (2014). Secure the Cloud Computing Environment from Attackers using Intrusion Detection System. *International Journal of Advanced Research in Computer Science & Technology (IJARCST 2014), 2(2), 181–186.*

Muniandy, B. (2010). Academic Use of Internet among Undergraduate Students : A Preliminary Case Study in a Malaysian University. *International Journal of Cyber Society Education, 3(2), 171–178.*

Kuldeep, T., Tyagi, S. S., &Richa, A. (2014). Overview - Snort Intrusion Detection System in Cloud Environment, *4(3),* 329–334.

Kumar, B. S., Sekhara, T. C., Raju, P., Ratnakar, M., Baba, S. D., &Sudhakar, N. (2013). Intrusion Detection System- Types and Prevention, *4(1),* 77–82.

Kumar, S., & Rai, S. (2012). Survey on Transport Layer Protocols : TCP

Li, M., Li, J., & Zhao, W. (2009). Experimental study of DDOS attacking of flood type based on NS2. *International Journal of Electronics and Computers, 1(500),* 143–152. Retrieved from http://www.umac.mo/rectors_office/docs/weizhao_cv/pub_refereed_journals/2009_ref_journals/IJEC_Dec 2009.pdf

Liao, H.-J., Richard Lin, C.-H., Lin, Y.-C., & Tung, K.-Y. (2012). Intrusion detection system: A comprehensive review. *Journal of Network and Computer Applications, 36(1),* 16–24. https://doi.org/10.1016/j.jnca.2012.09.004

Manna, M. E., & Amphawan, A. (2012). Review of Syn-Flooding Attack Detection Mechanism. *International Journal of Distributed and Parallel Systems (IJDPS), 3(1),* 1–19. https://doi.org/10.5121/ijdps.2012.3108

Orebaugh, A., Biles, S. & Babbin, J. (2005). *Snort Cookbook,* USA: O'Really.

Rani, S., & Singh, V. (2012). SNORT: An Open Source Network Security Tool for Intrusion Detection in Campus Network Environment. International Journal of Computer Technology and Electronics Engineering (IJCTEE), 2(1), 137–142. Retrieved from http://www.ijctee.org/files/VOLUME2ISSUE1/IJCTEE_0212_24.pdf

Reddy, G. N., & Reddy, G. J. U. (2014). A Study of Cyber Security Challenges and Its Emerging Trends on Latest Technologies. *International Journal of Engineering and Technology, 4(1),* 48–51.

Sanders, C. *Practical Packet Analysis: Using Wireshark to Solve Real-World Network Problems.* (2007). No Starch Press, USA: San Francisco.

SecTools.Org. (2017), *Hping3.*Retrieved March 10, 2017 from http://sectools.org/tool/hping/

Varga, A., & Hornig, R. (2008). An Overview of the OMNeT++ Simulation Environment. *Proceedings of the 1st International Conference on*

ISBN: 978-1-387-00704-2

Simulation Tools and Techniques for Communications, Networks and Systems & Workshops, 60:1--60:10. https://doi.org/10.4108/ICST.SIMUTOOLS2008.3027

Wuu, L. C., Hung, C. H., & Chen, S. F. (2007).Building intrusion pattern miner for Snort network intrusion detection system.*Journal of Systems and Software, 80*(10), 1699–1715. https://doi.org/10.1016/j.jss.2006.12.546

ISBN: 978-1-387-00704-2

Article 16

Web Application: Tele-education using Web Real-Time Communication (WebRTC)

Zulfikri Paidi, Wan Muhammad Aizuddin Wan Roslan
Faculty of Computer and Mathematical Sciences
Universiti Teknologi MARA Perlis Branch, Malaysia

Abstract
Distance learning can be described as the process of learning between lecturers and students from different locations over the Internet. This paper discusses about a web based video call application using WebReal-Time Communication (WebRTC). It allows lecturers and students to communicate in a real time through the web application for learning purposes. The web application enables users to perform a video call using web browser. However, sometimes the lecturers are not able to attend a class due to unforeseen circumstances. So, they need to find a suitable time to make a replacement class and gather all students to perform a video conference. With the availability of this web application, both students and lecturers can just make a replacement class through video conference. Besides, some students are usually busy with their activities and they do not have time to consult or make appointment with their lecturers. This video call application helps to address the problem by connecting both students and lecturers from different places through a web application. The objectives have been identified, which are to design and develop a web based video call application using WebRTC and to evaluate the performance and functionality of the web application. The result is gathered based on the test conducted, which shows that users will experience a smooth video streaming by using wireless LAN as compared to the broadband, which causes a sluggish video streaming.

Keywords: Web Application, Video call, Real-Time Communication, WebRTC, Learning

Introduction

Nowadays, online learning is a new method of gaining information through a web application. Lecturers can interact with their students for teaching and learning purposes on internet-based learning. Tele-education, also known as distance education, I is a situation where students and instructors are physically far away from each other and a two-way

ISBN: 978-1-387-00704-2

communication is included between them (Shepherd & Amoroso, 1998). Video conferencing is a transmission of video and audio back and forth between two or more physically separated locations. This communication can be accomplished through the use of web cameras, microphones and speakers.

The WebRTC is a media engine with Java Script API that has a capability to send and receive a real-time media and data in a peer-to-peer method between web browsers (Loreto, Romano & Pietro, 2012). The WebRTC provides ability of establishing a real-time communication capability such as audio, video and data communication into web browsers without the needs to install additional software (Zeidan, Lehmann & Trick, 2014). Therefore, this paper discuss on developing a web based video calls application using WebRTC.

Related Works
A.   Open Meetings as a Browsers-based Teleconferencing Tool for EFDA Laboratories
In the past few years, video conference was introduced to worldwide organization as a medium to communicate between organizations from different locations.   According to Santos, Castro, Santos, Gomes, Fernandes, Sousa and Varandas, (2011), Open Meetings is open source software that allows video conference via web browsers. Open Meetings does not require installation because it can integrate with current existing tools and customization of requirements.

B.   A video conferencing system based on WebRTC
The WebRTC is a browser based video chatting that does not require any third parties software or plug in. According to Chiang, Chen, Tsai and Yuan (2014), the WebRTC is an open project that grants a web browser with real-time communication (RTC) capabilities. There are many types of application programming interface that can be used to develop video chat application. To obtain and exchange media stream browsers, two API were needed, which are Media Stream and RTC Peer

ISBN: 978-1-387-00704-2

Connection. Media Stream is a type of API that functions to get audio or video from media stream from end device such as Webcam. RTC Peer Connection play an important role in providing connection establishment between two end users.

C.   Using Web Conference System during Lesson in Higher Education

According to this article, around 80% of students in Obuda University prefer education delivered in virtual way rather than classical way. Analysis has been made and the result is students seem more motivated in learning through virtual way. According to Kiss (2012), Big Blue Button is an open source web conference system used as consultation and presentation tools in education. The application allows instructors to deliver learning material and provide video conference between instructor and learners.

Methodology

The methodology involve in this project consist of two elements, which are WebRTC architecture and application development.

A.   WebRTC Architecture

The WebRTC technology grants a real-time voice and video communication from web browser or other peer node without demanding any third party software or servers between two endpoints. It requires components of a typical VoIP media engine into a browser or any peer endpoint with a simple API that a web server can control. Now users can experience voice and video calls that support browser to browser applications without the needs to download anything (Ellis,2015). Figure1 shows an overview of WebRTC.

ISBN: 978-1-387-00704-2

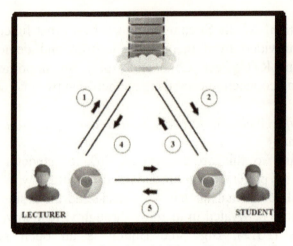

Figure1: Overview of Web Real-Time Communication

Figure1 illustrates the overview of how WebRTC works where it indicates that lecturers send message or data to students through the server and then students send a reply to the lecturer. Finally, the two peers communicate with each other. In WebRTC, the two types of API are required in order to acquire and exchange the media stream between browsers, which are Media Stream API and RTC Peer Connection API. Media Stream API is used to obtain audio and video media stream from local device, for example, the webcam and microphone, and to collect the input stream. Other than that, RTC Peer Connection is an API that gathers data from the output of Media Stream. RTC Peer Connection also provides connection establishment between the two users. The establishment of peer-to-peer connection requires Session Traversal Utilities for NAT (STUN) protocol and Traversal Using Relays around NAT (TURN).

B. Application development

This section explains the information on the development of the web application such as context diagram, prototype development and software requirement. Data Flow Diagram is a method for modeling system that displays how the input data is processed through the sequence of functions to produce an output. Context diagram is also part of the Data Flow Diagram. Context diagram

ISBN: 978-1-387-00704-2

is a diagram that represents an overview of the web application. The main entity for the web application is STUDENT and LECTURER. Figure2 illustrates the context diagram for the web application.

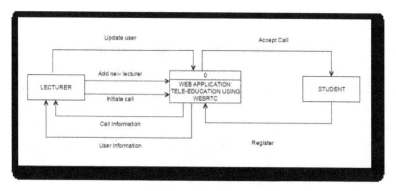

Figure 2: Context Diagram for Web Application

Besides, to develop the video call application, it follows several steps. The first step is to get the video and audio from device. This step requires Media Stream API, also known as "getUserMedia". It is a JavaScript API that allows to synchronize stream of media such as camera and microphone. Its function is to request access to the local camera video stream using the get User Media call. If this stream is setup successfully, then it is displayed on the local browser page in a video element and then added to the "peer_connection" object so that it can be sent to the remote peer's browser.

The second step is to create a user interface or video layout. The interface for the video call application is created using Cascading Style Sheet (CSS) language. The canvas size for the local and remote video is setup in this section. The size of remote video has been setup for 1024x768 pixels and the local video is 240x160 pixels. The button for 'dropacall' is also created in this section. This button functions to terminate the connection between two peers.

ISBN: 978-1-387-00704-2

The third step is to stream video with RTC Peer Connection. RTC Peer Connection is the WebRTC API used for video calling. This section requires to setup a Session Traversal Utilities for NAT (STUN). In this project, Google's Public Stun Server is used to check port address for incoming request and allow peer to pass on another peer by signaling mechanism.

The fourth step requires to setup signaling server. The "call_token" variable is a unique ID that links two users together. It is used to ensure that any signals passing through the signaling server are only exchanged between these two specific users. The"signaling_server" is a variable that represents the Web Socket API connection to the signaling server to which both the local users and remote users will be connected.

The final step requires configuring specific port for server.js. Server.js is a JavaScript file that allows to run a web server in Node.js application. In order to provide functioned web socket server, it is compulsory to create basicNode.js application. In this JavaScript file contains a web socket library. This section also defines port80, which is the standard for HTTP port.

After video call has been successfully developed, the web application will be deploy into cloud hosting. In this project, Heroku Cloud Application Platform is used to host the video call application. Heroku is a cloud platform as a service (PaaS), which supports JavaScript programming language. The video call application requires Node.js application. Heroku cloud application platform allows user to store the Node.js application, which can be run in the server.

Results and Analysis

The analysis is conducted by testing the performance and usability of the web application. Usability testing is conducted to determine the usefulness of the web application toward the potential users. The performance test is perform to measure the response time, round-trip time, the page load time and the

ISBN: 978-1-387-00704-2

smoothness of the video streaming based on different types of network.

A. *Usability testing*

Usability test was a test conducted to evaluate the usability of the web application. This test is measured by having roughly 30 respondents. In addition, each respondent was given a set of questionnaire consisting of 13 questions to test the web application. The questionnaire was created using Google Forms and was published on the Internet. All the information collected from the respondents was saved into a spreadsheet file. The analysis was evaluated based on the feedbacks from the questionnaire given. Table1 shows questionnaire that was given to the respondents to evaluate the usability of the web application.

Table1: List of usability test question

No.	Question
1.	User can register to the web application.
2.	User can login into the web application.
3.	Popup error message if user enter wrong details.
4.	User can display list of calls.
5.	When user click call button, popup window will appear.
6.	Video call application will generate link for student.
7.	User can save generated link and date.
8.	User can search call's record by date.
9.	When user click go button, popup window will appear.
10.	User can perform video call by clicking go button.
11.	During video streaming, user can view another user.
12.	User can click drop call button to end communication.
13.	When user click logout button, the web application will terminate the session.

Table1 shows the questionnaire that was distributed over the Internet. Based on the questionnaire, the respondents need to select whether successful or unsuccessful on each of the given questionnaire. Figure 3 shows feedback from the questionnaire

ISBN: 978-1-387-00704-2

after giving the ball to the respondents. The percentage shows that 100% of the respondents have successfully completed the usability test based on the given questionnaire, except for question 11 and question 12.

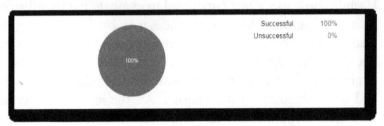

Figure 3: Usability testing –All question except Question11 and Question 12

Based on Figure 3, most of the respondents have successfully completed the test without any problem. However, several respondents were not able to complete question 11 and question 12. Figure 4 shows percentage for question11, which is during video streaming, the users are able to see another user on the video application.

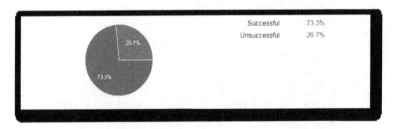

Figure 4: Usability testing for Question11

As seen on Figure 4, 73.3% of the respondents have successfully completed question 11 without any problems. Only 26.7% of the respondents are having problems with the video application. The problem might occur if the users use other than Google Chrome web browser. This is because, the WebRTC API can only support on the Google Chrome web browser. The video call interface will appear on the screen if the user uses other than

ISBN: 978-1-387-00704-2

Google Chrome web browser. However, the connection between two peers will not establish because the WebRTC cannots end and receive data from different web browser. Other possible problem might occur if the users have slow Internet connection. The web browser cannot load the video application because it requires a stable Internet connection to perform real-time communication. Figure 5 shows the percentage for question 12. Question 12 require user to click drop call button to terminate connection during video streaming.

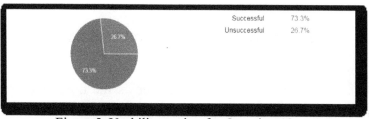

Figure 5: Usability testing for Question 12

Based on Figure 5, only 26.7% of the respondents did not successfully complete the usability test for question 12. However, 73.3% of the respondents were able to complete the test without having any problems. This problem actually related to the question 11. If the video application did not appear on the web browser, automatically the users could not see any button appearing on the application. The user will not be able to click on the button because the video application did not load into the web browser.

B.   Performance Testing

Web application response time was tested to measure how long does it takes for a web application to response back on user request. Figure 6 shows web application response time was tested using Blaze Meter testing tools.

ISBN: 978-1-387-00704-2

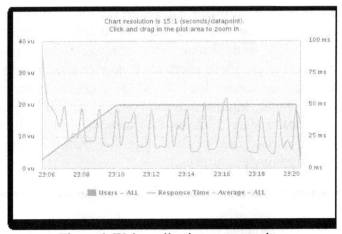

Figure 6: Web application response time

Based on the Figure 6, the graph shows the time taken for the application to response back on user's request. In addition, the web application was tested based on 20 virtual users. The minimum response time was 14 milliseconds and the maximum response time was 51 milliseconds. Based on the results, the higher the time taken, the longer users must wait for the web application to process request.

The next section will   discuss   about testing of web application from different types of network by using wireless LAN and broadband. Four tests were carried out during the test in order to gather all the data and the result was included in this section.

C.   Scenario1: Comparing the amount of round trip time with different types of network
Generally, round trip time is the amount of time it takes for a packet to reach its destination. A tool is used to capture the amount of time it takes from the moment a request is sent over network until a response is received. This test was conducted based on the different types of network by using wireless LAN and broadband. All the results were gathered in Table2. Figure 7 shows the amount of round trip time with different types of network.

ISBN: 978-1-387-00704-2

Table 2: Result of the test for scenario1

Type of Network	Test 1	Test 2	Test 3	Test 4
Wireless LAN	120	110	50	190
Broadband	300	160	150	329

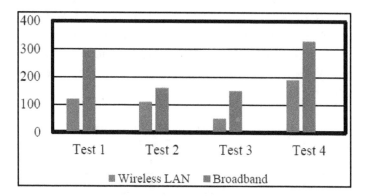

Figure 7: The total amount of round trip time in millisecond

Based on Figure 7, the amount of round trip time during test 1 for wireless LAN was 120 milliseconds, while for the broadband it took 300 milliseconds for the packet to reach its destination. For the second test, the amount of round trip time for wireless LAN was 110 milliseconds and 160 milliseconds according to the time taken for round trip time using broadband. The amount of round trip time reduces to 50 milliseconds for wireless LAN and 150 milliseconds for broadband during the third test. During the fourth test, round trip time was captured for wireless LAN was 190 milliseconds at the same time 329 milliseconds time taken for round trip time using broadband. Based on the results, the amount of round trip time taken for a packet to travel to a specific destination was longer by using a broadband compared to wireless LAN. As seen on Figure7, short period of time taken by a packet to travel to a specific destination and back again by using wireless LAN.

ISBN: 978-1-387-00704-2

D. Scenario2: Comparing the frame rate with different types of network

This test was performed to measure the frame rate of the video streaming from different types of network. The unit for frame rate is fps, which stands for frame per second. Technically, the smoothness of the video streaming can be analyzed from the frame rate of the video. All the recorded results are shown in Table 3. Figure 8 shows the frame rate for video streaming with different types of network. The higher the frames, the smoother the video will be (Tan & Chou, 2012).

Table3: Results of the test for scenario2

Typeof Network	Test1	Test2	Test3	Test4
Wireless LAN	40	34	41	47
Broadband	35	33	40	35

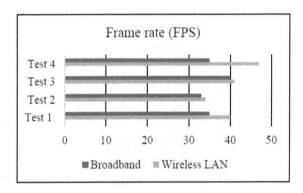

Figure 8: Frame rate with different types of network

Based on Figure 8, it shows the frame rate of video streaming by using different types of network. Four tests were conducted to measure the frame rate by using wireless LAN and broadband. The first test showed that the frame rate for video streaming was 40 fps using wireless LAN, while the frame rate for video streaming using broadband was 35 fps. During the second test, the result for frame rate using wireless LAN was 34 fps and for broadband was 33 fps. During this stage, both users might experience a sluggish video streaming as the frame rate was

ISBN: 978-1-387-00704-2

decreased. On the third test, both users have a smooth video streaming because the frame rate was 40 fps for wireless LAN and 41 fps for broadband. The final test showed that wireless LAN users have a smooth video streaming as the frame rate was around 47 fps, while the broadband users may experience a slow video streaming since the frame rate was 35 fps. Based on the test conducted, the results have been analyzed. If the frame rate of video was higher, then the user will experience a smooth video streaming. To have a smooth video streaming, it is recommended for the users to use wireless LAN as a network connection since the frame rate was higher.

Conclusion

The WebRTC stands for web real-time communication. It is a media engine with JavaScript API that has been used in the development of the video call application. In the video call application, two APIs have been used, which are the Media Stream API and RTC Peer Connection. The Media Stream API played a role in order to obtain the media data from the local device. The media data consists of device's camera and microphone. The RTC Peer Connection is also JavaScript code use to establish connection between two endpoints. Besides, the interface for the video call application was created using Cascading Style Sheet language (CSS).

Two experiments have been conducted to test the performance and usability of the WebRTC. Usability testing was conducted to determine the usefulness of the web application towards the potential users. The performance test was performed to measure the response and round-trip time, and to test the smoothness of the video streaming based on different types of network.

Based on the results, the amount of round trip time taken for a packet to travel to a specific destination was longer by using broadband compared to wireless LAN. While for testing the smoothness of the video streaming, if the frame rate of video was higher, then the users will experience a smooth video

ISBN: 978-1-387-00704-2

streaming. To have a smooth video streaming, it is recommended for the users to use wireless LAN as a network connection since the captured frame rate was higher.

References
Chiang,C.-Y.,Chen,Y.-L.,Tsai,P.-S.,&Yuan,S.-M.(2014).A Video Conferencing System Based on WebRTC for seniors. 2014 International Conference on Trustworthy Systems and Their Applications,51–56. http://doi.org/10.1109/TSA.2014.17

Ellis,L.(2015).The World of WebRTC.Multichannel News,36(4), 26.

Kiss,G.(2012).Using webconference system during the lessons in higher education.

Loreto,S.,&Romano,S.Pietro.(2012).Real-time communicationsin the web: Issues, achievements, and ongoing standardization efforts. IEEE Internet Computing, 16, 68–73.http://doi.org/10.1109/MIC.2012.115

Santos,B.,Castro,R.,Santos,J.H.,Gomes,D.,Fernandes,H.,Sousa, J., &Varandas, C. F. (2011). Open Meetings as a browser-based teleconferencing tool for EFDA

Shepherd,M.M.,&Amoroso,D.L.(1998).Designing adistance education program: theUniversity of Colorado at ColoradoSprings.Proceedings of theThirty-FirstHawaii International Conference on System Sciences, 6, 547–558. http://doi.org/10.1109/HICSS.1998.654815

Zeidan,A.,Lehmann,A.,&Trick,U.(2014).WebRTC enabled multimedia conferencing and collaboration solution,1–6.

ISBN: 978-1-387-00704-2

Article 17

Performance Evaluation of Dual Diversity Cognitive Ad-hoc Routing Protocol (D$_2$CARP) on Primary User (PU) Activation Time: A Simulation Approach

Rafiza Ruslan, Nur Maisarah Ab Rahman
Faculty of Computer and Mathematical Sciences,
Universiti Teknologi Mara Perlis Branch, Malaysia

Abstract
Cognitive Radio (CR) is known to solve spectrum scarcity that intent to improve spectrum utilization. In CR, secondary user (SU); also known as cognitive user need to ensure its transmission will not interfere primary user (PU) link. Link breakages among secondary users are due to PU activity that causing the degradation of network performance. Over the past decades, many routing protocol were developed for CR network. This paper focusses only on Dual Diversity Cognitive Ad-hoc Routing Protocol (D$_2$CARP) that jointly exploits path and spectrum diversity to provide multi-path and multi-channel solutions to SU. SU can switch to another channel or path if the current path breaks or the channel becomes unavailable. This project aims to provide a comparison network performance in different distributions running under the same routing protocol. The objectives of this project are to imitate a cognitive radio ad-hoc network using Network Simulator 2 (NS-2) and to create two scenarios in Exponential and Uniform distributions. The performance was analysed based on the percentage of packet drop, average packet delay and throughput. The results in both distributions show a slight difference. From the research, it can be concluded that D$_2$CARP is able to work well under random PU activation time as long as the SU number does not exceed the network capacity.

Keywords: *Cognitive radio ad-hoc network, routing protocol, primary user activation time.*

Introduction

Wireless technology requires electromagnetic spectrum to serve as their communication medium. Past studies by the Federal Communications Commission (FCC) stated spectrum bands allocated through fixed assignment policies are used only in bounded geographical areas or over limited periods of time which

ISBN: 978-1-387-00704-2

only results in between 15% and 85% spectrum utilization(Akyildiz, Lee, Vuran, & Mohanty, 2006). Another experiment by FCC also reveals that the spectrum usage is concentrated only on certain portions of the spectrum while a significant amount of the spectrum remains unutilized (Che-Aron, Abdalla, Abdullah, Hassan, & Rahman, 2015). Dynamic use of the spectrum bands in Cognitive Radio Ad-Hoc Networks (CRAHNs) create adverse effects on network performance if the same communication protocols which consider fixed frequency band are applied (Salim & Moh, 2013). In CRN, common scenarios that distinguish two types of users sharing the same portion of spectrum but implementing two different rules. Primary User is the licensed user that uses traditional wireless communication system. Whereas, the Cognitive User (CU) that equipped with CRs and exploits the Spectrum Opportunities (SOPs) to sustain their communication activities without interfering PUs (Cesana, Cuomo, & Ekici, 2010; Sengupta & Subbalakshmi, 2013).

Due to the decentralized infrastructure in CRAHNs, data routing encounters various challenges such as frequent topology changes, heterogeneous spectrum availability and intermittent connectivity caused by PUs activity. Most routing protocol did not jointly exploit the path and spectrum diversity. For examples, SEARCH routing protocol(K. R. . Chowdhury & Felice, 2009) is based on geographical forwarding and path and spectrum decision is made sequentially and not together while CRP routing protocol(K. R. Chowdhury & Akyildiz, 2011) selects the routing path in one preferred spectrum band only. A routing protocol should jointly exploit path and spectrum diversity to provide multi-channel and multi-path connection for SUs during the data transmission (Rahman, Caleffi, & Paura, 2012). D₂CARP routing protocol is the first protocol to jointly exploit path and spectrum diversity in 2012 and followed by FTCARP (Che-aron, Abdalla, Abdullah, & Md. Arafatur Rahman, 2014) and RACARP (Che-Aron, Abdalla, Abdullah, Hassan, & Rahman, 2015)routing protocol. Since

ISBN: 978-1-387-00704-2

D$_2$CARPis a new routing protocol, its performance in various condition such as random PU activation time remains unknown.

This project aims to provide a comparison network performance in two different distributions running under the same routing protocol. Hence, simulation on CRAHNs had been set up in Network Simulator 2 (NS-2) using D$_2$CARP routing protocol. The rest of the paper is organized as follows. Next section discusses related work. It follows with simulation methodology, experimental evaluation and finally the conclusion.

Related Works
Joseph Mitola(2000)introduced the term Cognitive Radio (CR) with the aim to employ underutilized spectrum in an opportunistic manner (Mansoor, Islam, Zareei, Baharun, & Komaki, 2014). Devices with cognitive capabilities can create CR network (CRN) as they can sense a wide spectrum range, dynamically discover currently unused spectrum blocks for data communication and intelligently access the unoccupied spectrum SOP (Cesana, Cuomo, & Ekici, 2011). They can change their transmitting parameters according to their surroundings. Hence, in the paradigm of CRAHNs, CUs can communicate with each other in an ad hoc manner through both licensed and unlicensed spectrum bands without relying on any pre-existing network infrastructure and in a non-intrusive manner to the licensed users(Che-aron et al., 2014).

There are many performance metrics used to measure network performance such as end-to-end delay, packet loss and throughput. D$_2$CARP measured packet delivery ratio (PDR), overhead, delay and hop count as the network performance metrics. Backup Channel and Cooperative Channel Switching (BCCCS) use channel interference(Zeeshan, Manzoor, & Qadir, 2010) while Local Rerouting and Channel Recovery (LRCR) also use network throughput as network performance metric (Tseng & Chung, 2013).

ISBN: 978-1-387-00704-2

Generator and seed are used to create random values in NS-2. If the seed is set to zero, the values generated will be totally random but if the seed is other than zero, the values generated will be based on the seed. Seed is the number vector used to initialize the random number generator. The values are generated based on its distribution type and there are five types of distribution in NS-2. They are Pareto, Constant, Uniform, Exponential and HyperExponential (Eitan& Jimenez, 2003). This project focused only two types of distribution Exponential and Uniform distribution to generate random PU activation time. Uniform distribution is defined through the minimum and maximum point configured while Exponential distribution is defined by its average value.

Simulation Methodology
The initial step was installing NS-2.34 on Fedora 20. Then, need to apply the required patches, which are multi-channel and D^2CARP patch in order to implement D_2CARP in NS-2. This project simulate the mentioned routing protocol under a random PU activation time by using Exponential and Uniform distribution to create two conditions; where PU is active at random time and PU is active at all the time during simulation. The network performances metric used in this project arepacket delay, packet dropped and throughput. Packet delay is defined as time taken by packets to be delivered across the network from source to destination, while packet dropped means amount of packet dropped or lost between the time link failure occurs to the time a new transmission route exists. The throughput is the ratio of the total amount of packet successfully received by destination before the packet delivery time expires.

Scenarios in this project were adopted from (Md Arafatur Rahman, 2013) and the simulation parameter were summarized in Table 1.

ISBN: 978-1-387-00704-2

Table 1: Simulation parameter

No.	Parameter Name	Value
1.	Simulation Area	1000m × 1000m
2.	Simulation Time	400 seconds
3.	Number of PUs	10
4.	Number of SUs	50
5.	Number of channel	4
6.	PU transmission range	150m
7.	SU transmission range	150m
8.	Mobility model	Random Way-Point model
9.	Traffic type	CBR
10.	Packet size	512 bytes
11.	Data packet interval	50ms
12.	Transport layer	UDP
13.	Checking interval for channel used by PUs	Every 5 seconds
14.	Data transmitting start time	60 seconds
15.	PU active time	100 seconds

The study was conducted in a simulation area of 1000m × 1000m. The simulation time was set to 400 seconds and channel number was set to 4. The number of PU was 10 while SU number was set to 50. Transmission range of both PUs and SUs was 150m and SU mobility model was set to Random Way-Point model. The traffic load was set as Constant Bit Rate (CBR) with 512 bytes of packet size sent every 50ms over UDP connection. SUs detection for channel used by PU's was set to every 5 seconds. Nodes started sending the packets when 60 seconds elapsed during the simulation.

Experiments setup
This project simulates three experiments with two scenarios in each experiment. Each experiment differs in terms of channel number, PU number and SU number. The first scenario uses the Exponential distribution while the second scenario use Uniform distribution. The first experiment involved increasing the number of channels available from 2 to 10 while the number of primary

ISBN: 978-1-387-00704-2

and secondary users was fixed to 10 and 50 respectively. The second experiment was created with different number of primary users ranging from 2 to 18 with the number of secondary users and number of channel became a constant variable. In the third experiment, secondary users became the manipulative variable with its number increased from 20 to 100 while primary users' number and number of channels became the fixed variables. With two scenarios in each experiment, the total scenarios for this project are six. Table 2 shows the experimentsetup in table form. The scenario that starts with the letter 'E' means the scenario uses Exponential distribution while for the letter 'U'indicates the scenarios are using Uniform distribution. The experiments were repeated for three times and average values were acquired.

Table 2: Experiment Setup

Experiment	Description	Exponential Distribution	Uniform Distribution
1	Increasing number of channels	Scenario E1	Scenario U4
2	Increasing PU numbers	Scenario E2	Scenario U5
3	Increasing SU numbers	Scenario E3	Scenario U6

Results and Analysis

Experiments result is summarized in Table 3 below. Packet drop is the highest during scenario E3 which is 71.71221 % because SU numbers were incremented. During scenario E2, PU activation time is totally random and PU number and channel is set to 10 and 4 respectively. Packet drop was the highest for this scenario because channel available is not enough to support SU data transmission. For scenario U6, which also varies in SU numbers but the PU is constantly active all the time during the simulation; the packet drop is 60%.

ISBN: 978-1-387-00704-2

Table 3: Experiment results

Scenario	Packet drop (%)	Packet delay (s)	Throughput (Kb/s)
E1	58.23641	1.577101	88.4
E2	63.02444	1.704249	68.33333
E3	71.71221	1.94233	57
U4	43.93694	1.519863	111
U5	50.71405	1.958137	92.55556
U6	60.58961	2.414777	77.4

This indicates extending SU numbers more than the network capacity lead to higher packet drop. The network performance between different PU activation time distribution shows small deviation. $D_2CARP$is able to work well under random PU activation time because the scenarios show same pattern of network performance regardless of the PU activation time. Figure 1 shows packet drop results across scenario in graphical form.

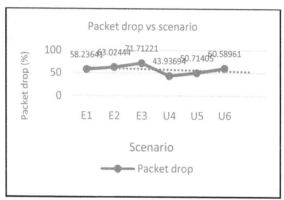

Figure 1: Packet drop vs scenarios

Packet drop for Exponential and Uniform distribution shows same pattern across the scenarios with the highest packet drop achieved was when SU number was increased in scenario E3 and U6. Figure 2 below shows packet delay in all scenarios in graphical representation. Scenario E1 to E3 uses Exponential

ISBN: 978-1-387-00704-2

distribution while scenario U4 to U6 uses Uniform distribution. Although the values are not the same for both distributions, it can be seen that both distribution have the same packet delay pattern across the scenarios.

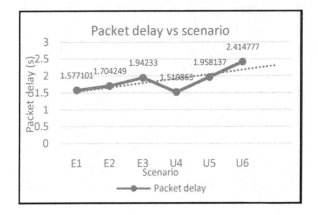

Figure 2: Packet delay vs scenarios

The highest delay achieved is in scenario U6 when SU numbers was increased and the PU is active all the time during the simulation. Scenario E3, which also involves varying SU numbers achieved an average of 1.94233 seconds of packet delay. This is because in scenario U6, the PU is active all the time while for scenario E3, the PU is set to be active at a random time. The smallest average packet delay is identified in scenario U4 and followed by scenario E1, which varies the channel numbers. The difference in average packet delay of scenario E3 and U6 is relatively small. Packet delay results also show the same pattern in both distributions. Figure 3 shows the network throughput across all scenarios in graphical form.

ISBN: 978-1-387-00704-2

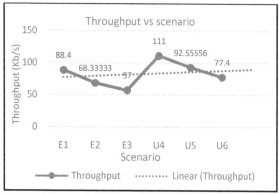

Figure 3: Throughput vs scenarios

Network throughput is the highest in scenario U4 because the scenario involves increasing the number of channels. Scenario E1 shows the second highest throughput because it also involves increasing channel number. The difference between scenario E1 and U4 is their PU activation time.

Discussion

Based on network throughput, D_2CARP has the capabilities to serve SU data transmission regardless of the PU activation time. Network throughput shows lower values when SU numbers was increased. Scenario U6 has the lower network throughput because SU has to compete with each other for idle channels and the PU is active all the time during the simulation. Packet drop is high when SU number exceeds the network capacity which is in scenario E3 and U6. Network throughput increase when the number of channel increased in scenario E1 and U4. The lowest percentage difference of packet drop achieved was 11.71 % in Experiment 3 and the shortest delay difference in both distributions was achieved in Experiment 1 which is 0.05 seconds. Highest throughput was achieved in Experiment 1 which was 111 Kb/s.

Conclusion

This paper has simulated two different distributions under random PU activity in D_2CARP routing protocol. The simulation

ISBN: 978-1-387-00704-2

from the two distributions: Uniform and Exponential are simulated against six scenarios based on packet drop, packet delay and throughput. As discussed in the earlier section, the network performance difference in both distributions shows small values and they also show similar network performance pattern across the simulation scenarios. It can be assumed that PU activation time has little effect to the network performance. In conclusion, D_2CARP is affirmed to work well under random PU activation time regardless of the scenario and condition created.

Acknowledgements

We would like to thank Assoc. Prof. Dr. Arafatur Rahman for assistance with the simulation methodology and helpful suggestions.

References

Akyildiz, I., Lee, W., Vuran, M., & Mohanty, S. (2006). NeXt generation/dynamic spectrum access/cognitive radio wireless networks: A survey. *Computer Networks, 50*(13), 2127–2159. https://doi.org/10.1016/j.comnet.2006.05.001

Cesana, M., Cuomo, F., & Ekici, E. (2010). Routing in cognitive radio networks: Challenges and solutions. *Ad Hoc Networks, 9(3),* (2010), 228–248. https://doi.org/10.1016/j.adhoc.2010.06.009

Cesana, M., Cuomo, F., & Ekici, E. (2011). Routing in cognitive radio networks: Challenges and solutions. *Ad Hoc Networks, 9*(3), 228–248. https://doi.org/10.1016/j.adhoc.2010.06.009

Che-Aron, Z., Abdalla, A. H., Abdullah, K., Hassan, W. H., & Rahman, M. A. (2015a). A Robust On-Demand Routing Protocol for Cognitive Radio Ad Hoc Network. *Mobile and Wireless Technology 2015, Lecture Notes in Electrical Engineering, 310,* 155–162. https://doi.org/10.1007/978-3-662-47669-7

Che-Aron, Z., Abdalla, A. H., Abdullah, K., Hassan, W. H., & Rahman, M. D. A. (2015b). RACARP: A Robustness Aware routing protocol for Cognitive radio Ad Hoc Networks. *Journal of Theoretical and Applied Information Technology, 76*(2), 246–257.

Che-aron, Z., Abdalla, A. H., Abdullah, K., & Md. Arafatur Rahman. (2014). FTCARP: A Fault-Tolerant Routing Protocol for Cognitive Radio Ad Hoc Networks. *KSII Transactions on Internet and Information Systems, 8*(2), 371–388. https://doi.org/10.3837/tiis.2014.02.003

Chowdhury, K. R. ., & Felice, M. D. . (2009). Search: A routing protocol for mobile cognitive radio ad-hoc networks. *Computer Communications,*

ISBN: 978-1-387-00704-2

32(18), 1983–1997. https://doi.org/10.1016/j.comcom.2009.06.011

Chowdhury, K. R., & Akyildiz, I. F. (2011). CRP: A Routing Protocol for Cognitive Radio Ad Hoc Networks. *IEEE Journal on Selected Areas in Communications,* 29(4), 794–804. https://doi.org/10.1109/JSAC.2011.110411

Eitan, A., & Jimenez, T. (2003). NS Simulator for beginners. Venezuela.

Iii, J. M. (2000). *Cognitive Radio An Integrated Agent Architecture for Software Defined Radio Dissertation.*

Mansoor, N., Islam, A. K. M. M., Zareei, M., Baharun, S., & Komaki, S. (2014). Cluster Modelling for Cognitive Radio Ad-hoc Networks Using Graph Theory. In *2014 International Conference on Applied Mathematics, Modelling and Simulation (ICAMMS)* (pp. 1–8).

Md Arafatur Rahman. (2013). *Cognitive Radio Ad-hoc Networks : A Routing Perspective.* University of Naples "Federico II."

Md. Arafatur Rahman's website (2011). *Implementation of D₂CARP in NS-2.* Retrieved fromhttp://wpage.unina.it/arafatur.rahman/D2CARP.html

Rahman, A., Caleffi, M., & Paura, L. (2012). Joint path and spectrum diversity in cognitive radio ad-hoc networks. *EURASIP Journal on Wireless Communications and Networking,* 1–9. https://doi.org/10.1186/1687-1499-2012-235

Salim, S., & Moh, S. (2013). On-demand routing protocols for cognitive radio ad hoc networks. *S. J Wireless Com Network (2013) 2013: 102.,* 1–10. https://doi.org/10.1186/1687-1499-2013-102

Sengupta, S., & Subbalakshmi, K. P. (2013). Open Research Issues in Multi-Hop Cognitive Radio Networks. *IEEE Communications Magazine,* (April), 168–176. https://doi.org/10.1109/MCOM.2013.6495776

Tseng, P., & Chung, W. (2013). Local Rerouting and Channel Recovery for Robust Multi-Hop Cognitive Radio Networks. In *2013 IEEE International Conference on Communications (ICC)* (pp. 2895–2899).

Zeeshan, M., Manzoor, M. F., & Qadir, J. (2010). Backup channel and cooperative channel switching on-demand routing protocol for multi-hop cognitive radio ad hoc networks (BCCCS). *Proceedings - 2010 6th International Conference on Emerging Technologies, ICET 2010,* 394–399. https://doi.org/10.1109/ICET.2010.5638455

ISBN: 978-1-387-00704-2

Article 18

Students Activities Notification System

Nur Khairani Kamarudin, Mohd Faris Mohd Fuzi,
Faculty of Computer and Mathematics Science,
Universiti Teknologi MARA Perlis Branch, Malaysia

Ahmad Haziq Abu Bakar
Brilliance Information Sdn. Bhd.
Bandar Sri Damansara, Malaysia

Abstract
Student portal is an official website of UiTM. The function of student portal is to spread the new information or activities for the current semester. The examples of information are date of course registration, date of validation, date of result final exam, faculty or club activities. From my survey, I found that it is hard to get new information. They have to log in into student portal to enable them to get the latest news. To solve this problem, an Android Mobile for Students Activities Notification System was being created using Android platform. This project was developed using hardware and software. The hardware is using mobile phone with Android operating system and personal computer for the server. Android SDK (System Development Kit) was used to develop the Android Mobile for Students Activities Notification System that compatible for Android operating system. These projects were conduct usability test and transmission of update information from server to client. As long as student is connected to the Internet, they can get the notification of new information that is being update. This project involve with server client communication. This project is important because it helps student to get or receive new update information without have to log in into student portal.

Keywords: GCM, UiTM, JXTA, JDK, SDK.

Introduction

In Mobile Application Architecture for Android Mobile for Student Notification System involve several steps to get the notification of the new information. The first step is student mobile phone must connect to the Internet to get connected to the web server. After that, admin were updating the new information on the web server and the information were stored in the data storage on the web server. After the new information was being

ISBN: 978-1-387-00704-2

updated, the web servers were use notification service to send the information to the mobile phone students. In the mobile phone students, their mobile were notified when they receive the new updated information.

Methodology

In methodology, there were three (3) process invloves in developing the system. First is the process of developing the Android mobile for students activities notification system which discuss the hardware and software used, followed by explanation on Android mobile application flow architecture. Lastly, is the design of Android mobile application to make sure the design meets user friendly interface.

1. Development of Android Mobile for Students Activities Notification System

Developing Android Mobile for Students Activities Notification System is using Eclipse. The languages that were used to develop this mobile application are Java and XML language. In this project, the connection is between servers to client connection. The web server is using php. The server is using 23.94.32.114 ip address. The server operating system is Centos 5.9. Servers were connected to the internet to get connected to mobile phone users. The mobile phone user is using Android 2.3 and above. Mobile phone users also were connected to the internet to get any updated information that being updated in web server. Figure 1shows the network topologies that were used in this project.

ISBN: 978-1-387-00704-2

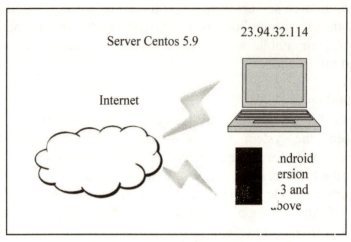

Figure 1: Network Diagram of Android Mobile for Students Activities Notification System

2. Android Mobile Application Flow Architecture

This phase explains the processes involved in designing and development the mobile application flow architecture. The computers were act as a server while mobile phone acts as a client as shown in Figure 2. The web servers were using PHP language. When the new information is being updated, the servers were connected to mobile application. At the client side, firstly the clients were connecting to the Internet. After that they download that mobile application on the mobile phone store. After finish download, the application were being installed on the mobile phone client. To use that mobile application, the client must login first. After login, to enable them receive the new updated information, they must register their mobile phone with GCM service.

The applications connected to the server to get any update information on the server. The connections were used wireless connection. The application only can get the new information went it connect to the internet. Figure 2 shows the mobile application flow architecture of this project.

ISBN: 978-1-387-00704-2

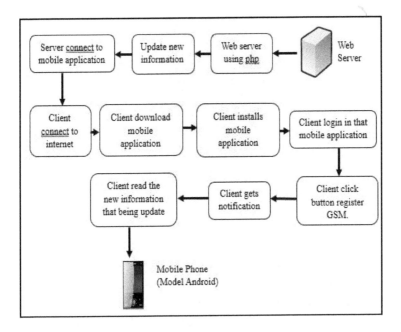

Figure 2: Mobile Application Flow Architecture

3. Design of Mobile Application Interface

Android Mobile for Students Activities Notification System has five interfaces which are introduction, login, GCM register, home and about us interface.

a) Introduction Interface

The first interface is introduction interface. The logo UiTM and welcome text were used to start the mobile application as a trademark of this mobile application. Figure 3 shows the introduction interface.

ISBN: 978-1-387-00704-2

Figure 3: Introduction Interface

b) Login Interface

The second interface is the login interface; two edit box and one login button were used for the user to login first before using this mobile application. The first edit box is student id. Student must enter their student id that is being given by the UiTM. The second edit box is student password. After student complete enter their student id and student password, enter the login button enable them to read the information that being updated. Figure 4 shows the login interface.

Figure 4: Login Interface

c) GCM Register Interface

The third interface is GCM register interface. The GCM register interface have three button which are home button, register gcm and unregister gcm and the status to show whether the mobile

ISBN: 978-1-387-00704-2

phone user is already register or not. The home button is link to home page interface. The register GCM button is to register the user device or mobile phone to enable them to receive notification when the new updated information was updated. The last button is the "unregister" button. This button is to stop the device from receive the notification. Figure 5 shows the GCM register interface.

Figure 5: GCM Register Interface

Experimentation
There are 2 scenarios experiments were conducted, which are Experiment 1 for the effect of response time to Android Mobile for Students Activities Notification System with multiple users (Table 2) and Experiment 2 for effect of response time to Android Mobile for Students Activities Notification System with different size of data (Table 2).

Table 1: Step of Experiment 1: The Effect of Response Time to Android Mobile for Students Activities Notification System with Multiple Users

NO.	DESCRIBTION
1.	Install Android Mobile for Students Activities Notification System to mobile phone 1, 2, 3, 4, 5.
2.	Start the experiment with mobile phone 1.

ISBN: 978-1-387-00704-2

3.	The new information was being updated in the web server.
4.	Time taken was being recorded when the mobile phone user receive the new information.
5.	Repeat step three and four for mobile phone 2, 3, 4, 5.

Table 2: Step of Experiment 2: The Effect of Response Time to Android Mobile for Students Activities Notification System with Different Sizes of Data

NO.	DESCRIBTION
1.	One mobile phone that was installed with Android Mobile for Students Activities Notification System was being connected to the web server.
2.	The new information was being updated in the web server with 215 Byte sizes of data.
3.	Time taken was being recorded when the mobile phone user receive the new information.
4.	Repeat step two and three using different sizes of data which are 802, 1299, 2953 and 3393 bytes.

Discussions

Experiment 1: The Effect of Response Time to Android Mobile for Students Activities Notification System with Multiple Users

In first testing, we use different size of data in Byte and send the data with one user only. The time taken is taken three times. As we can see, in Table 3 shows the result of the average time message receives to mobile phone users. From the data collected, it shows that the bigger the size, the longer the time. In this testing we not only depend on size of data but the time of message receive also depend on the speed of the Internet. Figure 6 show the graph of average time message receive against size of data.

ISBN: 978-1-387-00704-2

Table 3: Average time against size of data

Size Data(byte)	Time Message Receive(seconds)			Average Time Message Receive (seconds)
	First taken	Second taken	Third taken	
215	1.3	1.9	1.5	1.7
802	2.0	1.9	2.2	2.0
1299	2.5	2.2	2.9	2.5
2953	3.1	3.9	3.7	3.5
3393	3.5	4.1	4.0	3.9

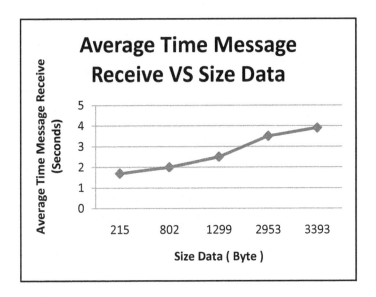

Figure 6: Graph of Average Time Message Receive against Size Data

Experiment 2: The Effect of Response Time to Android Mobile for Students Activities Notification System with Different Sizes of Data

For the second testing,which was tested in different number of users, this testing is using the same size of data which is 474 bytes. Table 4 shows the data collected in this testing. From the

ISBN: 978-1-387-00704-2

result of the testing, it can be conclude that when the number of users is increase, the time of message receive to mobile phone users are also increasing. In this testing also depend on speed of the Internet connection. The average time from five numbers of users is acceptable because it only take three to four seconds that the users to receive the message. Figure 7 shows the picture of time taken during both testing phase.

Table 4: Average Time against No. of Users

No. Of Users	Time Message Receive					Average Time Message Receive (seconds)
	First user	Second user	Third user	Fourth user	Fifth user	
1	1.2					1.2
2	3.84	2.3				3.1
3	4.6	2.8	2.5			3.3
4	4.1	4.3	3.5	4.2		4.0
5	4.2	3.6	3.0	4.9	4.4	4.0

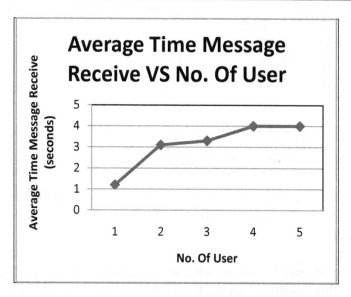

Figure 7: Graph of Average Time Message Receive against No. of Users

ISBN: 978-1-387-00704-2

Figure 8: Time taken during testing phase

Findings

The Android Mobile for Students Activities Notification System help the students in UiTM Perlis to get alert on important information that being update by UiTM admin in UiTM Student Portal. This mobile application also helps UiTM to spread their new information to student and their staff. Furthermore, by using this mobile application, it can reduce the probability of student miss some important information and it also wore make students to take immediate action to new information that they receive. The students directly received the information that being update in UiTM Student Portal in their mobile phone. This project also helps other developers of mobile application to make improvement or new application as a guideline to improve the education system.

Conclusion

From the observation on the experiment and feedback from students, the Android Mobile for Students Activities Notification System should be implemented in the UiTM Perlis to manage the information spreading. This is because it was made easier for the UiTM to spread their important information to students and staffs. It also can reduce the probability of student not receive or read the information and they can immediately take an action. In

ISBN: 978-1-387-00704-2

addition, it also can improve the education system to become more interesting. By improving the education system, students were getting motivated to study and easier to get new update about the important information. Besides that, by using this mobile application, spreading information was becoming more practical in conducting the information. Thus, it shows that this mobile application is the best way to spread the important information to UiTM Perlis students and staffs. It should be implemented in UiTM Perlis or others UiTM branch.

References

Ahmed M. G. (2013). How To Develop Smart Android Notifications using Google Cloud Messaging Service. Senior R&D Engineer-SECC.

Ben F. (2010). Mobile Application Development "The search for common ground in a divided market".

Chris A. (Red Hat), Shawn P. (Google) (2011). Understanding and UsingGit at Eclipse. Retrieved from http://eclipse.org/egithttp://www.eclipse.org/legal/cpl cpl-v10.html

Chris D. (2012). Type of Mobile Application. Retrieve from http://cdixon.org/2012/05/21/four-use-cases-for-mobile-apps/

Debajit G. (2010). Building Push Applications for Android.

Daniel S. (2010). Android Application Development. Senior Software Engineer, Google Inc.

ISBN: 978-1-387-00704-2

Article 19

Remote Web-based Cat Food Dispenser (DiCatDiHati)

Ahmad Faizwan bin Azmi, Mohammad Hafiz bin Ismail
Faculty of Computer and Mathematical Sciences,
Universiti Teknologi MARA Perlis Branch, Malaysia

Abstract
The Remote Web-based cat food dispenser is a design that will help the cat owners to monitor or to feed their cats even without their presence. Currently, most of the cat owner feed their cats manually and sometimes they forgot to feed their cats before leaving home. This attitude can lead their cats for having unbalanced "diet" because beside did not feed their cat, the food that they fill in on the eating plate early in the morning also will be unhealthy. That food will expose to the air and it is not fresh anymore to be eat. The objective of this project are to identify the requirement in building and develop Remote Web-based Cat Food Dispenser that interfaces both smartphone and computer. Remote Web-based Cat Food Dispenser may have multiple function like the cat owners can feed their cats, check the balance of food in the container and set a notification or alarm for them. The waterfall model concept was been used for the software development model. The waterfall model contains some consecutives phases where each phases must be completed before moving to next phase (Bassil, 2012). Two type of testing has been conducted to accomplish the third objective of this project which are User Acceptance Test and Usability Test. Most of the cat owner give high marks on the User Acceptance. This concludes that Remote Web-based Cat Food Dispenser can be implemented by the cat owners in order to help their cat having a balance diet.

Keywords: internet-of-things, iot, notification, cat feeder, remote activation

Introduction
Presently, cats have become one of the popular pet where in the New Zealand, 48% New Zealand's households owning an average of two cat. Cats also need to eat and drink in order to survive but their diet is incompatible with human diet). Besides that, the amount of food that a cat must eat should be enough and not too overly exceed to avoid overweight (Anand&Brobeck,

ISBN: 978-1-387-00704-2

1951). Through this project, cat owners can avoid the daily routine of remembering to feed their cat and can focus on other things.

Cat food dispenser is a device that helps the cat's owner to feed their cats. The cat food dispenser must have a container, a delivery plate and bottom lid (Lai, 2012). According to Lai (2012), at the bottom hole of the container, it must be covered with the bottom lid and has multiple through holes.

Remote web-based Cat Food Dispenser required numbers of hardware and software. Example of hardware needed in order to develop the Remote Web-based Cat Food Dispenser are LDR sensors, Raspberry Pi, Breadboard, Transistor, Capacitor and Servo Motor. While for software, FileZilla File Transfer, Adobe Dreamweaver and PuTTY are needed. This Remote will allowed the user to feed their cat, detect the level of the food in the container and set a reminder for them. The reminder are consist of three options which are Real time, Timer and Desktop Notification.

Related Works

i. Smart Pet Care System using Internet of Things

This article by Natarajan et.al (2016), discusses a new pet care system where the pet owners can feed the pets while the owners are not around and the owners can monitor the pets movement and status whether the pets eat the food or not. It also can control its excretion pad by the owner's smart phones.According to Natarjan et.al (2016), this project used Arduino as a platform since Arduino is cheaper and easier to use for every component. All of the devices are linked in a home network based on WIFI WLAN. The smart phone function is to monitor the status of smart pet care system and the user's smart phone also have to control the setting. In addition, to make the smart pets feeder work, the users need to set the feeding time and the amount of

ISBN: 978-1-387-00704-2

food to feed their cat based on the weight of the amount of single meal. The camera has been implemented with Raspberry Pi server. The other component is mobile web and APP for a smart phone. Users also can set the alarm to alert them about feeding time.

ii. *Pet Food Monitoring Using Raspberry Pi*

According to Ag (2016), this project used the image to monitor the amount of the food in the bowl to help the cat owners who love their pet but they are unable to monitor their pets eating habit due to a busy working schedule. As the platform for this project, the researcher used Raspberry Pi due to low power usage. Then, there are four main components that have been used to develop this pet food which is Raspberry Pi model A+, Wi-Pi wireless adapter, Raspberry Pi camera module and lastly Micro SD memory card 32GB. Furthermore, the interaction between the system and the user only occur if there is no food in the bowl. If there is food in the bowl, the system will not interact with the user. The system will send a notification like "NOTICE: food bowl is empty" to the user through email and the notification also can be sent through message (Ag, 2016). Hough Circle Transformation used to find the circle in an image and that circle is used to create a mask. The function of the mask is to detach the food bowl from the rest of the image so that the image analysis will be more accurate.

Construction of Prototype
A. Develop the Dispenser
This construction phase was more focused on the hardware where the researchers need to develop a container that can be filled with the food. That container was attached to the Raspberry Pi in order to make the servo motor and LDR sensor work. GPIO concept in the Raspberry Pi has been implemented for the interaction toward both servo motor and LDR sensor. All of the interactions between the hardware were using the Python languages.

ISBN: 978-1-387-00704-2

i. Servo motor

Servo motor was placed at the bottom of the container to allow the food flow. Raspberry Pi will connect to the servo motor, this phase need to be careful because servo motor is sensitive. If the researcher entered wrong amount of power to have control toward servo motor in the Raspberry Pi it will totally blow out the Raspberry Pi and it cannot be used anymore. The researcher need to test one by one the best amount of power needed to make the servo motor move to the right way and right speed (food flow is about 60-90 gram).

ii. Light Dependent Resistor (LDR) sensor

Four LDR sensors were placed in the food container. The first one represent the 100% level, second one is for 75%, third one for 50% and the fourth is represent 25%. Actually the function of LDR sensor is to detect the intensity of the light, better bright light around it the less intensity occur. So this concept has been applied to represent the food level where create an IF ELSE statement in the source code that state if the first LDR reading intensity is greater than 1500 it mean that the food still at the 100% level and if the LDR reading lower than 1500 it will pass to the second LDR. Same goes to other LDR sensor. Each LDR are connected to the different GPIO and GND. Each of the reading will be save in a txt file in the Raspberry Pi before it can be read through the PHP pages.

B. Create Interface

The interfaces of the remote were created using the PHP languages. Adobe Dreamweaver CS6 has been used in order to create it. Since this remote is a web-based remote so it is okay to combine the PHP languages and the Python Languages. Besides having PHP languages, some pageswere developed using Java Script Languages, for example, the reminder page that use the google API format. After all of the interfaceswere created, the file was transferred into the Raspberry Pi using the FileZilla File Transfer. Researcher only needs to pin the laptop with the Raspberry Pi IP Address, port number and the password of the

ISBN: 978-1-387-00704-2

Raspberry Pi in order to connect to it. Then, the researcher just needs to drag the file into the /var/www directory so the website can be publish through the internet.

C.   Create interaction between button in the web-page and hardware on the dispenser
The interaction over the button in order to have control of the hardware on the dispenser was created using the Python languages. For example, when the "FEED" button on the web-pages pressed it will make the motor move and allow the food flow. Same goes to the "FOOD LEVEL" button where it can return the LDR reading that already stored in the txt file of the Raspberry Pi. Each of the page that relate to the interaction must have "#!/usr/bin/env python" at the top of the page.

Testing and Evaluation
There are two types of testing that was conducted for this project, which are the Usability and User Acceptance tests. 25 respondents all together were selected by the researcher in order to test the Remote Web-based Cat Food Dispenser, 10 of them were tested under the Usability Test and the others 15 under the User Acceptance test.

Usability test was conducted to observe usability of Remote Web-based Cat Food Dispenser. There were no detail explanations about the function of this remote before the cat owners test the remote. A set of task was given to the cat owners based on the navigation, interaction and design of the remote.

While for the User Acceptance test, ten out of 15 of cat owners were the respondents who already done the usability test while the others are the new respondents. For the new respondents, developer has explained about the function of the remote and how it will work before the evaluation session begun. Then, for those who already did the usability test, they were able to explore the whole Remote Web-based Cat Food Dispenser. The content of the survey was divided into 4 parts, which are to test the

ISBN: 978-1-387-00704-2

Compatibility, Function, Navigation and Interface Design and General Feedback.

Table 1: Measurement Criteria for User Acceptance test

Stongly Disagree	Somewhat Disagree	Neutral	Somewhat Agree	Strongly Agree
1	2	3	4	5

Results and Discussion

a) Usability Test
Figure 1 shows that only three out of ten tasks were not completed by the user. For task 7, only four userssuccessfully completed the task and six more users have successfully completed task 8. Both tasks are option for the reminder whether they want to use the Real time or timer notification.

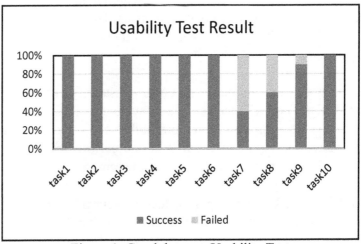

Figure 1: Graph base on Usability Test

b) Mean of User Acceptance Test
User Acceptance test with cat owners scored was 4.38. This means that the cat owners agreed to use the remote web-based cat

ISBN: 978-1-387-00704-2

food dispenser to help them to feed their cats. Mean score for each of the session can be referred to Table 2.

Table 2: Mean Score for User Acceptance Test

Criteria	Mean
Compatibility (C)	4.22
Function (F)	4.25
Navigation and Interface design Results (NID)	4.31
General Feedback (GF)	4.74

Prototype Circuit

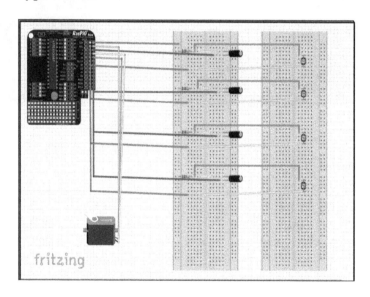

Figure 2: Figure of Prototype Circuit

ISBN: 978-1-387-00704-2

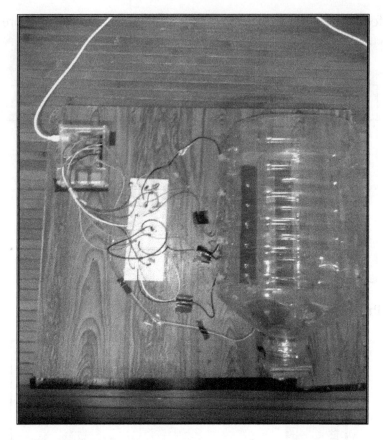

Figure 3: Images of the Prototype

Conclusion

Remote Web-based Cat Food Dispenser's objective was to identify the requirement in building and develop Remote Web-based Cat Food Dispenser that interfaces both smartphone and computer which can help the cat owners to feed their cat and detect the level of the food in the cointainer. Based on the observation and testing that was discussed it can be concluded that the main objective of this project is achieved.

References

Ag, K. (2016). Pet Food Monitor Using Raspberry Pi.

ISBN: 978-1-387-00704-2

Anand, B. K., & Brobeck, J. R. (1951). Hypothalamic control of food intake in rats and cats. The Yale Journal of Biology and Medicine, 24(2), 123–140.

Assignee, O., Citation, E., Krishnamurthy, S., & Krishnamurthy, S. (2002). Automatic pet food feeder.

Berntson, G. G., Potolicchio, S. J., & Miller, N. E. (1973). Evidence for Higher Functions of the Cerebellum: Eating and Grooming Elicited by Cerebellar Stimulation in Cats. Proceedings of the National Academy of Sciences, 70(9), 2497–2499. https://doi.org/10.1073/pnas.70.9.2497

Ferdoush, S., & Li, X. (2014). Wireless sensor network system design using Raspberry Pi and Arduino for environmental monitoring applications. Procedia Computer Science, (May), 376–381. https://doi.org/10.1016/j.procs.2014.07.059

Jeng, J. (2013). What Is Usability in the Context of the Digital Library and How Can It Be Measured. Information Technology and Libraries, 24(2), 47–56. https://doi.org/10.6017/ital.v24i2.3365

Lai, C. C. (2012). U.S. Patent No. 8,230,808. Washington, DC: U.S. Patent and Trademark Office.

Megat N.M. Mohamed Noor. (2013). Community based home security system using wireless mesh network. International Journal of Academic Research Part A; 2013; 5(5), 73-79. DOI: 10.7813/2075-4124.2013/5-5/A.9.

Maksimović, M., Vujović, V., Davidović, N., Milošević, V., & Perišić, B. (2014). Raspberry Pi as Internet of Things hardware : Performances and Constraints. Design Issues, 3(JUNE), 8.

Myers, F. (1983). United States Patent Sheet of 6.

Natarajan, K., Prasath, B., & Kokila, P. (2016). Smart Health Care System Using Internet of Things. Journal of Network Communications and Emerging Technologies (JNCET), 6(3), 37–42.

ISBN: 978-1-387-00704-2

Article 20

Digital Forensic Investigation of Trojan Attacks in Network using Wireshark, FTK Imager and Volatility

Muhamad Arif Hashim, Iman Hazwam Abd Halim, Mohammad Hafiz Ismail,
Norfaizalfarid Mohd Noor, Mohd Faris Mohd Fuzi, Abdul Hapes Mohammed,
Ray Adderley JM. Gining
Faculty of Computer Sciences and Mathematics
Universiti Teknologi MARA Perlis Branch, Malaysia

Abstract
Trojan attacks are the most common and serious threat to network users. It is a program that appears to be useful program but actually harmful one. It is difficult to detect Trojan attacks because it uses special techniques to conceal its activities from antiviruses and users. Thus, this research intends to retrieve and investigate of Trojan attacks on the network using digital forensic tools namely Wireshark, FTK Imager and Volatility. Two types of Trojan attacks called Remote Access Trojan (RAT) and HTTP Trojan (HT) are created and experimented in this research. These Trojans are sent to the targeted computer in the network through email. Wireshark is used to capture the network packets and then analyze the suspicious packets. FTK Imager is used to capture RAM data on targeted computer. Volatility is used to analyze the captured RAM data and extract suspicious process. This suspicious process is dumped into file and scanned using the Avast antivirus to check whether this process is running Trojan or otherwise. This research may benefit and contribute to the computer security and forensic domain. It can be extends to investigate other Trojan attacks such as Zeus, SubSeven or Back Orifice by using the same digital forensic tools.

Keywords:Digital forensic, Trojan attack, Wireshark, FTK Imager, Volatility

Introduction

The Trojan attack (Trojan) is one of the most notorious malware attacks(Al-Saadoon & Al-Bayatti, 2011). It is a program in which malicious code is contained inside the harmless program in such way that can control and cause some damage on the computer system (Al-Saadoon & Al-Bayatti, 2011). Trojan can cause

ISBN: 978-1-387-00704-2

massive harm to the computer system and can also crash computer system.

Mostly, Trojan infected the computer via the acts of downloading software, movie or music from unknown websites or an email attachment (Garcia, Reilly & Shorter, 2003). Trojan operates by hiding itself inside a useful software program(Al-Saadoon & Al-Bayatti, 2011). Once it is installed or executed in the system, Trojan begins its work by infecting different files in the computer. The user will notice that the computer has becoming slower and a window pop up may suddenly appears on the desktop(Al-Saadoon & Al-Bayatti, 2011). This phenomenon happens because of Trojan has already spread its virus to the computer's user. Later, this would cause their computer to crash and the computer is eventually no longer usable. Trojan also capable of stealing crucial information from the user's computer(Kumar, Upadhyay& Kumar, 2012).

Related Works
The analyzing a Trojan attack is tricky and crucial. It must include forensics analysis processes. Thus, Podile, Gottumukkala, & Pendyala (2015) highlight that forensic analysis is important for cases such as the analyzing of bank customer's computer that has been infected with Trojan. Forensic analysis may use FTK imager (FTK) and Digital Evidence Forensic Toolkit (DEFT) to collect evidence on registry files, internet history and events log files from the infected bank customer computer. Other than that, Volatility is also used to analyze RAM dump on infected machine.

Heriyanto (2012) performed forensic analysis to find and collect the evidence from Trojan banking malware for instance Cridex, Zeus and SpyEye. The tools that were used are Volatility and Wireshark. Volatility is used to seek the existence of Cridex and Zeus on the virtual machine while Wireshark is used to examine and capture the network traffic on Cridex, Zeus and SpyEye for evidence.

ISBN: 978-1-387-00704-2

Analysis and Results

The result obtained from the analysis, which has been carried out are as follow:

i.   Network Forensic Investigation

Network forensic performs analysis on network activities by collecting information associated with illegal activities(Xrysanthou& Apostolakis, 2006). Wireshark was used to captures network packet and analyses suspicious Trojan packet on the network.

Figure 1 and Figure 2 showed the resultsbased on Wireshark after a RAT and HTTP Trojan attack on victim's laptop. There was communication between attacker's laptop and victim's laptop when we filtered using the IP addresses 192.168.0.103 (attacker) and 192.168.0.100 (victim). This means that both attacks have already infiltrated the victim's.

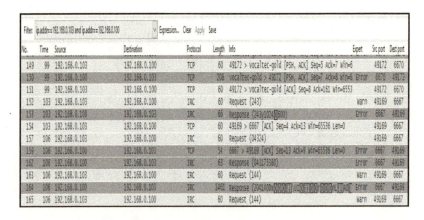

Figure 1 Packet captured after RAT attack

ISBN: 978-1-387-00704-2

No.	Time	Source	Destination	Protocol	Length	Info	Expert	Src port
2222	523	192.168.0.100	192.168.0.103	HTTP	1514	Continuation or non-HTTP traffic	Error	80
2223	523	192.168.0.100	192.168.0.103	HTTP	89	Continuation or non-HTTP traffic	Error	80
2224	523	192.168.0.100	192.168.0.103	HTTP	550	Continuation or non-HTTP traffic	Error	80
2225	523	192.168.0.103	192.168.0.100	TCP	60	50728 > http [ACK] Seq=407 Ack=2390 Win=65536 Len=		50728
2226	523	192.168.0.100	192.168.0.103	HTTP	634	Continuation or non-HTTP traffic	Chat	80
2227	523	192.168.0.103	192.168.0.100	TCP	60	50728 > http [ACK] Seq=407 Ack=3502 Win=64512 Len=		50728
2228	523	192.168.0.103	192.168.0.100	TCP	60	50728 > http [FIN, ACK] Seq=407 Ack=3502 Win=64512	Chat	50728
2229	523	192.168.0.100	192.168.0.103	TCP	54	http > 50728 [ACK] Seq=3502 Ack=408 Win=65536 Len=	Chat	80
2230	524	192.168.0.103	192.168.0.100	TCP	66	50730 > http [SYN] Seq=0 Win=8192 Len=0 MSS=1460 W	Chat	50730
2231	524	192.168.0.100	192.168.0.103	TCP	66	http > 50730 [SYN, ACK] Seq=0 Ack=1 Win=8192 Len=0	Chat	80

Figure 2 Packet captured after HTTP Trojan attack

ii. Memory Forensics Investigation

Memory forensic performs analysis on memory image taken from the victim's running computer (Sindhu &Meshram, 2012). Memory forensic is important in the investigation because it helps in extracting forensic artifacts from victim's computer's memory like network connection, running process and loaded module. Two memory forensic tools that was used to detect Trojan attacks are FTK Imager and Volatility.

Figure 3 and 4 showed the FTK imager has successfully captured RAM data on victim's laptop.

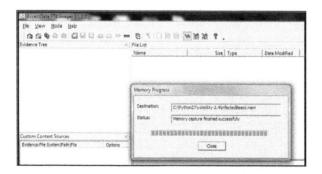

Figure 3 Successfully capture RAM data after RAT attack

ISBN: 978-1-387-00704-2

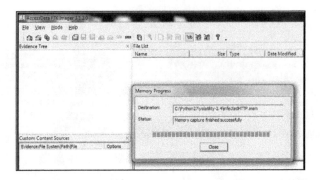

Figure 4 Successfully capture RAM data after HTTP Trojan attack

The memory files were saved as infectedBeast.mem for RAT and infectedHTTP.mem for HT. Once the RAM data has been captured, Volatility was used to perform memory forensic on the captured RAM data. Volatility analyzed the captured RAM data and extracted suspicious process from RAM data. Netscan plugin was used to extract information about the network connection held from and to the system with details included. Figure 5 showed the output of netscan plugin using the command "vol.py --profile=Win7SP0x86 netscan –f infectedBeast.mem" and Figure 6 showed the output of netscan plugin using the command "vol.py --profile=Win7SP0x86 netscan –f infectedHTTP.mem".

0x1487db00	TCPv4	192.168.0.100:6667	192.168.0.103:50000	ESTABLISHED	2432	beastserver.ex
0x164e8830	UDPv6	:::55107	*:*		3344	svchost.exe
0x1d2c7850	TCPv4	0.0.0.0:49154	0.0.0.0:0	LISTENING	572	lsass.exe
0x1d49ac40	TCPv4	0.0.0.0:49155	0.0.0.0:0	LISTENING	948	svchost.exe
0x1d50ca18	TCPv6	:::1:27275	:::0	LISTENING	1376	AvastSvc.exe
0x1d719188	TCPv4	0.0.0.0:49154	0.0.0.0:0	LISTENING	572	lsass.exe
0x1d719188	TCPv6	:::49154	:::0	LISTENING	572	lsass.exe
0x1d63d548	TCPv4	192.168.0.100:6674	192.168.0.103:50007	ESTABLISHED	2432	beastserver.e
0x21bddb98	TCPv4	192.168.0.100:6671	192.168.0.103:50004	ESTABLISHED	2432	beastserver.e
0x233a22c8	UDPv4	0.0.0.0:0	*:*		948	svchost.exe
0x23fe4a88	TCPv4	127.0.0.1:43227	0.0.0.0:0	LISTENING	1784	MBAMService.ex
0x24166828	TCPv4	0.0.0.0:49155	0.0.0.0:0	LISTENING	948	svchost.exe
0x24166828	TCPv6	:::49155	:::0	LISTENING	948	svchost.exe
0x23adec18	TCPv4	-:49581	10.0.7.12:443	CLOSED	3436	Wireshark.exe

Figure 5 List of network connection extracted from infectedBeast memory

ISBN: 978-1-387-00704-2

0x3e233488	UDPv4	0.0.0.0:0	*:*		1288	svchost.exe
0x3e233488	UDPv6	:::0	*:*		1288	svchost.exe
0x3e58f480	UDPv4	0.0.0.0:500	*:*		1000	svchost.exe
0x3e5ed7f8	UDPv4	127.0.0.1:49152	*:*		1376	AvastSvc.exe
0x3e257258	TCPv4	0.0.0.0:80	0.0.0.0:0	LISTENING	1180	HTTPSERVER.EXE
0x3e597888	TCPv4	0.0.0.0:554	0.0.0.0:0	LISTENING	1776	wmpnetwk.exe
0x3e700638	TCPv4	192.168.0.100:139	0.0.0.0:0	LISTENING	4	System
0x3f232c58	UDPv4	0.0.0.0:5355	*:*		1288	svchost.exe
0x3f25b2b8	UDPv4	0.0.0.0:5004	*:*		1776	wmpnetwk.exe
0x3f25b2b8	UDPv6	:::5004	*:*		1776	wmpnetwk.exe
0x3f25bbe8	UDPv6	::1:50473	*:*		2264	svchost.exe

Figure 6 List of network connection extracted from infectedHTTP memory

0x000000003e551020	smss.exe	272	4	0x3e555020	2017-06-09 05:07:05 UTC+0000
0x000000003e6f3528	ScreenRecorder	4128	2576	0x3e5555a0	2017-06-09 07:13:01 UTC+0000
0x000000003e7b3440	svchost.exe	1660	528	0x3e555300	2017-06-09 05:07:28 UTC+0000
0x000000003e7c0aa8	taskhost.exe	1724	528	0x3e555320	2017-06-09 05:07:28 UTC+0000
0x000000003e7cd390	backup.exe	1796	1604	0x3e555340	2017-06-09 05:07:28 UTC+0000
0x000000003e978a50	beastserver.ex	2432	2352	0x3e555680	2017-06-09 07:14:39 UTC+0000
0x000000003f2f3030	wmpnetwk.exe	5944	528	0x3e5555e0	2017-06-09 05:10:12 UTC+0000
0x000000003f36bb90	svchost.exe	3344	528	0x3e555600	2017-06-09 05:10:22 UTC+0000
0x000000003f576bb0	System	4	0	0x00185000	2017-06-09 05:07:05 UTC+0000

Figure 7 List of hidden process extracted from infectedBeast memory

There was an active network connection between IP address 192.168.0.100 and 192.168.0.103 on victim's laptop. Network connection to the IP address 192.168.0.103 was made by the PID 2432 and the process that was associated with PID 2432 is beastserver.ex. PID 2432 was used as a cover process for some hidden processes which are being carried out on the victim's laptop. Figure 7 showed the output of psscan plugin using the command "vol.py --profile=Win7SP0x86 psscan –f infectedBeast.mem".

It showed that one of the processes beastserver.ex with the PID 2432 looked suspicious because the beastserver's extension was different from the other processes' extension whereas the other

ISBN: 978-1-387-00704-2

processes had the same .exe extension. These suspicious beastserver.ex process was dumped into files and was scanned using Avast antivirus to confirm that it is Remote Access Trojan (RAT). The result exhibited that Avast antivirus detected beastserver.ex process as Win32:BeastDoor-AA [Trj]. RAT used beastserver.ex process to hide it activity on victim's laptop so that victim cannot detect its present.

```
0x00000000271040f8 dumpcap.exe      4020   1952 0x3e5b5540 2017-05-23 00:35:43 UTC+0000
0x000000002eca2d40 AvastUI.exe      1996   1932 0x3e5b5480 2017-05-23 00:16:50 UTC+0000
0x000000003cc36498 explorer.exe     1516   1456 0x3e5b52c0 2017-05-23 00:16:42 UTC+0000
0x000000003cccf660 spoolsv.exe      1588    572 0x3e5b52e0 2017-05-23 00:16:44 UTC+0000
0x000000003cd45530 svchost.exe      1648    572 0x3e5b5320 2017-05-23 00:16:45 UTC+0000
0x000000003cd4a530 taskhost.exe     1668    572 0x3e5b5340 2017-05-23 00:16:45 UTC+0000
0x000000003cd4c030 HTTPSERVER.EXE   1180    316 0x3e5b56a0 2017-05-23 00:36:30 UTC+0000
0x000000003cd6fd40 wmpnetwk.exe     1776    572 0x3e5b5560 2017-05-23 00:18:57 UTC+0000
0x000000003cd9fd40 svchost.exe      2264    572 0x3e5b5280 2017-05-23 00:18:59 UTC+0000
0x000000003cdc5950 Wireshark.exe    1952   1516 0x3e5b51e0 2017-05-23 00:35:39 UTC+0000
0x000000003cde7c78 RtHDVCpl.exe     1884   1516 0x3e5b53c0 2017-05-23 00:16:48 UTC+0000
```

Figure 8 List of hidden process extracted from infectedHTTP memory

The result showed that there was no active network connection detected between IP address 192.168.0.100 and IP address 192.168.0.103 on the victim's laptop. Based on Figure 8, the HTTPSERVER.EXE process was running on victim's system but the source and destination IP address is 0.0.0.0. Figure 8 showed the output of psscan plugin using the command "vol.py --profile=Win7SP0x86 psscan –f infectedHTTP.mem".

It showed that HTTPSERVER.EXE process with the PID 1180 looks suspicious. This suspicious HTTPSERVER.EXE process had been dumped into files and was scanned using Avast antivirus to confirm that whether this process is a HTTP RAT. The result showed that Avast antivirus was unable to detect the HTTPSERVER.EXE process as a HTTP Trojan. This Trojan was considered dangerous because it uses a special technique to make their detection more difficult. Table 1 showed the result obtained from the Avast antivirus scanning.

ISBN: 978-1-387-00704-2

Table 1 Avast Scanning Result

Trojan	Process ID	Dumped file	Avast antivirus
RAT	beastserver.ex 2432	2432.dmp	Win32:BeastDoor-AA[Trj]
HTTP Trojan	HTTPSERVER.EXE 1180	1180.dmp	No thread found

Conclusion

This research seeks to explain the importance of network forensic and memory forensic investigations on Trojan malware incidents. It has achieved its objectives to retrieve and investigate the evidence of Trojan attack using digital forensic tool like Wireshark, FTK Imager and Volatility. Based on the research results, it can be concluded that Wireshark is very useful in an investigation because it successfully detects both a RAT attack and a HTTP Trojan attack on the network. Volatility is a very powerful memory forensic tool that contains a great set of features and options which can help in detecting a Trojan attack. Volatility along with FTK Imager can be considered as a great memory forensic duo when performing an investigation of a Trojan attack. Both FTK Imager and Volatility can detect a RAT attack while the HTTP Trojan is quite difficult to be detected because Volatility cannot detect the communication between the IP address of the attacker and the IP address of the victim. It only shows the processes that are running on the victim's.

References

Al-Saadoon, G. M. W. & Al-Bayatti, H. M. Y. (2011). A Comparison of Trojan Virus Behavior in Linux and Windows Operating Systems. *World of Computer Science and Information Technology Journal (WCSIT), 1*(3), 56–62.

Garcia, H. J., Reilly, R. & Shorter, J. D. (2003). Trojan horses: They deceive, they invade, they destroy, 136–142.

Heriyanto, A. P. (2012). What is the Proper Forensics Approach on Trojan Banking Malware Incidents? In Proceedings of the 10th Australian Digital Forensics Conference, pp. 10-20. Edith Cowan University, Western Australia.

Kumar, K., Upadhyay, H. & Kumar, R. (2012). Trojan: Infection and precaution. *BPR Technologia: A Journal of Science, Technology &*

ISBN: 978-1-387-00704-2

Management, 1(1), 54–61. Mabuto, E. K. & Venter, H. S. (2011). State of the art of Digital Forensic Techniques. Conference : Information Security South Africa Conference 2011. South Africa

Podile, A., Gottumukkala, K. & Pendyala, K. S. (2015). Digital Forensic Analysis Of Malware Infected Machine - Case Study. *International Journal of Scientific & Technology Research, 4*(9).

Sindhu, K. K. & Meshram, B. B. (2012). Digital Forensic Investigation Tools and Procedures. *I. J. Computer Network and Information Security*, (4), 39–48.

Xrysanthou, A. & Apostolakis, I. (2006). Network Forensics : Problems and Solutions. In Conference : E-Democracy: Challenge of the Digital Era, pp   307-318. Greece.

ISBN: 978-1-387-00704-2

Article 21
Noise Reduction in Audio

Zulfikri Paidi, Nurhasyimah Idrus
Faculty of Computer and Mathematical Sciences
Universiti Teknologi MARA Perlis Branch, Malaysia

Abstract
Noise reduction in audio is a process of minimizing the presence of noise in the audio signal. Noise reduction approach helps user understand how to remove noise from the signal. Audio is very susceptible with noise and it presence will give impact on two major ways; first it will degrade the quality of information being transfer and second limit the capacity of data being transmit. There are lot of noise reduction techniques been proposed as to remove noise from audio signal such as wiener filter and average filter. In this project, wavelet theory implementation is proposed for reducing noise from audio signal. The main objective is to identify and remove the presence of noise in the signal. Furthermore, measurements of noise signal pattern are recorded before and after the noise reduction process. To be specific, this project will focus on speech type of audio. Speech acquisition of the participant were recorded in two types of environments; controlled and uncontrolled environments. Types of speech recorded in each environment are normal, whispering and angry speech. Speech signal patterns are analysed using cross-correlation between three wavelets families consists of Coiflet 5, Daubechies 10 and Daubechies 9 in order to determine best fit the original signal.

Keywords -Audio, Noise, AWGN, Wavelets, Cross-correlation

Introduction

Noise is referred to signal, which is unable to convey any useful information arising due to some sort of disturbance and cause the interference in the communication or the measurement of signal (Villanueva-Luna, Adrian, Jaramillo-Nuñez, Alberto, Sanchez-Lucero, Daniel, Ortiz-Lima, Carlos, Aguilar-Soto, Gabriel, Flores-Gil, Aaron, & May-Alarcon, 2011). In order to acquire the required information without the presence of noise especially in audio files such as speech recording files, the noise reduction must be used. There are various kinds of tools and software available which can be used to improve the signal contain of noise in the audio files such as Wiener filter, Average filter, and

ISBN: 978-1-387-00704-2

subspace transformation (Benesty, Jingdong, Chen, & Huang, 2008). In this project, MATLAB is used to develop a system that can remove the noise since the result of the technique recovers signal with higher correlation.

In ideal situation, audio recordings are free from the distorted or noisy speech signal. Besides, the quality of information signal is not corrupted and the capacity of information transmission is high in audio recordings. However, like any signal, audio recordings are very susceptible with noise. Noise is determined as a corruption in the communication that degrades the quality of information signal and limits the capacity of data transmission (Goel, Roopali, Jain, & Ritesh. (2013). Without the reduction of noise in the signal, it will limit the ability of user to identify the information transfer in audio files contain of noise (JaiShankar, & Duraiswamy, 2012).

The importance of this project is to implement the noise reduction technique in audio files contain of speech. In addition, noise reduction can solve major problems such as unclear audio files and in many applications such as cellular mobile communication, speech recognition, image processing, medical signal processing, radar, sonar, and any other applications where the desired signals cannot be isolated from noise.

Noise Reduction in Audio Theory
There are large amount of research and engineering concern in noise reduction in order to obtain a clean speech without interference of noise (Villanueva-Luna, et. al., 2011); (Aggarwal, Rajeev, Karan, Jai, Kumar, Vijay, Rathore, Sanjay, Tiwari, Mukesh, Khare, & Anubhuti. 2011); (Benesty, et al., 2008). As well as this put an interest to those researchers, this project comprehends the theory and implementation of the noise reduction technique. First and foremost, this project describes the audio theory continues with the noise theory and wavelets theory.

ISBN: 978-1-387-00704-2

A. *Audio Theory*

In the age of digital information, audio data has been becoming an essential part in various modern computer applications. Audio classification has become a focus in the research of audio processing and pattern recognition (Dhanalakshmi, Palanivel, Ramalingam, & Vennila, 2009). Audio is a representation of sound in which sound is referred to vibrations that travel through the air or another medium whether solid, liquid, or gaseous and can be heard by human ears (McLoughlin, 2009). All vibrations of sound are known as sound waves. The frequency of the waves is dependent on the frequency of the vibrating source. The high frequency of the vibrating source impresses the sound wave to have a high frequency (Vijaykumar, Vanathi, & Kanagasapabathy, 2007). In addition, frequency is defined as rate or the number of times per second, which a sound wave cycles from positive to negative and to positive again (Villanueva-Luna, et. al. (2011). Frequency is measured in cycles per second or Hertz (Hz).

Meanwhile the audio signal is the form of sound that represents longitudinal variations of pressure in a medium to be synthesized directly or originate at a transducer such as a microphone to convert the audio signal into the electrical signal (Villanueva-Luna, et. al. (2011). Transducer functions as a device used to convert the signal from one form of energy into another form of energy (Seiça, 2012). The main advantage of converting the signal into electrical signal is the signal can then be processed or also known as signal processing.

Signal processing occurs as audio signal can be represented in digital or analogue signal (Mihov, Doychev, & Ivanov, 2009). Digital signal is converted into encoded digital data stream by using a digital-analogue converter (DAC) through an amplifier and a speaker. Digital audio in general is categorized as speech, music and noise which in this project analyzing on speech signal since speech is important in delivering information in communication (Vijaykumar, et al., 2007). Alternately, analogue

ISBN: 978-1-387-00704-2

signal applied analogue-digital converter (ADC) to convert into encoded digital data stream.

Speech is the most basic means to human communication (Gold, Morgan, & Ellis, 2011). Throughout the years, speech has been well applied into many areas of technology include database access service, speaker verification, identification of vocal-related illnesses and telephone banking (Muangjaroen, & Yingthawornsuk, 2012). In natural environment, speech signal generally immersed in noise and it is essential for speech processing system to implement noise reduction techniques to extract the desired speech signal (Russo, Stella, & Rozic, 2012). There are some characteristics of speech signals such as auditory quality, characterization of different sounds and problems that might occur. For further information, vowel "a" and "n" have a relatively regular shape, while "t" pronounced as a single letter and especially the sibilant "s" which consists of fast oscillating parts that look very similar to noise. Therefore, it is clear that noise reduction will be very sensitive for speech parts (Wieland, Urban, & Funken, 2009).

B. *Noise Theory*

Generally, noise often present in transmission of signals, which can cause major problems in communication (Goel, et al., 2013). Noise is defined as an unwanted signal that interfere the communication or measurement of another signal (Villanueva-Luna, et. al. (2011). Noises present in communication channels are disturbing the original signals from path without any noise (JaiShankar, & Duraiswamy, 2012). Besides, noise disturbs in the communication which degrades the quality of information signal (Goel, et al., 2013). Over the past few decades there is an increase in the level of environmental noise which is due to growth of technology whereby the noise coming from various factors such as vehicles, noisy engines, and heavy machines (Chavan, Chavan, Manjusha, & Gaikwad, 2010). Noise is further classified into several categories depending on its frequency spectrum or time characteristics (Di Bert, Luca, Caldera, Peter,

ISBN: 978-1-387-00704-2

Schwingshackl, David, Tonello, & Andrea 2011). Several categories are further shown in Table 1.

Table 1: Categories of Noise

Types of Noise	Characteristics
White noise	A pure random noise that has an autocorrelation function and consists of frequencies in a flat power spectrum
Band-limited noise	Noise that has same characteristics as the white noise with a limited bandwidth that covers the limited spectrum of signal and contains a sin-shaped autocorrelation
Narrowband-noise	A type of noise that contain a narrow bandwidth such as 50/60 Hz from the electrical supply
Colored-noise	A non-white noise or wide-band noise that has a non-flat shape of spectrum. Examples are brown noise and pink noise
Impulsive noise	Noise that contain a short-duration pulse of random amplitude, time of occurrence and duration
Transient noise pulses	A noise that consists of long duration noise pulses such as clicks and burst noise

Although there are various categories of noise, this project is only investigating on removal of white noise in speech signal due to white noise is a common source of noise which consists in all frequencies (O'Haver, Prof. Tom. 2013). White noise is defined as the random signal contains equal power of spectrum within a fixed bandwidth at any centre frequency which refers to a statistical model for signals and signal sources rather than any specific signal (Aggarwal, et al., 2011), (Vijaykumar, et al. 2007). White noise is a type of noise which presents in which all frequency components, ranging from zero frequency (DC) to infinite frequencies (Anwar, Umer Hassan, & Sabieh, 2008).

Additive White Gaussian Noise Model (AWGN) is a channel model in which the only impairment to communication, an addition of independent White Gaussian Noise samples to the input signals (MathWorks, 2014a). Besides, an AWGN channel adds White Gaussian Noise to the signal that passes through this AWGN model.

ISBN: 978-1-387-00704-2

C. *Wavelets Theory*

Since there is a problem in the presence of noise in the speech signal, wavelets can help to minimise the problem (Aggarwal, et al., 2011). Over a decade, various de-noising techniques have been proposed for the removal of noises from audio signal such as Wiener filter, Average filter, VisuShrink and BayesShrink(Aggarwal, et al., 2011), (Benesty, et al., 2008). However, recently, wavelet methods are mostly used in removal of noise in the signal processing due the high effectiveness in the reduction of noise in the signal (Aggarwal, et al., 2011). Wavelets are referred to nonlinear functions and do not remove noise by low-pass filtering like many traditional methods where this low-pass filtering can blur the sharp features in a signal and makes it difficult to separate the noise from the signal (Aggarwal, et al., 2011). Furthermore, wavelets are able to significantly reduce noise from speech without degrading the quality of speech signal or introducing any audible artefacts (Nongpiur, 2008).

Wavelets consists of a huge number of wavelets families which have several different wavelets having a high number of vanishing moments and capable of representing complex polynomials (Ratnakar, Sunil. Singh, & Nitisha 2009). Wavelets with more vanishing moments should be selected as it provides better reconstruction quality and introduce less distortion into processed speech and concentrate more signal energy in few coefficients.

There are three wavelets families; Daubechies 10, Daubechies 9 and Coiflet 5 that have high vanishing moments. Theoretically, vanishing moment is referred to scaling function which is able to represent complex signal accurately (Villanueva-Luna, et. al., 2011). Daubechies wavelets are widely used in solving a broad range of problem such as signal discontinuities and fractal problems (Ratnakar, Sunil. Singh, & Nitisha 2009). Daubechies wavelets are family of orthogonal wavelets of discrete wavelet

ISBN: 978-1-387-00704-2

transforms which is characterized by a maximal number of vanishing moments for some given support.

Coiflet 5 is discrete wavelets function to have scaling functions with vanishing moments. This Coiflet 5 wavelet is generally used in many applications using Caldeon-Zygmund Operators. These wavelets families are implemented in measurement of the project by using cross-correlation in order to determine best fit between the original signal and the ones that have been processed. Cross-correlation is referred to measure of similarity of two waveforms as a function of a time-lag applied to one of them. This concept of cross-correlation is a need and widely used for signal processing applications in digital communications (Anwar, et al. 2008).

Methodology
The initial phase for this project is information gathering on noise reduction in audio whereby the objective, method, project requirement, and the significance of the project were determined. Speech was prepared and recorded. A participant was given the same speech and recorded speech was collected as samples of speech data. Speech acquisition of the participant were recorded in two types of environments; controlled and uncontrolled environments. Types of speech recorded in each environment are normal, whispering and angry speech. The overall samples used in this project are 48 speech data. Graphical User Interface Development Environment (GUIDE) in MATLAB was used for developing noise reduction system in speech development.
The speech signals can be processed, transmitted or stored once in digital domain. Since the Audio Device Block enables experimentation and processing of digital signals, From Audio Device in MATLAB Simulink was implemented to read audio data from an audio device in real time. From Audio Device Block was selected with To Multimedia File in MATLAB Simulink for the purpose to save the audio acquired by a given time. The From Audio Device Block buffers the data from audio device using the process illustrated in Figure 1.

ISBN: 978-1-387-00704-2

The Figure 1 shows the From Audio Device GUI, where this project selected a 5 seconds queue period. The audio device begins writing the input data to a buffer at the start of the simulation. This input data has data type specified by the Device data type parameter. When the buffer is full, the From Audio Device block writes the contents of the buffer to the queue. The size of the queue specified by using the Queen duration (seconds) parameter. The From Audio Device Block pulls data from the top of the queue to fill the Simulink frame as the audio device appends audio data to the bottom of the queue. This data has the data type specified by the Output data type parameter. This file is used in this project to experience de-noise method using wavelets.

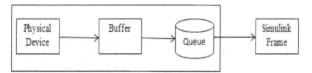

Figure 1: The From Audio Device Block

In addition, the Multimedia File Block write video frames, audio frames or both to a multimedia (.avi, .wav, .wma, .mp4, .ogg, .flac, or .wmv) file. Cross-platform supported file formats for audio files are WAV, FLAC, OGG, and MPEG4 (only for Window 7 and MAC OS X)In this project, MATLAB programming used the *wavread* function to load a WAVE file specified by the string filename which returning the sampled data in y. If the filename does not include an extension, *wavread* appends a .wav extension.

In this project, MATLAB programming used the *wavread* function to load a WAVE file specified by the string filename which returning the sampled data in y. If the filename does not include an extension, *wavread* appends a .wav extension. Furthermore, Waveform Audio File Format (WAVE) or commonly known as WAV due to its filename extension is a Microsoft and IBM audio file format standard for storing an

ISBN: 978-1-387-00704-2

audio bit stream on personal computer (PC). This audio file format is selected for this project since it is the main format used in Windows systems for raw and typically uncompressed audio and consists of simple structure, which is easy to exchange sound files among different programs. Some radio broadcasters especially which adopted the tapeless used uncompressed WAV files for transmitter simulation and receiver testing.

Experimentation and Results
Experiments were constructed using different types of speech signal; normal, whispering and angry signal in each control and uncontrolled environments. Three wavelet families of Coiflet 5, Daubechies 10 and Daubechies 9 had been analysed through the experiments to de-noise the presence of noise in three speech signals. From each experiment, the main objective is to first identify noise from the speech recorded and then remove the presence of noise in speech using wavelets techniques. In addition, White Gaussian Noise was added at level AWGN 0, AWGN 5, AWGN 10 and AWGN 15 into the speech signals before the noise reduction take places. Patterns of speech signal were collected and recorded inside spreadsheet.

Analysis of results obtained from the experiments is further shown in Figure 2. This figure showed that when the value of AWGN is increased until it reached the maximum AWGN 15, the pattern of signal become constant. The signals de-noised by Coiflet 5, Daubechies 10 and Daubechies 9 showed the constant result when reached AWGN 15.

ISBN: 978-1-387-00704-2

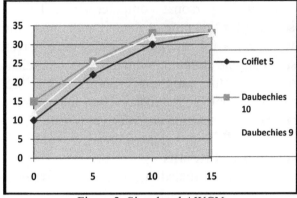

Figure 2: Signal and AWGN

Another finding acquired from the experiments is different expression of speech voices from recording which consists of normal, whispering and angry speech did not affect the AWGN. When the AWGN were reaching the maximum AWGN 15, the pattern of signal remain constant whether the experiments are using normal, whispering or angry speech signal.

Conclusions

This project had achieved its two objectives; to identify and remove the presence of noise in normal, whispering and angry signal in controlled and uncontrolled environments. Then, second objective is to measure the pattern of the normal, whispering, and angry signal before and after the noise reduction using cross-correlation technique. By comparing the experiment result between normal, whispering and angry signal in controlled and uncontrolled environments, it can be further concluded that Daubechies 10 and Daubechies 9 shows better result when de-noise the signal. In addition, the higher the amount of White Gaussian Noise (AWGN) is added to the signal, the better the signal can be de-noised. Based on the observation and analysis from the experiments conducted, the uncontrolled environment shows better result in de-noising process compared to in controlled environment.

ISBN: 978-1-387-00704-2

References

Aggarwal, Rajeev, Karan Singh, Jai, Kumar Gupta, Vijay, Rathore, Sanjay, Tiwari, Mukesh, & Khare, Anubhuti. (2011). Noise reduction of speech signal using wavelet transform with modified universal threshold. *International Journal of Computer Applications, 20*(5), 14-19.

Anwar, Umer Hassan and Sabieh. (2008). Statistical properties of White Noise (Electronics & Signal Processing).

Benesty, J., Jingdong, Chen, & Huang, Y. A. (2008). On the Importance of the Pearson Correlation Coefficient in Noise Reduction. *Audio, Speech, and Language Processing, IEEE Transactions on, 16*(4), 757-765. doi: 10.1109/TASL.2008.919072

Chavan, Mahesh S, Chavan, Mrs Manjusha N, & Gaikwad, MS. (2010). Studies on implementation of wavelet for denoising speech signal. *International Journal of Computer Applications, 3*(2).

Dhanalakshmi, P, Palanivel, S, & Ramalingam, Vennila. (2009). Classification of audio signals using SVM and RBFNN. *Expert Systems with Applications, 36*(3), 6069-6075

Di Bert, Luca, Caldera, Peter, Schwingshackl, David, & Tonello, Andrea M. (2011). *On noise modeling for power line communications.* Paper presented at the Power Line Communications and Its Applications (ISPLC), 2011 IEEE International Symposium

Goel, Roopali, & Jain, Ritesh. (2013). Speech Signal Noise Reduction by Wavelets. *International Journal of Innovative Technology and Exploring Engineering (IJITEE), ISSN-2278-3075, 2.*

Gold, Ben, Morgan, Nelson, & Ellis, Dan. (2011). *Speech and audio signal processing: processing and perception of speech and music*: Wiley. com.

JaiShankar, B, & Duraiswamy, K. (2012). AUDIO DENOISING USING WAVELET TRANSFORM.

MathWorks. (2014a). AWGN Channel. from http://www.mathworks.com/help/comm/ug/awgn-channel.html

McLoughlin, Ian. (2009). *Applied speech and audio processing*: Cambridge University Press.

Mihov, Slavy, Doychev, Doycho, & Ivanov, Ratcho. (2009). *Practical Investigation of Specific Types of Noise Signals for the Purpose of Suppression in Hearing-Aid Devices.* Paper presented at the XLIV International Conference ICEST-2009, B.

Muangjaroen, Supavit, & Yingthawornsuk, Thaweesak. (2012). *A Study of Noise Reduction in Speech Signal using FIR Filtering.* Paper presented at the International Conference on Advances in Electrical and Electronics Engineering.

Nongpiur, R. C. (2008, March 31 2008-April 4 2008). *Impulse noise removal in speech using wavelets.* Paper presented at the Acoustics, Speech

ISBN: 978-1-387-00704-2

and Signal Processing, 2008. ICASSP 2008. IEEE International Conference

O'Haver, Prof. Tom. (2013). Signals and noise. From http://terpconnect.umd.edu/~toh/spectrum/SignalsAndNoise.html

Ratnakar Madan, Prof. Sunil Kr. Singh, and Nitisha Jain2 (2009). Signal Filtering Using Discrete Wavelet Transform. 2.

Russo, Mladen, Stella, Maja, & Rozic, Nikola. (2012). Noise reduction in speech signals using a cochlear model. *Advances in Smart Systems Research, 2*(1), 7.

Seiça, Álvaro. (2012). The Transducer Function: An Introduction to a Theoretical Typology in Electronic Literature and Digital Art. *Journal of Science and Technology of the Arts, 4*(1), 71-79.

Soto, J Gabriel, Flores-Gil, Aaron, & May-Alarcon, Manuel. (2011). De-Noising Audio Signals Using MATLAB Wavelets Toolbox.

Vijaykumar, VR, Vanathi, PT, & Kanagasapabathy, P. (2007). Modified adaptive filtering algorithm for noise cancellation in speech signals. *Electronics and Electrical Engineering.–Kaunas: Technologija*(2), 74.

Villanueva-Luna, Adrian E, Jaramillo-Nuñez, Alberto, Sanchez-Lucero, Daniel, Ortiz-Lima, Carlos M, Aguilar- Wieland, Bernhard, Urban, Karsten, & Funken, Stefan. (2009). *Speech signal noise reduction with wavelets*. Diplomarbeit an der Universität Ulm.

ISBN: 978-1-387-00704-2

SECTION III:

INFORMATION
TECHNOLOGY
&
SYSTEM
SCIENCES

Article 22

Construction of i-KCare: Kidney Failure Self-Care Multimedia Courseware

Arifah Fasha Rosmani, Nur Atikah Adzman
Faculty of Computer and Mathematical Sciences
Universiti Teknologi MARA Perlis Branch, Malaysia

Abstract
Kidney failure is a condition where the kidney is unable to function normally. Currently, most of kidney failures patients are not aware of the importance of at home self-care and this may affect their health and consequently, sooner or later it will decline. The patients should be conscious of their proper diet, daily activities that they can perform, and other related information to avoid their kidney from worsening. The kidney failure patients need to understand all this information to help them in taking care of themselves at home. Thus, this multimedia courseware is designed and constructed for these patients to increase their knowledge and awareness on the disease. This project has applied one of the System Development Life Cycle (SDLC) models, which is Prototype Model and it had been tested using Acceptance Test and Heuristic Test. The participants for the tests are kidney failure patients, their family members, and nurses in dialysis centers. This courseware is expected to increase their knowledge and awareness on the disease, hence, helping them to have a better self-care at home.

Keywords: kidney failure, self-care management, multimedia courseware

Introduction

In 2014, World Health Organization (WHO) states that kidney failure is one of the diseases that causes the death rate to arise annually since the last 20 years, and currently, obesity is one of a compelling risk factors for the development of kidney disease. It escalates the risk of developing major risk factors of Chronic Kidney Disease (CKD) (World Health Organization, 2017).

A general term for kidney disease is heterogeneous disorder that gives impact to the function and structure of the kidney (Levey & Coresh, 2011). The kidney function is very important, to clean

ISBN: 978-1-387-00704-2

and filter blood, control blood pressure and keep the bones strong. Most people are not aware and do not realize the importance of having healthy kidneys and, what are the factors and symptoms of kidney failure.

Kidney failure patients are required to undergo kidney dialysis to survive, either through hemodialysis or Continuous Ambulatory Peritoneal Dialysis (CAPD). However, Clarkson and Robinson (2010) found that dialysis that is accompanied by restriction of dietary, fluids intake, fatigue and other causes that might limit the patients' activities. The patients should know what activities that they can do or cannot do to avoid their kidneys from deteriorating. Besides, there is a big challenge in improving their wellbeing with healthcare costs reduced (Coughlin, Pope, Leedle, 2006).

To help increase the public's awareness, a courseware has been developed to spread information about kidney failure and it is expected that the patients will have a better understanding of their health status, be more alert when a problem occurs, and pay less visit to hospitals. This courseware has utilized multimedia elements as multimedia technology can excite people to produce strong interest in learning (Chen, 2012), thus leading to better understanding.

Background of Research
Some people who are suffering this disease are unaware of the importance of having good self-care at home. They need to know information about dietary habits, choices for treatment and symptoms (Ormandy, 2008), the activities that they can and cannot do. Self-care means that patients take care of their health and well-being on their own, while accepting support from people whether they are involved or not in the patients' care management (Ong, Jasal, Porter, Logan, Miller, 2013). Knowing the importance of self-care is the key to the exploration to a better quality of life for these patients (Sato, Yamamoto, Hirakawa,

ISBN: 978-1-387-00704-2

2011). Self-care could enhance compliance with medical level, stimulate, aware of the early physical changes and facilitates the patients' autonomy (Hagger & Orbell, 2003; Lorig& Holman 2003). It is vital for the patients to know about dietary habits and activities or routine that they should do or avoid as it may affect their health. For example, food intake including grains, fruits and vegetables are essential, but they need to limit or avoid whole grains and certain fruits, and not to drink too much water as these can harm them, and so on. The patients need to know this information as a precaution to maintain and take care of their kidneys and their current health.

They need to know about kidney failure disease to understand more about the disease and help them to have a better self-care at home. Therefore, a multimedia courseware was developed as one of the ways to improve the understanding about kidney failure. Multimedia technology has been integrated in this courseware and it means a technology that included different types of information such as text, animations, videos, images, sounds, or graphics by using computer are included to establish human-computer interaction and logical relationship (Chen, 2012). Multimedia can influence users to have strong interest in gaining knowledge. These multimedia elements were used in the courseware design and developed with the aims to help people increase their awareness and gain knowledge about kidney failure disease and help the kidney failure patients to have a better self-care at home. This project is a significant endeavour in improving the kidney failure patients', and the other users' knowledge and awareness about kidney failure, thus helping them to have a better self-care at home. Other than that, the users' family members also can use the courseware to learn more about the disease.

ISBN: 978-1-387-00704-2

Related Works

i. CAPD (Continuous Ambulatory Peritoneal Dialysis) eBook
This eBook is developed to help the patients to adapt CAPD in their daily life by using multimedia elements, for example text, sound, animation, and graphics to make its users easier to learn during the learning process (Rosmani, Shalahudin, Ahmad, Ismail, 2012). CAPD is one of the treatments that kidney failure patients can choose to eliminate wastes from their body, such as extra water and chemicals. It is a continuous treatment that has four to five dialysis exchanges daily, which connects tubes and solution bags to manipulate the gravity to fill and drain the peritoneal cavity (Zabat, 2003). One of the advantages of this application is that it can help the kidney patients to learn and perform CAPD. By adapting the Persuasive Technology principles, this application is able to enhance its users' learning process. This is proven based on the results of the tests. For the usability test, it was conducted to measure the multimedia application criteria, such as, objectives of the application, content, interactivity, interfaces, sound and navigation. Most of the results gained the mean value 4.20 and above. On the other hand, according to the Heuristic Test result, 33.3 percent of the participants chose "strongly agreed", and 66.6 percent chose "agreed" for the effectiveness of the Persuasive Technology principles adaption. However, one of the disadvantages of this application is it is in the Malay language. Non-Malay who do not understand Malay may find it difficult to understand the application content. The content should be in English or both Malay and English.

ii. i-KS: Composition of Chronic Kidney Failure Disease (CDK) Online Informational Self-Care Tool
This courseware aims to develop a multimedia application that will help kidney failure patients by providing guidelines in managing themselves. The guidelines are essential to monitor the patients' health and to make sure they can live like normal people (Rosmani, Mazlan, Ibrahim, Zakaria, 2015). Two tests were used

ISBN: 978-1-387-00704-2

to evaluate this application, which were Usability Test and Heuristic Evaluation, to make sure it meets its goals. This courseware offers a user-friendly courseware as the interfaces are attractive and easy to understand. This will ease users whether elderly or young people to understand and use the courseware. By providing attractive and understandable interfaces, it also attracts users' attention to learn more. However, it demands users to use internet access and it will be difficult to use if there is no internet access or slow internet connection.

Methodology

To develop the courseware, one of the SDLC models is chosen. The chosen model is Prototyping Model (Kumar, Zadgaonkar, Shukla, 2013), and this model was mapped to the methodology. The basis of this model has six phases, which are requirement gathering, quick design, building prototyping, customer evaluation, refining prototype, and engineer prototype. Prototype models provide flexibility for the users as they always interact with the developer. Hence, this reduces risk of failure, as potential risks can be identified early and actions can be taken to remove that risk (Ji & Tiwari, 2015).

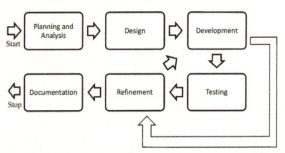

Figure 1: Methodology (based on Prototyping Model)

- Planning and Analysis: Find information about kidney failure and understand the user requirements.
- Design: Change the requirements details description into structure.

ISBN: 978-1-387-00704-2

- Development: Create a flow chart and storyboard to design the multimedia courseware interface and its content.
- Testing: Users will evaluate the courseware and give feedback.
- Refinement: Refine the entire design and development. If there are errors or problems, the problems or errors need to be solved.
- Documentation: Document all the activities as a project report

Though, this paper will focus only on the main part of this courseware which is the design and development phase.

i. Storyboard Design

Storyboard is a graphic organizer, such as a sequence of illustrations or images, showed in series (Rosmani, Wahab, 2011). Storyboard was created in design phase to demonstrate the idea visually and as guidance for development phase so that the development process will be maintained on its track. It gives us ways to make decision on how we will control and manage the project. This storyboard was created using sketchbook, based on information collected before proceeding with the development phase.

ISBN: 978-1-387-00704-2

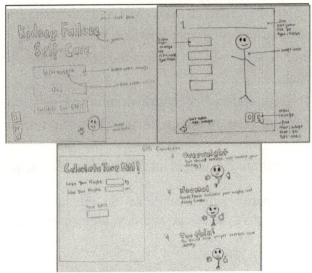

Figure 2: Storyboard examples

ii. Project Development

In the development phase, some information needed was collected for this multimedia courseware to make sure that it meets all the requirements. The information collected was gained through the internet, and a hospital. After that, the design phase began by sketching the interfaces using a sketchbook and a pencil. Then, the development phase was started using Adobe Flash software.

There are 3 main sections in this courseware as shown in Figure 3 below which are: 1) Information section, 2) Quiz, and 3) BMI Calculator

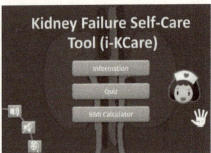

Figure 3: Main Sections of Kidney Failure Self-Care Tool (i-KCare)

ISBN: 978-1-387-00704-2

This is the home page where users can choose whether to click on "Information" to know about kidneyfailure disease, "Quiz" to answer few questions about kidney, and "BMI Calculator" to calculate BMI.

i. Information Section

In the information section, as shown in Figure 4, users can choose which kidney disease information they want to read. They can read about what kidney failure is, kidney failure factors and symptoms, people who tend to get the disease, ways to detect it and its effects if it is not detected early, ways to prevent it, activities the patients can do, food that they can and cannot eat, and information about blood test.

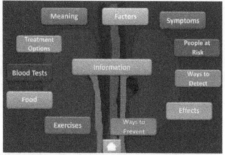

Figure 4: Information Section of i-KCare

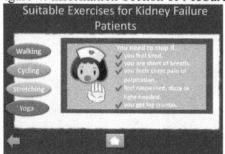

Figure 5: An example of information in Information Section in i-KCare

This is one of the interfaces for the kidney information section and it allows users to click the home button to go back to the

ISBN: 978-1-387-00704-2

home page, back and next buttons to go to the previous page and next page.

ii. Quiz

The front page for "Quiz" is as shown in Figure 6. When users click on "Start Now!" button, it will start the quiz. The back button will go to the home page. For this page, users choose the answer by clicking on one of the answer provided. The next button will bring users to the next question, and the back button will bring users to the previous page. The quiz section will automatically calculate marks for the correct and false answers.

 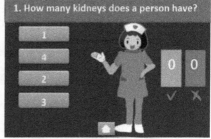

Figure 6: Quiz

iii. BMI Calculator

BMI calculator will calculate its users' BMI weight. Users need to insert their height in centimeter (cm) and weight in kilogram (kg). Then, users need to click on "Calculate" button to know the result. The result will show in the result text box as shown in Figure 7.

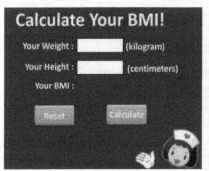 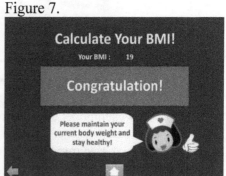

Figure 7: BMI Calculator

ISBN: 978-1-387-00704-2

Findings and Discussion
To identify users' feedback and suggestion about this project, 2 tests were conducted, which were Heuristic Testing and Acceptance Testing. Heuristic Test was conducted on UiTMCawangan Perlis lecturers from Computer Science Department and Acceptance Test, was conducted on a few non-patients and patients of Zaharah Dialysis Centre, which is located in Kangar, Perlis.

i. Heuristic Test
It is a method where a group of experts evaluate a user interface for design problems based on usability principles or heuristics (Manzari& Christensen, 2006). By conducting this evaluation, developers can gain early feedback during the design process (usability.gov, 2017). Thus, this testing can help in improving the user interfaces and the ease of use to the courseware users. This evaluation is conducted with the help of four examiners, who are lecturers of UiTMCawanganPerlis. The examiners are given some time to use the courseware and after that, they were given a questionnaire to answer. The examiners agree that most of the contents, text, colours, and images used are appropriate.

Here are the percentages of users' satisfaction based on the appearance of i-KCare. 75%of the participants agreed that the objectives or goals are clear, 50% agree that i-KCare employed a clean and simple design, pleasing colour scheme, and consistent in the used of text and colour. Next, 25% of them agree that the courseware's icons were easily understood, the images usedwere meaningful and purposeful, and all the users strongly agree that the design is consistent. From the result, most users were satisfied with i-KCare appearances. Next is the results on text used, 50% agree that text used is minimum, buttons are clear and follow its convention, and it was easy to findneeded information. Other than that, 25% of the respondents agree that the title is easy to understand, and the terminology used is clear and finally,75% of

ISBN: 978-1-387-00704-2

them strongly agree that the courseware load easily, support undo and redo, and easy in finding related information.

Conclusion and Recommendation

In conclusion, most of the users, including both patients and non-patients, were satisfied and they did not have any problem to use i-KCare and strongly agree that the courseware can deliver positive impacts in their daily life, thus, it shows that this project has achieved its objective, which is to increase knowledge and awareness about kidney disease. Hence, hopefully this project can give benefits to its users by helping them enhance their knowledge and awareness, and have a better self-care at home. Some of the recommendations for future works are to provide multiple languages that can be chosen by its users as some of the users might not understand English, especially the elderly, more interactivity with its users, and use of more pictures instead of text as users might get tired of reading and a commercial look for its use in the health industry.

References

Chen, Q. (2012). Research for Influence of Physical Education Multimedia Teaching on Sports Motivation of Students.*AISS: Advances in Information Sciences and Service Sciences, 4(16)*, pp. 14-22.

Clarkson, K., & Robinson, K. (2010). Life on dialysis: A lived experience. *Nephrology Nursing Journal, 37(1)*, pp. 29-35.

Coughlin, J.F., Pope, J.E., and Leedle, B.R. Old Age, New Technology, and Future Innovations in Disease Management and Home Health Care.*Home Health Care Management & Practice 18, 3 (2006)*, pp. 196-207.

Hagger, M., & Orbell, S. (2003).A Meta-Analytic Review of the Common-Sense Model of Illness Representations.*Psychology & Health,18(2)*, pp. 141-184.

Ji. H., Tiwari, A., (2015). Comparative Review of Software Development Life Cycle Models.*International Journal of Engineering Science & Advanced Research (IJESAR)*, 1(1), pp. 51-54.

Kariyuki, S., Washizaki, H., Fukazawa, Y., Kubo, A., & Suzuki, M. (2011). Acceptance testing based on relationships among use cases. *Proc. of 5th world congress for software quality.*

Kumar, N., Zadgaonkar, A.S., & Shukla, A. (2013). Evolving a New Software Development Life Cycle Model SDLC-2013 with Client

ISBN: 978-1-387-00704-2

Satisfaction. *Proc. of International Journal of Soft Computing and Engineering (IJSCE)*, 3(1), pp. 216-221.

Levey, A. S., & Coresh, J. (2012).Chronic kidney disease.*The Lancet, 379(9811)*, pp. 165-180.

Lorig, K. R., & Holman, H. R. (2003). Self-management education: History, definition, outcomes, and mechanisms.*Annals of Behavioral Medicine, 26(1)*, pp. 1-7.

Manzari, L., Christensen, J. T., User-Centered Design of a Web Site for Library and Information Science Students: Heuristic Evaluation and Usability Testing, *Information Technology and Libraries*, 2006, pp. 163-169.

Ong, S.W., Jassal, S. V, Porter, E., Logan, A. G., & Miller, J. a., Using an electronic self-management tool to support patients with chronic kidney disease (CKD): a CKD clinic self-care model. *Seminars in Dialysis, 2013. 26(2)*, pp. 195-202.

Ormandy, P. (2008). Information topics important to chronic kidney disease patients: a systematic review. *Journal of Renal Care, 34(1)*, pp. 19-27.

Wang, W., Rövekamp, T. J., Brinkman, W. P., Alpay, L., van der Boog, P., &Neerincx, M.A. (2012, August). Designing and evaluating a self-management support system for renal transplant patients: the first step. *Proc. of the 30th European Conference on Cognitive Ergonomics.ACM*, pp. D15-D19.

Zulkifli, A. N., Noor, N. M., Bakar, J. A. A., Mat, R. C., & Ahmad, M. (2013, September).A conceptual model of interactive persuasive learning system for elderly to encourage computer-based learning process.*Proc. of IEEE International Conference on Informatics and Creative Multimedia (ICICM), 2013*, pp. 7-12.

Rosmani, A. F., Mazlan, U., H., Ibrahim, A., F., Zakaria, D., S. (2015, April). i-KS: Composition of chronic kidney disease (CDK) online informational self-care tool. *Proc. of 2015 International Conference on Computer, Communications, and Control Technology (I4CT)*, pp. 379-383.

Rosmani, A. F., Shalahudin, N. F., Ahmad, S. Z., & Ismail, M.H. (2012, June). CAPD eBook: Evaluating multimedia application for Continuous Ambulatory Peritoneal Dialysis (CAPD) users. *Proc. of 2012 IEEE Symposium in Humanities, Science and Engineering Research (SHUSER)*, pp. 939-942.

Rosmani, A. F., Wahab, N. A. (2011, May). i-IQRA': Designing and constructing a persuasive multimedia application to learn Arabic characters. *Proc. of IEEE Colloquium on Humanities, Science and Engineering (CHUSER)*, 2011, pp. 98-101.

ISBN: 978-1-387-00704-2

Usability.gov (2017), *Heuristic Evaluations and Expert Reviews.* Retrieved
from:https://www.usability.gov/how-to-and-tools/methods/heuristic-evaluation.html

Sato, Y., Yamamoto, K., Hirakawa, M., Doi, S., & Yamamoto, Y. (2011, August). Support of self-management for chronic kidney failure patients. *Proc. of the 2011 Visual Information Communication-International Symposium, ACM*, pp. 6.

World Health Organization (2017), *2017 Theme: Kidney disease & obesity.* Retrieved from: http://www.who.int/life-course/news/events/world-kidney-day-2017/en/

Zabat, Eden. (2003). When your patient needs peritoneal dialysis, *Nursing 2003*, 33(8).

ISBN: 978-1-387-00704-2

Article 23

Mobile Application for Calendar Events of UiTM Perlis Branch (CEPS)

Muhammad Nabil Fikri Jamaluddin, Ummaira Abd Saad, Mahfudzah Othman,
Shukor Sanim Mohd Fauzi, Alif Faisal Ibrahim, Ray Adderley JM Gining
Faculty of Computer and Mathematical Sciences
Universiti Teknologi MARA Perlis Branch, Malaysia

Abstract

Smartphone nowadays has become a must for everyone to communicate and retrieve important information. Various information about products, events and almost everything are accessible from the fingertips. Recently, method of dissemination of information regarding events in UniversitiTeknologi MARA (UiTM) Perlis Branch, is conducted thru posters, flyers and social networking sites. This method of spreading information is not reliable since it still fails to reach the whole community even students, lecturers and staff of the campus. Thus, lead to less number of participation. This project aims to introduce an innovative way of spreading information about events to communities via mobile application. Valuable information includes name of events, date, target audience, organizer and its location will be made available in the application for user. Data is stored in the MySQL database and JSON is used to manipulate it and pass to mobile application to be represented in user interface. User acceptance testing is conducted via questionnaire to check the capability and deliverables of the mobile application to the end users. The overall result shows that the application developed is acceptable and applicable to be used in by the community of UiTM Perlis.

Keywords:*Mobile Application, Calendar of Events, Information Dissemination, Events Calendar, Events Announcements.*

Introduction

Smartphone applications are meant to allow users to carry them anywhere they go, easy access to the information and completing simple tasks while on the go. Usage of smartphone is increasing nowadays where people spend more time to accomplish tasks beyond from basic communication needs(Cao & Lin, 2016). The delivery of smartphones had increased from 1.44 billion in 2015 to 1.49 billion in 2016 which mark a growing trend with three

ISBN: 978-1-387-00704-2

percent(Sui, 2017). The spread of information thru mobile application is becoming very effective due to its number of users in community. Thus, it is beneficial to develop an application to disseminate the information regarding events in mobile phone.

A successful event, require an organizer to attract large crowds. Earlier method of dissemination of information regarding events is thru spreading words, posters, flyers, social network sites and advertisementswhich is not reliable since it still fails to reach the whole community. There are multiple events conducted in UiTM Perlis at a time, which could lead to misleading information about the events. The information posted on social network sites is not effective due to unfiltered information on the newsfeed of the target audience and creates redundant information. Unorganized method of information delivery cause the information not delivered to target audience and same problem will be faced by new students.

This paper presents a mobile application for viewing and listing events organized in UiTM Perlis named as Mobile Application for Calendar Events of UiTM Perlis Branch (CEPS) with the assistance of Global Position System (GPS) for marking the specific location on the map. The mobile application lists current and future events held in UiTM Perlis and its details, including event names, time, venue, organizer, target and number of participant and location. It also able to pin and display the location of events on the real map using Google Maps Application Programming Interface (API) and Android Operating System (OS).

Related Works
iii. OHIO University: Calendar of Events
Figure 1 below shows a calendar of events of OHIO University. This university provides an electronic calendar for their students to inform the events which were organized in this university. Clicking on the date form calendar, users are able to know details

ISBN: 978-1-387-00704-2

of events' information such as type of events, times, date, location, and website of the events. Moreover, students can browse events' activities based on week of month.

Figure 1: Calendar of Events from OHIO University website (Ohio University, 2013).

iv. University of Illinois Urbana Campaign

Students or users are able to search current events by clicking the date. The advantage about this calendar of events is, it allows users to search events based on all, grid, month, week, day using search tool. Upon the click of events, it will be highlighted in red color. The details of information such as Speaker, date, time, location, cost, sponsor, contact, e-mail, phone, registration, views are attributes of the information of the related event will be displayed.

Figure 2: Calendar of events of University of Illinois Urbana Champaign
(University of Illinois Urbana Campaign, 2013).

ISBN: 978-1-387-00704-2

Research Methodology

This research applies repetitive development process (Figure 3) adapted from a Waterfall Model consists of six phases. The flow progress works in repetition until each phase satisfies and may revert to the previous phases. Activities, techniques and deliverables are explained as follows:

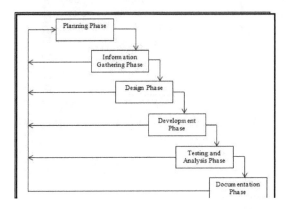

Figure 3: Waterfall Model (Repetitive).

i.   Planning Phase –Includes the feasibility study to identify area, scope significance and outcome of the project based on related journal, research articles and text books.

ii.   Information Gathering Phase – Search for required information related to the topic, collect relevant data and information from the discussion with person in charge and available resources and materials. All required software are determined in this phase.

iii.   Design Phase – Includes the database design and flow of application logic. This phase ends with the prototype frame work produced.

iv.   Development Phase – Development of the mobile application for Android platform using Android Studio, database development using PhpMyAdmin and php editor using Dreamweaver.

ISBN: 978-1-387-00704-2

v. Testing and Analysis Phase – Developed application is evaluated to test the delivery and user's acceptance by allowing the random person to test the application and fill up the survey form. Results obtained from survey areanalyzed.

vi. Documentation Phase – Involves writing a documentation of the project.

Mobile Application Framework and Implementation

In general, the mobile application utilizes JavaScript Object Notation (JSON) for reading data from database. Based on Figure 4, mobile application begins with requesting data to Hypertext Preprocessor (PHP) web service, and it will direct the request to the database. Data returned by the database is represented in a form of JSON using PHP standard library and pass back to mobile application. Finally, mobile application represents the data in a graphical user interface (GUI). Database developed for this project consists of two simple tables purposely to store data for the events and details about the developers.

Implementation of this project involved the use of mobile application as a client and a laptop as a server for storing and manipulating data. Data conversion into JSON format is done at the server side after received a request from the client (mobile application). The connectivity between these two devices is thru the network of wireless router. Client should properly set the address of the server in order to establish a connection.

ISBN: 978-1-387-00704-2

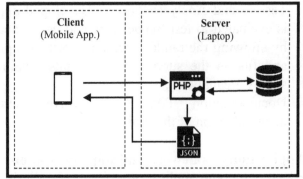

Figure 4: Framework for mobile application CEPS.

Development
i. Home and events interface

Figure 5(a)   Figure 5(b)

Figure 5: (a) Main interface. (b) List of events from the CEPS application.

Figure 5 (a) shows main interface of Calendar Events UiTM Perlis (CEPS)mobile application with a button named 'Events' which will be directed to second interface.Figure 5 (b) shows the second interface of CEPS android application. In this page, it has a navigation tab consist of HEA (Hal EhwalAkademik), HEP (Hal EhwalPelajar) and ABOUT US information. Both HEA and HEP shows current and future events will be held in UiTM Perlis. It has information about the event's name, open for and date of

ISBN: 978-1-387-00704-2

the events. About us section shows information regarding CEPS developer. Users can return to the home page of the application by clicked the back-arrow navigation at the top of CEPS application.

ii. Event Details and Map Location Interface

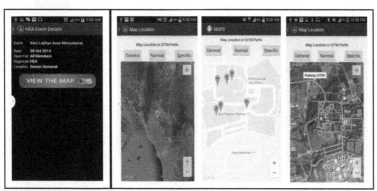

Figure 6(a)   *Figure: 6(b)*

Figure 6(a) Details of selected events. (b) Specific location of events on the map.

Figure 6 (a) shows the event details after users tapone of the event listed in the main interface either from HEA or HEP tab, name of event, date, open for (target audience), organizer and location of the event are displayed. One button ('View The Map') is available for users to view specific location on the map where the image of the map is provided by Google API. Figure 6.b shows specific location of the event chosen on the map based on pin in red color. Users also provided with options to view the map either in 'general', 'normal' or 'specific' mode.

Results and Analysis
Survey on user acceptance testing is carried out to check acceptance and deliverables of product to end user. To complete the study, 30 respondents are selected randomly among

ISBN: 978-1-387-00704-2

UiTMPerlis students, lecturers and staffs. Two main parts of testing, which are effectiveness and satisfaction.

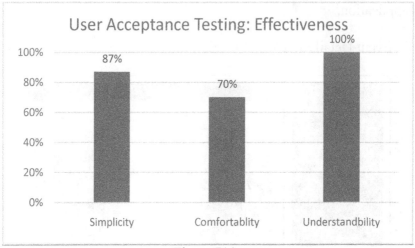

Figure 7(a)

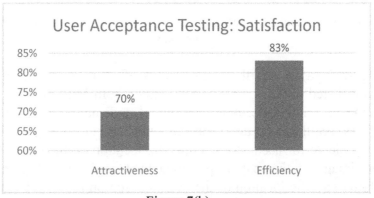

Figure 7(b)

Figure 7: (a)User acceptance testing: effectiveness (b) User acceptance testing: satisfaction

The first part of the user acceptance test begins with effectiveness of CEPS which is presented in the bar chart in Figure 7(a). This part is divided into three categories which are simplicity,

ISBN: 978-1-387-00704-2

comfortability and understandability. Among 30 respondents, 87% agree that this mobile application is simple and easy to use. 70% of them believe it is comfortable to use and all of respondents agree it easy to understand. From the figures presented, it shows majority of the respondents agree that the CEPS is effective.

Results for the second part of the testing are presented in Figure 7(b), where it is divided into two categories which are attractiveness and efficiency. 70% respondents agree CEPS is attractive and 83% of them believe it is efficient for real usage. Results from two categories showed that the average satisfaction is obtained for CEPS.

Conclusion and Future Works

Effective way of dissemination of information about certain event is very crucial in organizing a successful event to attract participation of big crowds. CEPS mobile application is introduced to make the information available and easy to access for the UiTM Perlis community such as students, lecturers and staff. Centralized and organized information in single mobile application introduces an innovative way of information dissemination. Details of events and specific locations provided allow the potential participants to well informed with the event. Results from user acceptance testing shows majority of the respondents agree that the CEPS is effective for real usage. While in term of user's satisfaction, it shows the average results. This suggests, a few improvements should be taken into consideration.

The future works for this project should consider the user's satisfaction criteria such as attractiveness and efficiency. Currently CEPS provides information solely about the events, in order to attract more users to the mobile application, other information can be provided such as announcements, news, exam schedules and contact information on each department in UiTM Perlis. Features such as filtering can be implemented in the

ISBN: 978-1-387-00704-2

mobile application, so that the users able to filter certain events based on their preference. Recommendation of events to the users can be implemented based on user's interest. For the enhancement of the project, web based system can be developed for admin to manage the data about the events.

As a conclusion, this project has achieved the objectives to develop a mobile application with a list of current and future events held in UiTM Perlis. It is accepted by majority of users who tested the application and received positive feedbacks. CEPS introduces an innovative and organized way of presenting the information about the events.

References

Cao, H., & Lin, M. (2016, June). Mining smartphone data for app usage prediction and recommendations: A survey. *Pervasive and Mobile Computing*, pp. 1–22. http://doi.org/10.1016/j.pmcj.2017.01.007

Ohio University. (2013). Calendar of events. Retrieved December 22, 2013, from https://calendar.ohio.edu/

Sui, L. (2017). Strategy Analytics: Global Smartphone Shipments Hit a Record 1.5 Billion Units in 2016. Retrieved August 22, 2017, from https://www.strategyanalytics.com/strategy-analytics/news/strategy-analytics-press-releases/strategy-analytics-press-release/2017/01/31/strategy-analytics-global-smartphone-shipments-hit-a-record-1.5-billion-units-in-2016#.WZuzaSgjG70

University of Illinois Urbana Champaign. (2013). Research Park Events. Retrieved December 22, 2013, from https://illinois.edu/calendar/month/7

ISBN: 978-1-387-00704-2

Article 24

Development and Evaluation of Mandarin Language Exploration Game for Non-native Speakers

Aznoora Osman , Siti Nabilah Abdul Malek
Faculty of Computer and Mathematical Sciences
Universiti Teknologi MARA Perlis Branch, Malaysia

Abstract
This paper discusses the development and evaluation of an exploration game for Mandarin language. The game focuses on mastering basic vocabularies in Mandarin for non-native speakers. Emphasis is given on word recall and pronunciation of Chinese characters. The evaluation consisted of testing session with students to discover the effects of the game towards the students' confidence in word recall and pronunciation of Chinese characters. The target audience of the project is students in UiTMPerlis Branch, who undertake Level 1 Mandarin language course. The research methodology that was used in this project is spiral model. There are four phases in the spiral model which are game idea specification, game design prototype, playtesting and evaluation. Game interface was designed by using Unity 3D software. The exploration game was constructed by integrating two elements from Octalysis' game framework into the exploration game which are ownership and avoidance. Ownership is the element where players are inspired to complete the game when they have sense of owning something. Avoidance element is based on the avoidance of negative circumstances. Testing phase employs user testing which was conducted with 19 bachelor degree students from Level 1 Mandarin language class. From the results, it was discovered that generally, the exploration game has positively influenced the students' confidence to recall and to pronounce Chinese characters. This could signify that exploration game is a promising tool in elevating confidence among language learners.

Keywords: Exploration game, Mandarin language, Non-native speakers, Unity 3D, Gamification framework

Introduction

Gamification is a process of employing game-thinking and game mechanics to engage users and solve problems (Nah, Telaprolu, Rallapalli&Venkata, 2016). Gamification is apparently a trend in many areas, including business, authoritative management, in-

ISBN: 978-1-387-00704-2

service training, health, interpersonal set up, and education (Caponetto, Earp & Michela, 2014). Many students play (computer) games in their relaxation time, thus acquiring abilities which can easily be utilized when it comes to showing more advanced knowledge (Erenli, 2013). Gamification has drawn the attention of academics, practitioners and business experts in spaces as various as training, information studies, human–computer interaction, and wellbeing (Seaborn&Fels, 2014). Gamification has been demonstrated as a significant idea and has given confirmation of its effectiveness as a tool for motivating and connecting with users in non-entertainment contexts (Seaborn&Fels, 2014).

Currently, in UiTM, students learn Mandarin using textbooks and workbooks. Unfortunately, learning a foreign language could be very difficult for non-native speakers, especially to recall and to pronounce the Mandarin characters. This could be due to the nature of Mandarin language that uses characters, thus resulting in difficulties to learn to read as compared to language that uses alphabets (Cao, Khalid, Lee, Brennan, Yang, Li, Bolger & Booth, 2010).

Therefore, in this study, an exploration game about basic vocabulary in Mandarin was developed and testedto evaluate its effectiveness in enhancing recall and pronunciation of Chinese characters.

Development Methodology
Spiral model is a suitable methodology for design-oriented project (Wheelwright and Clark, 1992; Shenhar, 1988) and each cycle helps someone to understand the phases better and refines certain requirements as well as project development. Four noteworthy phases which are game idea specification, game design prototype, playtesting and evaluation has been adapted in this spiral model. The spiral model begins with the Game Idea Specification document, in view of which the Prototyping activity

ISBN: 978-1-387-00704-2

is directed to deliver Game Design Prototype. In the following phase which is Playtesting, potential players of the game try different things with the model under recreated conditions with discovering design flaws, giving knowledge, and giving criticism. The Evaluation activity involves assessing the game score calculation and accuracy.

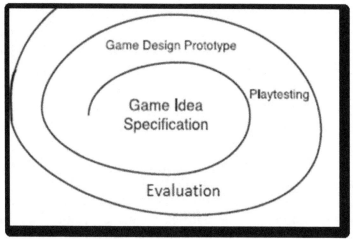

Figure 1. An adapted Spiral Model (Wheelwright and Clark, 1992; Shenhar, 1988)

The game was developed by using a software called Unity 3D. The target audiences of the game are students in UiTMPerlis Branch, who undertake Level 1 Mandarin language course. The game focuses on word recall and pronunciation of Chinese characters in the Mandarin language.

To spark interest of players, the game was designed to resemble Chinese look and feel. Therefore, the background image of its main menu screen comprised of an ancient Chinese palace, and the background music used traditional Chinese song. There is a button that user can click to start the game. Players would be given instructions and description of the mission of the game. The game was set with time limit and equipped with a scoreboard. Since the game was developed to mimic an

ISBN: 978-1-387-00704-2

exploration, a recreation park scene was chosen as the basis of its game environment. Along the journey, players are required to answer questions pertaining to Mandarin language. There are also hints and tips that could assist them in improving their vocabulary while playing.

Players are required to find 10 objects in the park. When an object is hit, its corresponding quiz questions would be displayed on the screen. The quiz contents encompass topics such as family member, numbers, days and telling time. For every correct answer, player would get 5 points that add up to the total score. In contrast, for every incorrect answer, 5 points will be deducted from the total score. When a player gave incorrect answer, the correct anwer would be shown on the screen, which helped them learn from their mistakes.

Game Evaluation and Findings
A total of 19 students in a Mandarin Level 1 class at the university voluntarily participated in the evaluation session to play with the game and measure the game's effectiveness in enhancing self-efficacy belief in language learning. It was followed by game evaluation of fun. Subjects were given briefing about the main contents of the game and the purpose of the testing session. In the beginning, subjects were given five minutes to navigate around the game to familiarise themselves with the environment. Then, as the session started, they were allocated roughly around 20 minutes to play with the game. All of them had successfully played the exploration game until the end.

An instrument for self-efficacy belief evaluation and fun evaluation was developed by the researchers. It was administered immediately to the subjects after they underwent the treatment via the exploration game. The instrument has two sections, where the first section focuses on self-efficacy belief and the second section focuses on fun evaluation. The answer to each item was

ISBN: 978-1-387-00704-2

in the form of a Likert scale, with range specified from 1 to 5 where 1 holds the lowest value which is strongly disagree while 5 holds the highest value that is strongly agree. Subjects were requested to choose the most suitable answers that represented their opinions or feelings after having exposure to the game.

There were five items that need to be rated in the first section of the instrument which is about self-efficacy belief evaluation. This is related to subjects' confidence in practising Mandarin language. The purpose is to discover whether respondents have confidence to recall and to pronounce Chinese characters in Mandarin language after playing the game. Another five items in the second section revolves around game fun evaluation. The purpose is to reveal the subjects' sense of enjoyment in playing the exploration game while also learning.Based on Table 1, all mean scores indicated that the exploration game generally received positive feedback from participants with regards to their confidence in mastering the language. It indicated that they gainedmore confidence to recall and to pronounce Chinese characters in Mandarin language after having exposure to the game. In addition, the exploration game has also made them more confident to read Mandarin sentences and would be able to use the knowledge gain for their Mandarin test.

Table 1. Mean Score Self-Efficacy Belief Evaluation

	I feel more confident to recall Chinese characters after playing the game.	I feel more confident to pronounce Chinese characters after playing the game.	I feel more confident to read Mandarin in sentences.	The game met my Mandarin educational needs.	I can apply the Mandarin knowledge in my Mandarin test.
Mean	4.11	4.00	4.21	4.37	4.32
N	19	19	19	19	19
Std. Deviation	.737	.667	.631	.496	.582

ISBN: 978-1-387-00704-2

Mean scores in Table 2 indicates that subjects had enjoyful experience with the game in which they understood the rules and mission of the game, and were also able to manouvre while completing the game within its time limit. From this finding, it can be concluded that the exploration game had successfully fulfilled fun and enjoyment elements to the players.

Table 2. Mean Score of Game Fun Evaluation Report

	I understand the rules and mission of this game.	I can move and control this game by using keyboard and mouse.	I enjoy playing the game while learning.	The time limit of this game was about right.	I can adapt with the game environment after entering it.
Mean	4.11	4.53	4.37	4.21	4.21
N	19	19	19	19	19
Std. Deviation	.737	.513	.831	.976	.855

Conclusions

Exploration Game of Mandarin Language for Non-native Speakers is a digital game-based learning that can be used as supplemental learning materials for students who undertake Mandarin language course at university level. Two elements from the Octalysis game framework which are ownership and avoidance were successfully integrated into the game. Ownership element influenced the players to complete the game since they had sense of owning something. Avoidance element is based on avoidance of negative circumstances; for example, in this game, players would carefully give their answers to all questions along the journey to avoid losing scores. The game has been evaluated for its effectiveness in enhancing confidence to recall and to pronounce Chinese characters among non-native speakers. It has also been evaluated for fun measurement. It was discovered that while playing educational game, subjects also enjoyed

ISBN: 978-1-387-00704-2

themselves and this has helped them to finish the game, thus indirectly boost their coonfidence in practising Mandarin language.

References

Cao, F., Khalid, K., Lee, R., Brennan, C., Yang, Y., Li, K., ... Booth, J. R. (2011). NeuroImage Development of brain networks involved in spoken word processing of Mandarin Chinese. NeuroImage, 57(3), 750–759. https://doi.org/10.1016/j.neuroimage.2010.09.047

Caponetto, I., Earp, J., Ott, M., & Cnr, I. T. D. (2014). Gamification and Education : A Literature Review, (2009), 50–57.

Erenli, K. (2013). The Impact of Gamification - Recommending Education Scenarios. International Journal of Emerging Technologies, 8(1), 15–21.

Nah, F.F., Telaprolu, V.R., Rallapalli, S. and Venkata, P.R. 2013. Gamification of education using computer games. In *Proceedings of the 15th international conference on Human Interface and the Management of Information: information and interaction for learning, culture, collaboration and business - Volume Part III* (HCI'13), Sakae Yamamoto (Ed.), Vol. Part III. Springer-Verlag, Berlin, Heidelberg, 99-107. DOI=http://dx.doi.org/10.1007/978-3-642-39226-9_12

Seaborn, K., & Fels, D. I. (2014). Gamification in theory and action: A survey. International Journal of Human Computer Studies, 74, 14–31. https://doi.org/10.1016/j.ijhcs.2014.09.006

Wheelwright, S. C., and K. B. Clark (1992).*Revolutionizing Product Development: Quantum Leaps in Speed, Efficiency and Quality*. New York: Free Press.

ISBN: 978-1-387-00704-2

Article 25

Cybercrime Awareness: Development and Evaluation of an Adventure Game

Aznoora Osman, Nurul Syarafina Azizan
Faculty of Computer and MathematicalSciences
Universiti Teknologi MARA Perlis Branch, Malaysia

Abstract
This paper discusses the design and development of an adventure game about cybercrime. This game uses variety of multimedia elements including text, animation, image and 3D objects. The theme of this game focuses on identity theft and phishing. Therefore, the purpose of the game is to educate the learners about cybercrime and enhance their awareness towards online activities that could victimised them. This would ensure that they take precautions of their safety while using the Internet. In this research, agile method is used as the development methodology. It includes five phases which are brainstorm, design, development, quality assurance and deployment. The completed game was used as a treatment in a user testing involving 26 students from UiTMCawangan Perlis from different ages, gender, course and faculty. After treatment, subjects were administered with two instruments to measure their perception of awareness towards cybercrime and their perception of fun for the game. It was revealed that most subjects agreed that they had an increase in awareness after exposure to the game. The game was also positively perceived as fun, with regards to its graphical and instructional design, contents relevance with the theme and suitability of game duration. Some recommendations for future enhancements are also discussed.

Keywords: Gamification, Cybercrime, Awareness, Phishing, Identity Theft.

Introduction

Gamification describes the broad trend of employing game mechanics to non-game environment such as innovation, marketing, training, employee performance, health and social changes (Arnold, 2014). Gaming techniques in educations are very helpful in learning wider, longer and deeper ways, which in turn could help to motivate and improve learning performance (Morillas Barrio, Munoz-Organero, & Sanchez Soriano, 2016).

ISBN: 978-1-387-00704-2

The internet and technology are going fast along the growth of living people and almost all the people relying on the machines (Dashora & Patel, 2011). As of 2015, Internet users in Malaysia, including those in urban and rural areas, have reached 20.1 million people(BERNAMA, 2016). With Internet connectivity, users gain benefits that enrich their lives, communication, entertainment, education and information seeking. Nevertheless, Internet also poses a threat to the community, for example exposure to cybercrime. Cybercrime is characterized as an expected demonstration including the utilization of PCs or different innovations and the criminal action must happen in a virtual setting (Singleton, 2013). Five cases of cybercrimes are duty discount extortion, corporate record takeover, fraud, robbery of touchy information and burglary of licensed innovation (Singleton, 2013). Cybercrime issue develops as fast as the progress of technology and the number of attacks increase sharply; however, many people are unaware how to protect themselves (Weber, 2009).

In Malaysia, 95% of parents are worried about their children safety online, with 60% of them admitted that their kids were cybercrime victims and 48% acted on their fears (Chin, 2016). Manasrah, Akour, & Alsukhni, (2015) revealed that university students were not only the victims of cybercrime, but they were also the cyber attackers.

Therefore, there is urgent need to educate university students about cybercrimeso that they could protect themselves from becoming the victims or the criminals. An adventure game is deemed the most suitable technique because gamification system increases student motivation (Domínguez, Saenz-de-navarrete, & Pagés, 2014) and games promote creativity and productivity during learning, through reward and badges in the games (Herro & Clark, 2016).

ISBN: 978-1-387-00704-2

This project employs a game based learning to educate learners via computer games. The game was developed using software called Unity 3D. The development methodology used for this project is agile method. The game was then used as a treatment with target users to test its effect towards perception of awareness and perception of fun. The data was collected by using an awareness instrument and a fun evaluation instrument.

Methodology

Based on research carried out in early 2014, the methodology phase found by Rickinson& May (2009) are scoping, searching, selecting, analyzing, synthesizing and reporting were used in developing gamification (Caponetto, Earp, & Ott, 2014). For this project, agile method was chosen to develop an adventure game.

Agile method is focusing on fast production in working code and it is incremental development software ("Assumptions Under lying Agile Softwar e Development Pr ocesses," 2005). Steps involved in agile methodology are brainstorm, design, development, quality assurance and deployment.

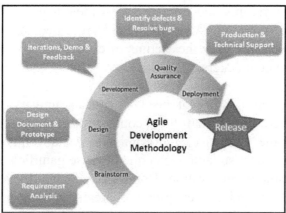

Figure 1: Agile Development Methodology

ISBN: 978-1-387-00704-2

a) Brainstorm

In this phase, it focuses on defining the topic, identifying the problem statement, objective, and scope of the project. The method that was used is to find related journals and articles about cybercrime, gamification, educational learning and online safety. The deliverables are problem statement and current issues of the project topic and aims and objective. Also, relevance tree and the related table were formed.

b) Design

This phase includes design document. For the design, the document needs to developing the initial content idea, storyboard was created for the project flow, plan the task for challenges in the games and prepare a script. For developing the initial content idea, a framework from Nah et.al was adapted for this project development. In this project, C# will be used for the script language in Unity 3D. The deliverables for this phase are the interface design, storyboard, and contents related to cybercrime.

c) Development

In development phase, the project has been developed by using a software named Unity 3D and Adobe Photoshop. Both of the software use for graphic and multimedia purpose.The hardware requirement is a computer processor Core i5, RAM size is 4.00 GB and windows edition is Windows 10 Pro which can support this project. The user also has to give a feedback after using an application. The method for measure a feedback is use fun evaluation which measures how much fun one's having or had while playing games. The deliverable is cybercrime awareness the educational games for university students.

d) Quality Assurance

Quality assurance means to identify defect and resolve bugs. This phase follows the development phase so that improvement can be done for this game application. The method uses for identifying defect and bugs through usability test. After finding the defect

ISBN: 978-1-387-00704-2

and bugs, a developer has to improve and update the application. The deliverable is updated and improve the project.

e) Deployment

The last phase in agile development methodology is deployment which means updated and fix the defects or error before. After fixing all the errors and defects, the application is ready to use. The adventure game about prevention of cybercrime is ready to be released. This phase also includes documentation project. All the documents from the first phase has been documented in detail by using Microsoft Word and Mendeley for reference manager.

Game Environment and Contents

The game environment was designed to resemble an actual office that is equipped with common office furnitures and computers. The main screen has a cartoon-like background image of a police officer holding a magnifier to scheme through a person who is portrayed as a cybercriminal. There is a button labeled "Play Now" that brings the player to a 3-D game scene. In this scene, players could view how to play the game by choosing the "How to Play" button. It gives instructions about specific keyboard keys to be used, and the role of mouse to control the movement of the actor.

Rules and mission of the game are presented in dialog callouts to mimic a conversation between a spy and the boss. The mission of the game is to catch a cybercriminal. The prime suspect is described by the boss to be one of the employees at the office. The suspect is not known by the players; however, it is their mission to correctly identify the employee, by embarking on the exploratory journey.

The game uses exploratory approach to complete the mission. The players embark on an adventure to capture a cybercriminal. The game requires players to maneuver around an office space,

ISBN: 978-1-387-00704-2

hit certain animated objects and answer the corresponding questions pertaining to identity theft and phishing, which are two of the most common cybercrimes. The answers were in multiple choice. Players would earn some points to their score when they answer each question correctly. The instructional contents were subtly embedded into the game via these questions. With every answer (correct and incorrect), it comes with a hint of who the criminal is. A correct answer entitles the players to a worthier hint, while an incorrect answer leads to vague hint. To proceed with the journey, players with incorrect answer were enforced to keep on choosing the answer until they get it right. The purpose is to make sure that they gain some understandings about cybercrime while playing. There is also a time countdown that indicates the remaining time to complete the mission. The game was developed to be accomplished within 10 to 15 minutes. This is to ensure players motivation and interest to complete the game is maintained.

Towards the end of the game, players are required to identify the criminal by choosing a picture of an employee from all pictures in the screen. With correct answer, players are congratulated and given a trophy image on the screen, as well as a display of score points. Additionally, an image of the criminal is portrayed to be miserably locked up in prison. The game can be played again by hitting the "Play Again" button, or hitting the "X" button to exit from the game.

User Testing and Findings

An experiment with a sample of target users was conducted with 26 students from UniversitiTeknologi MARA (UiTM) Perlis Branch, who were enrolled in different courses, aged between 19 and 21 years old. The researchers, who acted as the facilitators, started the session with a brief introduction about the experiment, the game contents and the instruments that subjects were supposed to answer. The session took about 50 minutes, where 5 minutes was allocated for briefing, 5 minutes for subjects to

ISBN: 978-1-387-00704-2

explore the game before actual treatment started, 30 minutes for treatment (playing with the game) and 10 minutes for subjects to answer the instruments. As a token of appreciation, all participants were presented with small gifts after completing the session.

The purpose of awareness evaluation was to discover end user's opinion and awareness of issues in cybercrime, mainly identity theft and phishing. The purpose of fun evaluation was to evaluate the game with regards to its design, contents and play duration. It was employed to discover subjects' perception of fun after playing with the game. Table 1 describes the analysis of results for both instruments.

Overall, it was revealed that the game received positive response for its ability to enhance level of awareness about cybercrime. Before exposure to the game, about 65% of subjects were not aware about cybercrime issues. After treatment, about 80% of subjects agreed that their awareness has increased. This could be an indicator that game based learning has an impact in enhancing general knowledge among its users/players. Meanwhile, for fun evaluation, every item received convincing response, with more than 50% of subjects agreed and strongly agreed to the statements, such as the clarity of instructions, contents that complement the theme, suitability of graphics/illustrations and duration of the game.

Table 1: Description of User Testing and Results – Awareness and Fun

Items	Analysis
Before playing the game, were you aware about the cybercrime issues?	65.4% of the respondents vote for yes and 34.6% vote for no about their awareness on cybercrime issues before playing the game.
After playing the game, have your awareness increased?	38.5% of the respondents strongly agreed, 42.3% agreed, 7.7% neither agreed nor disagreed and 11.5% disagreed about the increased of awareness level.

ISBN: 978-1-387-00704-2

The instructions given are clear	38.5% of the respondents strongly agreed, 26.9% agreed, 30.8% neither disagreed nor agreed and 3.8% disagreed the instruction given is clear.
The game test my general knowledge about cybercrime	65.4% of the respondents strongly agreed, 30.8% agreed and 3.8% disagreed the game test their general knowledge about cybercrime.
I like the graphics/illustration	7.7% of the respondents strongly agreed, 46.2% agreed, 30.8% neither agreed nor disagreed and 15.4% disagreed that they liked the illustration or graphics.
How many minutes did it take you to finish the game?	76.9% of the respondents answered below then 10, 19.2% between 10 to 20 minutes and 3.9% is between 21 to 30 minutes.
Was the game too short, too long or just right?	57.7% of the respondents thinks the game was just right, 38.5% it is too short and 3.8% too long.
How much did you like the game?	7.7% of the respondents strongly agreed, 46.2% agreed, 30.8% neither agreed nor disagreed and 15.4% disagree about their feeling towards the game.
Were the questions in game related with the theme?	96.2% of the respondents chose yes and 3.8% chose no.

Some recommendations were given by subjects, as enhancements in future work. These includes adding relevant background sound to trigger excitement to complete the game, enlarging the game window and reducing the walking speed of the actor in the game so that players could keep pace.

Conclusions

As a conclusion, the study has achieved it objectives which are to identify the issues in cybercrime, to investigate the gamification framework to support the development of the project, to develop adventure game about cybercrime, to evaluate the game effectiveness in enhancing awareness of cybercrime and to

ISBN: 978-1-387-00704-2

measure in terms of fun evaluation. 3D animated objects, graphics (such as buttons, background image, characters image), texts and spoken sound were successfully integrated into the game. All the multimedia elements have purpose to gain attention from the players and to sustain their motivation. In addition, it enriched the learning experience while playing the game. It can be concluded that, despite some of its shortfall, the exploratory game has demonstrated its capability to create awareness about serious issue like cybercrime.

References

Assumptions Under lying Agile Softwar e Development Pr ocesses. (2005), *16*(4), 62–87.

Caponetto, I., Earp, J., & Ott, M. (2014). Gamification and Education: A Literature Review. *Proceedings of the European Conference on Games Based Learning, 1*(2009), 50–57. Retrieved from http://www.scopus.com/inward/record.url?eid=2-s2.0-84923559781&partnerID=tZOtx3y1%5Cnhttp://search.ebscohost.com/login.aspx?direct=true&db=eue&AN=99224935&site=ehost-live

Dashora, K., & Patel, P. P. (2011). Cyber Crime in the Society: Problems and Preventions. *Journal of Alternative Perspectives in the Social Sciences, 3*(1), 240–259.

Domínguez, A., Saenz-de-navarrete, J., & Pagés, C. (2014). Computers & Education An empirical study comparing gami fi cation and social networking on e-learning. *Computers & Education, 75*, 82–91. https://doi.org/10.1016/j.compedu.2014.01.012

Herro, D., & Clark, R. (2016). An academic home for play: games as unifying influences in higher education. *On the Horizon, 24*(1), 17–28. https://doi.org/10.1108/OTH-08-2015-0060

Manasrah, A., Akour, M., & Alsukhni, E. (2015). Toward improving university students awareness of spam email and cybercrime: Case study of Jordan. *2015 1st International Conference on Anti-Cybercrime, ICACC 2015.* https://doi.org/10.1109/Anti-Cybercrime.2015.7351955

Morillas Barrio, C., Munoz-Organero, M., & Sanchez Soriano, J. (2016). Can Gamification Improve the Benefits of Student Response Systems in Learning? An Experimental Study. *IEEE Transactions on Emerging Topics in Computing, 4*(3), 429–438. https://doi.org/10.1109/TETC.2015.2497459

Singleton, T. (2013). The top 5 Cybercrimes, (October), 17.

ISBN: 978-1-387-00704-2

Article 26

Asma Ul Husna Interactive Courseware: Adaptation of Multimedia Learning Principles

Arifah Fasha Rosmani, Ray Adderley JM. Gining, Asiraa Angwar
Faculty of Computer and Mathematical Sciences
Universiti Teknologi MARA Perlis Branch, Malaysia

Abstract
Asma Ul Husna interactive courseware has been developed as an assistive tool intended for primary school students to learn about the 99 names of Allah SWT. The interactive courseware implemented multimedia elements such as text, graphic, audio and animation to assist users' learning process. Additionally, as it is presented with the absence of the traditional face-to-face method, the materials are required to be engaging to the users. The 'engaging' requirement is achieved by adopting several multimedia learning principles. The principle of multimedia learning consists of variety of principles which are utilised to develop the design and organisation of multimedia presentations. User Acceptance test has been carried out among primary school students to determine the overall level of acceptance and understanding towards the courseware. Other than that, this test is also conducted to assess the effects of the multimedia learning principles being adopted. The impacts shown by the results are significant as to confirm its benefits to its target users.

Keywords:cognitive theory ofmultimedia learning, multimedia learning principles, interactive courseware

Introduction

Asma Ul Husna is known as the names of Allah SWT which are in total of 99 names. According to Nurul Murtadho (2012), Asma Ul Husna definition is divided by two; which is, Asma defined as a name and Husna described as beautiful. Therefore, the whole meaning of Asma Ul Husna is the most beautiful names owned by Allah SWT. As a Muslim, memorising the names of Allah SWT is a necessary knowledge as it refers to all the benefits of His Creation and His attribute. It is also meaningful for a Muslim when they correctly understand its meaning and follow the moral

ISBN: 978-1-387-00704-2

behind the attributes of Allah SWT in their daily life. In general, Asma Ul Husna is widely practised by schools in Malaysia, especially in Islamic religious schools as it is believed to be beneficial to its practitioner. Generally, Asma Ul Husna is learned and memorised by students in their early childhood. Usually, this information is easily forgotten as the approach of learning and memorising used is often incorrect.

Currently, the Asma Ul Husna are available through songs called 'nasyeed', a variety of books, and from Al-Quran & Translation. It is a challenge for the students to study and memorise Asma Ul Husna through songs and texts. The reason being, in songs, the pronunciation is not identical with how it should be primarily pronounced. Moreover, Asma Ul Husna reading material is usually presented as books or cards which include its translation, benefits and Zikr. As an example, bookstore provides such material which filled with only texts, and it lacks the elements to ease the learning process; thus, it is not suitable as a material for learning and memorization.

Therefore, to promote the learning process of primary school students in learning and memorizing Asma Ul Husna, a better alternative of interactive courseware is introduced. This courseware is incorporated into several selected multimedia learning principles - to enhance the courseware elements to produce an engaging and efficient education product. Through this courseware, the users will be able to control, learn and use the courseware according to their comfort and pace. Moreover, with the aid of the adopted principles, its design and content are formed in a way that it can be used at ease.

Principle of Multimedia Learning
The principles of multimedia learning are introduced by Mayers (2001). These principles guide in producing an engaging multimedia courseware without the traditional face-to-face method. It primarily focused on the courseware design and

ISBN: 978-1-387-00704-2

organisation. There are a wide variety of multimedia learning principles discussed by Mayer (2016) which supported by research distinguishing different multimedia learning situations to decide which results in better student learning. In this paper, four most appropriate principles are studied, which are, Segmenting Principle, Modality Principle, Multimedia Principle, Voice Principle and Image Principle.

i.   Segmenting Principle
    Segmenting is an elementary principle involves breaking down a large chunk into smaller chunks. Information segmentation is a process of breaking down the information into bite-size segments - in a way that it can easily be absorbed. The application of this principle in multimedia learning is such a way that complex or lengthy lessons are separated into smaller parts, which are delivered one at a time (Clark & Mayer 2011).

ii. Multimedia Principle
    Multimedia Principle highlights the ability of learners to experience deeper learning from the combination of words and pictures than solely from words. By providing both verbal and visual information which complement each other, it encourages a faster rate of learning, more thoroughly, efficiently and stays longer in learner's memory (Mayer, 2016). Communicating with verbal or visual alone decreases the learning rate as the information is only processed by one of our information processor channel, which is the auditory and visual channel.

iii. Voice Principle
    Voice Principle promotes active learning and learner engagement through stimulating social responses in a way that delivering information by speaking naturally with good tempo. (Mayer, 2016). The definition of 'natural' speaking depends on the targeted audience. Audiences who are used to

ISBN: 978-1-387-00704-2

US English accent should be able to feel natural and comfortable to learn information in their accent compared to other accents. Currently, text-to-speech technology is widely used in multimedia learning, but it violates the Voice Principle as it does not output a natural voice. Using human voice is a way better as it is natural for the learner to associate the information to and process it.

iv.   Signalling / Cueing Principle
The Signalling / Cueing Principle idea is on emphasising what is important in the material presented (Mayer, 2016). The emphasising technique used can be graphically or verbally. In technical terms, signalling means emphasising using verbal. Meanwhile, cueing means highlighting using graphics. The techniques used in Signalling involved using a higher tone of voice in audio or using bold font in written texts. In Cueing, the technique used is by highlighting important parts by using circles, arrow or zooming effect.

Methodology

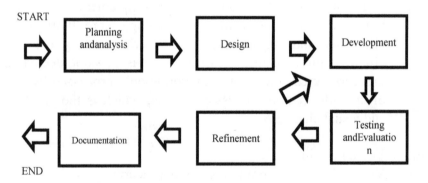

Figure 1: Methodology

ISBN: 978-1-387-00704-2

The project has been conducted based on the research model presented in the figure below. It involves six phases; 1) Planning and analysis, 2) design, 3) development, 4) testing and evaluation, 5) refinement, and 6) documentation.

1) Planning and Analysis: Identifying the field of study (Courseware and Multimedia learning principles), problem statement, research objectives, project scope, project significance and the expected outcome.

2) Design: Change the user requirement description into a structure in the form of a storyboard and adapt selected multimedia learning principles into the design and content of the coursework.

3) Development: Create the courseware using selected hardware and software by following the design that has been prepared.

4) Testing and Evaluation: Users will evaluate the courseware and provide feedback.

5) Refinement: Enhance the design and development based on the previous testing and evaluation. Fix any error and problems.

6) Documentation: Documents all the activities involved in the project in a form of report.

Adaptation of Multimedia Learning Principle in Asma Ul Husna Courseware

This project offers an alternative way of learning and memorising the Asma Ul Husna (99 Names of Allah) - through computer application called Asma Ul Husna Courseware. The adaptation of the principles of multimedia learning is disseminated throughout the module provided by this courseware. Adaptation of the principles is crucial as it will determine whether the users will be able to understand and use the courseware at ease. The three most important modules provided in this courseware are; Info, Asma Ul Husna List, Du'a Collection and Quizzes.

ISBN: 978-1-387-00704-2

The first principle of Segmenting Principle adaptation is reflected in the Asma Ul Husna List module. This principle is focused on breaking down large chunk information into smaller one. Displaying the 99 names in one page is violating the Segmenting Principle. In this courseware, the 99 Names of Allah are divided by some pages, as in one page only five names are listed. Furthermore, the user needs to click the names listed to see the details of each name - as the users will be able to focus on the content one at a time.

Figure 2: Adaptation of Segmenting Principle on Asma Ul Husna module

The Multimedia Principle is concerned about presenting both audio and visual material to the users to increase their learning rate. Engaging multiple users' information processing channel promotes a faster rate of learning. Thus, in this courseware, some of the module presented uses both images and audio supports to enhance users learning rate. In the AsmaUlHusna Lists module, the audio can be heard by clicking on the visual of the names.

ISBN: 978-1-387-00704-2

Figure 3: Clicking on the displayed text produces audio

The third principle, the Voice Principle is closely related to the Multimedia Principle as it also focuses on audio. A natural voice is believed to be a good stimulation for the user's social responses. The audio used to vocalize the names in this courseware is a natural voice - a human voice. Thus, it is more comfortable for the users to learn instead of learning the pronunciation from machine voice.

The last principle which is Signalling/Cueing principle adaptation can be seen especially in the video provided for the Du'a Collection module. The emphasising effect of Signalling and Cueing used in this video is by highlighting the texts with different colour as to shows various content presented. Other than that, the zooming effect is used highlight the content to provide a clear view. The Asma Ul Husna view also adopting the emphasis effect by showing that the name is interact-able by showing pop-up.

ISBN: 978-1-387-00704-2

Figure 4: Zooming effect and usage of different colour applying
Signalling / Cueing Principle

Results and Discussion

Usability Testing was conducted to measure all the multimedia applications criteria such as its objectives, content and interactivity. Two criteria focused on this test are on Learnability and Satisfaction - referring to the usability theories introduced by Jacob Nielsen. Learnability is measured on how natural for a new user to learn the new information provided in the application. Meanwhile, satisfaction is studying in how the user scale their experience while using the application. The test participants (primary schoolers) will rate their experience on given questionnaire.

Table 1: Usability Testing Questionnaire

No	Statement	No	Statement
1	The text use is clearly seen and suitable	5	Music sound is clear and suitable
2	I can easily understand the information given.	6	Color used is in the courseware is attractive.
3	The graphics and image use are suitable and pleasing.	7	Easy to remember where to find information.
4	I can understand the video content.	8	I understand on how to use the application.

ISBN: 978-1-387-00704-2

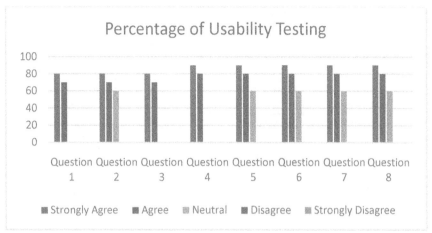

Figure 5: Results of Usability Testing

The usability test aimed to measure the Learnability and Satisfaction criteria towards the courseware. There are five scales used; Strongly agree, Agree, Neutral, Disagree and Strongly Disagree. By referring to the figure above, the users did not scale any answers below the Neutral scale - most of them either agreeing to the questions and a smaller percentage are neutrals. The result shows that the courseware has successfully fulfilled its purposes of implementing the multimedia criteria.

Other than that, User Acceptance test has been conducted and participated primarily by primary school students. According to Kariyuki (2011), this test is conducted to measure how successful the developed application captures the users' requirements. The goal of this testing is to determine the user level of acceptance and understanding of the courseware content. Moreover, to assess the effects of multimedia learning principles adapted to the courseware, this test is significant.This test is conducted on a group of primary school students. The students are given the opportunity to go through the courseware and answers list of questions provided regarding the test.

ISBN: 978-1-387-00704-2

Table 2: User Acceptance Test Questionnaire

No	Statement	No	Statement
1	I understand the courseware content	6	The courseware background is satisfactory.
2	I understand the meaning of AsmaUlHusna	7	The content in this courseware is clear
3	I can use the courseware easily	8	Colour used is satisfactory.
4	The navigation button provided is suitable	9	The text (font) is clear and understandable.
5	This courseware is suitable for primary schoolers	10	I can answer the quiz provided in this courseware.

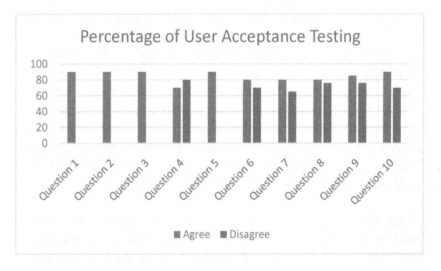

Figure 6: Results of User Acceptance Test

The figure above shows the results of the User Acceptance Test. There is only two scales used which are; Agree and Disagree. With this minimum scale used, the results should make it very clear whether the courseware is acceptable or not. Most of the students (90%) agreed with the half of the questions listed (Q1, Q2, Q3, Q5 and Q10) and the rest of question (Q4, Q6, Q7, Q8, and Q9) had an average of 80% of participant agreed.

ISBN: 978-1-387-00704-2

Majority of the students can use the courseware with ease. The multimedia learning principles adopted in this course enhance the effectiveness of its design and content. Half of the questions which has 90% students agreed with are focusing on the overall understanding of the content delivered which shows that the intent on emphasizing the content is satisfied. The rest of the questions which got 80% agreement is focusing on the overall design is satisfactory, as there are several enhancements can be applied to it which is addressed in the recommendation part in this paper.It can be concluded that most of the test participants are satisfied with the courseware presented and can use it with ease.

Conclusion and Recommendation
In conclusion, based on the User Acceptance test result that has been conducted, the participant was satisfied, and they can use the AsmaUlHusna courseware with ease. The multimedia principles selected has been successfully adopted in the courseware resulting in a satisfactory courseware regarding its design and content. This project focuses on adopting the selected multimedia principles to the AsmaUlHusna courseware specifically targeted to the primary schoolers in the hope of offering a better way of learning the 99 Names of Allah. Some recommendations for future works are to consider for more multimedia learning adaptation in the courseware to maximise its potential as an efficient, appealing and engaging courseware. Completion of this courseware is encouraged as it can be utilised in the future, and also includes some other types of assessment (puzzles) to improvise the learning rate. Furthermore, this courseware can be devised by offering multiple languages so it can be used in its user's language.

References
Alsumait, A.,& Al-Osaimi, A. (2010). Usability heuristics evaluation for child e-learning applications. Journal of Software, 5, 654-660

ISBN: 978-1-387-00704-2

Clark, R. C., & Mayer, R. E. (2011). E-Learning and the Science of Instruction: Proven Guidelines for Consumers and Designers of Multimedia Learning (3rd ed.). San Francisco, CA: John Wiley & Sons.

Kariyuki, S., Washizaki, H., Fukazawa, Y., Kubo, A., & Suzuki, M. (2011). Acceptance testing based on relationships among use cases. *Proc. of 5th world congress for software quality.*

Manzari, L., Christensen, J. T., User-Centered Design of a Web Site for Library and Information Science Students: Heuristic Evaluation and Usability Testing, Information Technology and Libraries, 2006, pp. 163-169.

Mayer, R. E. (2001). *Multimedia learning.Multimedia learning. New York: Cambridge University Press.* New York: Cambridge University Press.

Mayer, R. E. (2016). *The Cambridge Handbook of Multimedia Learning, 2nd Ed.* New York: Cambridge University Press.

ISBN: 978-1-387-00704-2

Article 27

Online Car Rental System using Web-Based and SMS Technology

Mohd Nizam Osman, Nurzaid Md. Zain, Zulfikri Paidi, Khairul Anwar Sedek, Mohamad NajmuddinYusoff
Faculty of Computer and Mathematical Sciences
Universiti Teknologi MARA Perlis Branch, Malaysia

Mushahadah Maghribi
Department of Information Technology and Communication,
PTSS Perlis, Malaysia

Abstract
The motivation behind this research is the growing popularity of web-based systems and the need to explore the Short Message Service (SMS) technology that industries could tap into to enhance their services to the customers. This paper described a notification-based content alert and web-based system using SMS technology. It was specifically developed for the alert notification to the customers about the car rental information, and the availability of the car reserved. The main purpose of developing SMS-based content alert for car rental system is to reduce the cost and time consumed, which is beneficial to the car rental agencies and customers. Therefore, the system was designed automatically to send an alert SMS to the customers about the availability of the car reserved. This system was developed based on System Development Life Cycle (SDLC) using the waterfall model as a methodology. A user acceptance testing was conducted with thirty (30) respondents to determine the effectiveness of the system by evaluating the questionnaire which was categorized into three (3) parts includes user interface design, usefulness, ease of use and usability and alert system function. Results of the system evaluation showed that overall were satisfied with all categories respectively. Hence, the system using web-based and SMS technology is accepted by customers, convenient, economic and reliable method of notification for the car rental agencies.

Keywords: *Web-based system, SMS technology, car rental system, SDLC, user acceptance test.*

ISBN: 978-1-387-00704-2

Introduction

Car rental or car hire agencies are private companies that provide short time leasing vehicles for a specified time with a fee to their customers. In Malaysia, car rental service increasingly becomes the preferred option for most people, especially among students in campuses and universities. This occurs because not all students can afford having their own vehicle and perhaps the university bus service doesn't always help. Besides, the raising taxi fares and inconsistent bus arrivals in Malaysia continue to discourage people from taking up the public transport. Therefore, car rental service continues to grow in Malaysia, hence it required an improvement and good monitoring system.

Many organizations used web-based system that can be integrated with SMS technology because most people often used mobile phone that gives convenience to the users who are familiar with SMS technology. The technology has been implemented into the wide-range different sectors, such as education (Song & Fox, 2005; Vera & Comendador, 2016; Verma & Gupta, 2013), health organization(Gurol-Urganci, de Jongh, Vodopivec-Jamsek, Atun, & Car, 2013; Wang & Andoh-Baidoo, 2017), government (Onashoga, Ogunjobi, Ibharalu, & Lawal, 2016; RoshanTharangga et al., 2013) and private sectors(Ghoreishi & Shajari, 2010).

Many revolutionaries have changed from manual to the online system,especially in the workflow and type of resources that are stored in the car rental services. The changed from the traditional car rental system to the digital system is predictable. Besides, at the end of 2006, total of car rental companies has more than six thousand around the world and in the year 2013, statistics showed that almost 2 million cars were rent in United States (Yang, Jin, & Hao, 2009).Currently renting services are given based on manual work, which includes a lot of time and resources required is also increased because each process requires different resources. Besides, the user will have to go manually at the

ISBN: 978-1-387-00704-2

centreor must first contact the car rental company for the desire vehicle. Therefore, the online car rental system integrated with SMS notification was provided and supported the customer for the reservation, assist management in knowing rental car inventory at a specified time and notify the customers about the availability of the car reserved, which support the satisfactory service to customer and support the company's operational processes.

The earlier studies shown that Management Information System (MIS) could be used to manage car rental, expected to accelerate the processes and services to customers (Busse et al., 2017; Li, 2013; Qurratul, 2012). Meanwhile, the used of the web-based system become a popular trend due to the services can be accessed remotely by using web browser and can be accessible from anywhere in the world. Besides, a mobile phone is an essential medium to communicate, interact or device to gain knowledge (Asmara & Aziz, 2011). Nowadays, SMS technology can be implemented with the web-based system in the more convenient way. SMS text message is also possible to be send from computer to recipients by using GSM modem and SMS gateway as a transmitting device.

With the growing popularity of mobile phones and SMS, the technology should be seriously considered because most people have high usage of mobile technologies. It becomes a need of the generation as it makes the work faster and hazel free. The challenge will be to determine the nature of services that the car rental agencies should deliver via SMS and to come up with solutions to their various challenge mobile phone technologies currently present to ensure satisfactory services to its customer. Furthermore, many car rental agencies are still using traditional methods by manually notifying the customer using phone calling. Hence, it considered time-consuming and the worst case, the information is not delivered to the customer at the right time. Most of the car rental agencieshave no automation system to

ISBN: 978-1-387-00704-2

notify the customer to return the car and take the reservation of the car when it is available. Therefore, taking this into consideration, the service at the car rental agencies is enhanced through the development of the web-based system integrated with SMS notification for making it simple for the customers.

Methodology
The web-based car rental system integrated with SMS technology has a very user-friendly interface. By using this system, employees can manage bookings, payment, vehicle issues and SMS notification to the customers within a few clicks only. The new data can be added or an existed data can be edited or deleted too by administrators. Thus, there is no delay in the availability of any information, whether needed, can be captured very quickly and easily. For security purposes, all customers need to create a new account before logging in or he/she can log into the system with his/her created account before they can make a reservation for a car. Then, the customer will be notified the availability of the car reserved through SMS. This system becomes very helpful for employees, administrator and customers. Figure 1 shows the car rental system architecture for the proposed system.

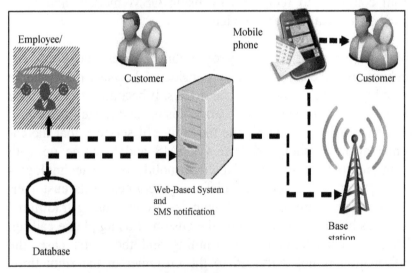

Figure 1: Car Rental System Architecture

ISBN: 978-1-387-00704-2

The Software Development Life Cycle (SDLC) was used to develop the web-based system and SMS notification. SDLC is a framework that describes all activities and processes in a software development project. The process is associated with the waterfall model which consisted of five phases such as planning, analysis, design, development, and evaluation.

i.   *Planning.*
     In this phase, all information, data and problems about the project were gathered by read articles, journal, and thesis from previous research. From the information gathered, all the requirements and opportunities were recognized. The aims to find the core problems and constraints occur on the current car rental system and to formulate goals of analysisconstruction, and system development that focuses on online car rental system and SMS technology.

ii. *Analysis.*
     Analysed the current car rental system management workflow, looked for problems occurs in the current car rental system, car rental procedures and car rental data processing. Besides, the activities included were the identification of the hardware and software requirement in the development system, scope of project, schedule of activities such as Gantt chart and the total budget.

iii. *Design.*
     In this phase, the researcher designed the requirement needed in system development. Included were the system components, system architecture, contextual diagram, data flow diagram, entity relationship diagram, user interface design and system flowchart.

iv. *Development*
     Layouts of interfaces for the web-based development were created using HTML and PHP coding through Adobe

ISBN: 978-1-387-00704-2

Dreamweaver CS6 and notepad++. PHP language is used to execute the system and MySQL is used for the database, while Apache runs as a web server software using Xampp package. Then, SMS Gateway script by iSMSwas embedded in the web-based to make the system able to send the message to the customer's mobile phone.

v. *Evaluation*

Debugging and testing of the program for fixing bugs or errors of the design were also done in this phase. Free from error is a necessary testing to find errors that may occur as in the language error, logic errors and error analysis program. Then, the system was evaluated to determine the system performance and to ensure all requirements accomplished. User acceptance testing was done by testing the system on users to ensure that users can perform the tasks respectively.

In the development SMS system notification, the researcher was used SMS gateways and mobile phone, which are connected to the web-based system. The SMS gateways served as the gateway to connect with the mobile phone users and the system for sending the alert message automatically to the customers about the availability and the status of the customers' car reservation. The mobile phone was used for receiving the text messages and alert messages about the booking status from the system.

The system was tested and conducted to the targeted respondents. For this study, the targeted respondents were university studentsaround Perlis. In order to evaluate the effectiveness of the system, user acceptance testing was conducted. A quantitative approach was taken, and a survey questionnaire was the data collection instrument for this study. A total of thirty (30) survey questionnaires were distributed and received for the analysis. The questionnaire consisted of three (3) parts. The first part was comprised of user interface design. The second part of the questionnaire investigates the usefulness, ease of use

ISBN: 978-1-387-00704-2

andusability, whereas the third part, evaluate the SMS alert function. The data were analysed using arithmetic mean technique based on the ranking score value.

Research Results

To evaluate the user acceptance testing on the Web-based and SMS System, the study was tested to thirty (30) respondents. The study has successfully done to evaluate the effectiveness of the system which contains seventeen (17) questions overall and categorized into three (3) parts respectively. The score value with scale one (1) to five (5) was given for every type of criteria identified. Every scale represents from strongly disagree(1), disagree(2), average(3), agree(4) and strongly agree(5).

Table 1: Analysis and mean on the effectiveness of the system

No.	Criteria	Score (1-5)					Mean
		1	2	3	4	5	
User interface design							
1	The characters of the system are easy to read.			2	9	19	4.57
2	The terms used in the system are consistence.			3	18	9	4.20
3	The interface of the system is pleasurable.			5	15	10	4.17
4	I like the interface of this system.			5	15	10	4.17
5	Message displaying error of the system is helpful.			2	14	14	4.40
6	Performing tasks in this system is clear.				13	17	4.57
					TOTAL MEAN		4.35
Usefulness, ease of use and usability							
7	Using the system helps me to rent faster.		1		9	20	4.60
8	Using the system saves my time.			2	10	18	4.53
9	This system is easy to use.			1	12	17	4.53
10	I am satisfied when using this system.			2	12	16	4.47
11	I am comfortable using the system.			3	12	15	4.40
12	It is easy to find information needed in the system.		1	5	12	12	4.17

ISBN: 978-1-387-00704-2

13	The system has all functions and capabilities I want.		1	5	13	11	4.13
14	I found various functions in the system were working well.			3	17	10	4.23
					TOTAL MEAN		**4.38**
SMS alert function							
15	The SMS alert system used in the system is appropriate and relevant.			1	14	15	4.47
16	I found that the SMS notification system is helpful to the users.			1	16	13	4.40
17	Overall, I am satisfied with this system.			1	13	16	4.50
					TOTAL MEAN		**4.46**

In order to evaluate the effectiveness of the system, the study has successfully done for each type of the criteria. Table 1 summarized the results for the identified criteria. The mean for every question and total mean for each category was calculated respectively. The overall results shown that respondents were satisfied with the system that integrated with SMS alert function, and it can help them completed their task easier and faster. This can be proven when the total mean for the criteria was calculated as the highest which is 4.46 for the SMS alert function. Besides, most participants were accepted and satisfied with the system since each of the question categories grades were above 4.0.

Conclusion

This paper has presented some insight on user technology to construct and integrating the web-based system with SMS technology to enhance the service provided by the car rental agencies. The system helped the workers to notify the customers through SMS system by sending a reliable message to alert the customers about the bookingstatus,and the availability of thecar reserved. Thus, the system provides a convenience way of notification through the use of mobile phone, which is a common personal communication medium for most people. Besides, this system makes it easy to get car information, book a car and quickly rent a car.

ISBN: 978-1-387-00704-2

To measure the effectiveness of the system, user acceptance testing was conducted to evaluate the performance of the system used questionnaire method. Based on the results and analysis, the overall system was measured to be acceptance by the users. From the testing session, the system functions are well-functioned and most of the respondents were satisfied with the system.

In conclusion, the integration of web-based and SMS technology in the car rental agencies is the best way to take the advantages of today technology, in order to enhance the productivity and efficiency of organization. In reality, SMS has been adopted by many users and has in fact, become extremely popular. Despite their limitations, mobile devices,especially mobile phones have become a natural part of the everyday life of a huge number of people, especially the younger generation growing up with computing and Internettechnologies.

References

Busse, M., Busse, M., Swinkels, J., Swinkels, J., Merkley, G., & Merkley, G. (2017). Enterprise rent-a-car. *Kellogg School of Management Cases*, 1–15. https://doi.org/10.1108/case.kellogg.2016.000112

Ghoreishi, N., & Shajari, M. (2010). Web-Based SMS Passenger Application: New Approach to Inform Passengers via SMS in Airlines.In *Proceedings of the International Conference on e-Education, e-Business, e-Management, and e-Learning 2010*.

Gurol-Urganci, I., de Jongh, T., Vodopivec-Jamsek, V., Atun, R., & Car, J. (2013). Mobile phone messaging reminders for attendance at healthcare appointments. *The Cochrane Database of Systematic Reviews*, (12), CD007458. https://doi.org/10.1002/14651858.CD007458.pub3

Li, Z. (2013). Design and realization of car rental managerment system based on AJAX+ SSH. *Information Technology Journal*, *12*(14), 2756–2761.

Onashoga, A., Ogunjobi, A., Ibharalu, T., & Lawal, O. (2016). A Secure Framework for SMS-Based Service Delivery in M-Government Using a Multicast Encryption Scheme. *African Journal of Science, Technology, Innovation and Development*, *8*(3), 247–255. https://doi.org/10.1080/20421338.2016.1156837

Qurratul, A. (2012). Development Of Car Rental Management Information System (Case Study: Avis Indonesia). In *proceedings intl conf information system business competitiveness* (pp. 104–105).

ISBN: 978-1-387-00704-2

RoshanTharangga, J., Samarakoon, S. M. S., Karunarathne, T. A., Liyanage, K. L. P., Gamage, M. P. A., & Perera, D. (2013). Smart attendance using real time face recognition. In *SAITM-RSEA 2013* (pp. 41–44).

Song, Y., & Fox, R. (2005). Integrating m-technology into Web-based ESL vocabulary learning for working adult learners. In *Wireless and Mobile Technologies in Education (WMTE), 2005* (pp. 5–9). IEEE.

Vera, M. C. S., & Comendador, B. E. V. (2016). A Web-Based Student Support Services System Integrating Short Message Service Application Programming Interface. *International Journal of Future Computer and Communication, 5*(2), 77–82.

Verma, P., & Gupta, N. (2013). Fingerprint Based Student Attendance System Using GSM. *International Journal of Science and Research (IJSR), 2*(10), 128–131.

Wang, Y., & Andoh-Baidoo, F. (2017). Design of Integral Reminder for Collaborative Appointment Management. In *Proceedings of the 50th Hawaii International Conference on System Sciences* (pp. 910–919).

Yang, Y., Jin, W., & Hao, X. (2009). Dynamic Pool Segmentation Model and Algorithm in the Car Rental Industry. *Journal of Computers, 4*(12), 1202–1208. https://doi.org/10.4304/jcp.4.12.1202-1208

ISBN: 978-1-387-00704-2

Article 28

Game-based application for normalization learning

Nik Nuru Izzasalwani Nik Pa, Dr. Norfiza Ibrahim, Azmi Abu Seman
Faculty of Computer and Mathematical Sciences
Universiti Teknologi MARA Perlis Branch, Malaysia

Abstract
Normalization is a relational database design for the organizing data process to minimize redundancy. The main aim for this study is to develop a game application for normalization learning. Besides, the study also focusing on identifying the preferred learning technique for normalization, the suitable multimedia and game-based elements for the development of a game application for normalization learning, and measuring the applicability of the application. Design science research methodology was implemented throughout the study which consists of five phases. Unity 3D software is used to develop a game-based application for normalization learning. The application has applied the Multimedia Principles, Game Based Principles and Marczewski's Gamification Framework in the development. Game-based environment provides an alternative on how to learn database normalization interactively. There are two types of testing used in measuring the application; heuristic evaluation and user acceptance at public university and were analyzed based on statistical analysis. The analysis from heuristic evaluation indicates that the game-based application is usable and practicable for normalization learning while analysis by user acceptance shows that the respondents are strongly agrees on the technical aspects in the application and they are ready to use this application. Therefore, the research has achieved its objective. Besides, the application will enhance the student's ability to easily recognize the various normal forms and will be skillful in the hands-on process of database normalization.

Keywords: Game-based, game application, gamification, multimedia, normalization

Introduction

Normalization is operationally defined as method used to design relational database tables for reducing duplication of information and protecting the database (Georgiev, 2008). Database normalization is the main topic in database theory and a good understanding on the matter important for students.

ISBN: 978-1-387-00704-2

Eessaar(2016) stated that database normalization process helps database developers to reduce data redundancy and thus avoid certain update anomalies. The major problem emerged when students are unable to receive purely theoretical subject (Georgiev, 2008). However, most of the students in the university are taught using textbooks and additional materials like presentation slides to learn database normalization. This learning technique will disrupt their learning due to the lack of good tools which could aid the students in database normalization.

On the other hand, a study by Nik NurulIzzasalwani (2017) found that 90.9 % of the respondents strongly agreed that they prefer to use multimedia presentation compared to text. It can be suggested that through the use of a game application, students can improve their understanding besides it is easy to learn. Therefore, this research is intended to create a game-based application for normalization learning. This game-based application will enhance the student's ability to easily recognize various normal forms of normalization. As a result, students will have more skills and interactive hands-on in the process of normalization. Besides, games also can be used by students, and teachers in any institutions for the learning process. The research is important as it will provide an alternative on how to learn database normalization in interactive ways. The game application for normalization learning will help the students to learn normalization more easily and quickly.

Thus, technique for identifying games based on learning normalization must be investigated. The methods used are web based learning and interactive multimedia. Interactive Multimedia (IMM) package has a higher potential of supporting an individual to inherent strength of media characteristics (Kulasekara, Jayatilleke, &Coomaraswamy,2008). With multimedia technology in education, traditional educational materials will be translated into interactive electronic form through the use of multimedia authoring tools.

ISBN: 978-1-387-00704-2

Database normalization is very important because it is a process in the database for organizing data. Database normalization process helps database developers for diminishing the data redundancy to avoid update anomalies featured (Eessaar, 2016) because there are combinatorial effects between propositions that are recorded in a database. Combinatorial effects mean that inserting, updating, or deleting of additional propositions in the same table or other tables. According to Demba (2013), Edgar F. Codd is a creator of the database relational model in 1970 and introduced the theory of normalization in the database. Normalization is a relational database design for the process of organizing data to minimize redundancy. Normalization is a method of producing good relational database designs (Bahmani, Naghibzadeh, &Bahmani,2008). There are three stages of the normalization called first normal form (1NF), second normal form (2NF) and third normal form (3NF).

Meanwhile, there are four game-based principles which are intrinsic motivation, authenticity, self-reliance and autonomy and experiential learning created by Perrotta, Featherstone, Aston, and Houghton (2013). Firstly, the learning must have intrinsic motivation where it is the game or one voluntary activity. In addition, it is also the best game for learning in the context of an invitation rather than coercion. Secondly, authenticity is a must have which involves the true nature of the learning and distinct from imitation or decontextualized forms of learning that are placed in schools as stated by Perrottaet.al (2013). Thirdly, the learning environment must be self-reliance and autonomy. There are many aspects of the game based including the basic technical skills like programming, writing, painting and music. Fourthly, experiential learning is important in order to create game-based learning (Perrottaet.al, 2013). The experience of learning is a very long and influential in the educational field.

ISBN: 978-1-387-00704-2

Principles

There are five game elements to create a game-based like Intro Page, Instructional Support, Game Board, Assessments at each level, and Rapid Feedback (Athmika, 2016) but there are three game elements that were used to develop a game application for normalization learning like Intro Page, Instructional Support and Assessments at each level. The researchers choose these elements in order to give a good first impression to users. A big logo will attract player's attention to the next step, which is the intro page. A nice logo attracts users to keep and play. Moreover, Instructional Support is applied to tell the player the rules before start the games and to know the overall value of what they have learned (Athmika, 2016).

Besides, Marczewski's gamification framework(Andrzej Marczewski, 2015) is adapted to determine and designing the game-based application. There are 5 of 8 parts of Marczewski's gamification framework were chosen;i) what is being gamified, ii) why is it being gamified, iii) who are the users, iv) how is it being gamified, and v) tested with users. The first part of Marczewski's gamification framework is what is being gamified. Learning activities is being gamified into an application to students understand better about normalization using game application. The second part is why it is being gamified. Gamification can increase motivation its users. The game application for normalization learning will help the students to learn normalization more easily and quickly. People who use (third part) are the users from Faculty of Computer and Mathematical Sciences (FSKM) students who are going to learn normalization using game application. The fourth part is how it being gamified. As mentioned previously, the elementsthat need to be in the game-based application are intro page, instructional support, game board, assessments at each level and rapid feedback (Athmika, 2016). Another element is computer-controlled integration of text, graphics, drawings, video, animation, audio, and any other media where every type of

ISBN: 978-1-387-00704-2

information can be represented, stored, transmitted and processed digitally. The fifth part of Marczewski's gamification framework is tested with users during the research. The testing is conducted in Evaluation Phase. There are some improvement were made to the game-based application based on the given feedback.

As far as multimedia development is concern, two of the multimedia principles were used in developing a game-based application; Spatial Contiguity and Temporal Contiguity Principle. Spatial Contiguity principle can facilitate the people when text and graphics placed at the same screen, while Temporal Contiguity Principle can help people to learn better through graphics (Mayer, 2009). Wherein for multimedia elements are color, text, graphics, animation, audio and design screen.

Related Works
i. Learn Database Normalization
A web-based environment for learning normalization of relational database schemata is developed to give interactive hands-on experience to students on normalization process (Georgiev, 2008). Concepts of web-based learning environment, called Learn Database Normalization (LDBN). One of the reasons for this is the lack of good tools which could aid the students during the learning process of relational database normalization. Thus learning environment was developed in order to give students the ability to easily and efficiently test their knowledge of the different normal forms in practice. The concept of assignments is a major difference between LDBN and the other normalization tools, which only provide one possible solution (decomposition) to the users, without users having the ability to test the structure themselves (Figure 1). On the other hand, LDBN can be used for checking the correctness of any proposed decomposition. This method could be useful to lecturers who need to test handwritten assignments.

ISBN: 978-1-387-00704-2

Figure 1: Learn Database Normalization (LDBN)

ii.   NORMIT

Mitrovi (2005) claimed that NORMIT is a Web-enabled tutor with a centralized architecture. It is also a constraint-based tutor that teaches data normalization. Database normalization is a procedural exercise as depicted in Figure 2. So the students can go through steps provided to analyze the quality of a database. Basically, NORMIT requires students to determine candidate keys, a set of attributes, prime attributes and functional dependencies to determine normal forms. NORMIT will give a general description of the error, specifying what general domain principles have been disrupted.

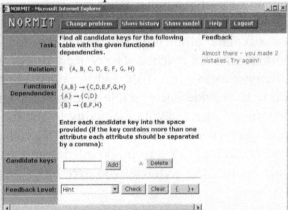

Figure 2: NORMIT Exercise

ISBN: 978-1-387-00704-2

iii.   NERD

NERD is a learning tool for learning ERD development and normalization (Cortez, 2014) and this application is developed using Java. The advantages of this application are four functionalities like generating ERD from text, performing normalization process, display the topic to students and giving students a set of questions such as quiz as shown in Figure 3. NERD application allows students to identify database problem specifications and provide learning through examples to enable students to learn.

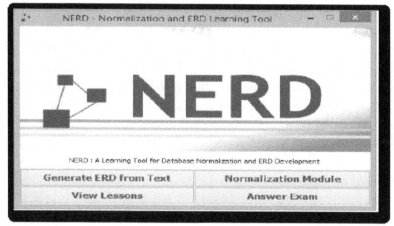

Figure 3: NERD

Research Methodology

This research consists of five phases of the design science research methodology adapted from Peffers, Tuunanen, Rothenberger, and Chatterjee (2007) which are Awareness of Problem, Suggestion, Development, Evaluation and Conclusion. In the first phase, the activities for the problem to be identified consist of preliminary study, literature study, content analysis, as well as comparative study normalization technique and game application for learning. The second phase of the study is to provide some suggestions to solve the problem consist of expert's feedback on normalization learning among lecturers and

ISBN: 978-1-387-00704-2

integration of database normalization using multimedia and game-based learning.

Then, phase three of thedevelopment comprises the proposed normalization learning using game-based application. The evaluation phase contains a few actions such as the development of evaluation strategies, test the proposed game application using evaluation strategies and test the applicability of the game application. Conclusion phase is the final stage in the game application development which consists of analyzed result from evaluation strategies as well as report writing.

The software that has been used in the game-based application construction is Unity3D, and Adobe Photoshop is used for creating images and text. There are some features and functions that have been built and developed for game-based application for normalization learning like Home screen, Tutorial Site, Home, Game and Page Score Construction.

Results and Findings
There are two types of testing on the game-based application (Figure 4) were conducted during the evaluation phase which are heuristic evaluation and user acceptance test. Heuristic evaluations were carried out by seven experts who are the IPT lecturers. Meanwhile, user acceptance was tested to 40 students of FSKM,UiTM Perlis and the result from the testing was analyzed based on the questionnaire.

ISBN: 978-1-387-00704-2

Figure 4: One of the scene in the game-based application

From the conducted testing,heuristic evaluation indicates that the game application is usable for normalization learning and practicable. In addition, user acceptance shows that the multimedia and game elements that were used had fulfilled of elements requirement in the game application. Besides, most of the respondents are strongly agreed to use this application.

The game-based application has achieved its target because it is usable to be one of the effective learning methods. Therefore, it can be concluded that the users satisfied with this game-based application for normalization learning.

Conclusion
As the conclusion, the research has achieved its objective. The game application has been successfully developed using multimedia elements and games elements that are suitable such as text, audio, animation, graphics. Besides, the game application will enhance the student's ability to easily recognize the various normal forms of normalization and will be skillful in the hands-on process of database normalizationlearning.

ISBN: 978-1-387-00704-2

References

Andrzej Marczewski, (2015). *Gamified UK Gamification Consultancy.* Retrieved October 20, 2016, from https://www.gamified.uk/gamification-framework/

Athmika, T.(2016). *5 Must have Elements of Game-based Mobile Learning Courses.* Retrieved October 7, 2016, from http://blog.commlabindia.com/elearning-design/elements-of-game-based-mobile-learning

Bahmani, A. H., Naghibzadeh, M. and Bahmani, B. (2008).*Automatic database normalization and primary key generation.* Canadian Conference on Electrical and Computer Engineering, Niagara Falls, ON, 2008, pp. 000011-000016. doi: 10.1109/CCECE.2008.4564486

Cortez. (2014). *NERD: A Learning Tool for Database Normalization and ERD Development.* Department of Physical Sciences and Mathematics

Demba, M. (2013).*Algorithm for Relational Database Normalization Up to 3NF.*International Journal of Database Management Systems (IJDMS) Vol.5, No.3, June 2013. pp. 39–51.

Eessaar, E. (2016). *The Database Normalization Theory and the Theory of Normalized Systems: Finding a Common Ground.* Baltic J. Modern Computing, Vol. 4 (2016), No. 1, 5-33.

Kulasekara, G.U., Jayatilleke, B.G., &Coomaraswamy, U. (2008).*Designing Interface for Interactive Multimedia: Learner Perceptions on the Design Features.* Asian Association of Open Universities Journal, Vol. 3 Issue: 2, pp.83-98, https://doi.org/10.1108/AAOUJ-03-02-2008-B002.

Georgiev, N. (2008). *A Web-Based Environment for Learning Normalization of Relational Database Schemata,* Computing Science Master Thesis.Ume°a University, Sweeden.

Mayer, R.E. (2009). *Multimedia Learning (2nd ed.).*Cambridge University Press, New York, NY, USA.

Mitrovi, A. (2005). *Scaffolding Answer Explanation in a Data Normalization Tutor.*Facta Univ. Ser. Elec. Energ. vol. 18, No. 2, August 2005, 151-163.

Nik NurulIzzasalwani (2017), *Developing a Game Application for Normalization Learning.*Bachelor of Information Technology Thesis.UniversitiTeknologi MARA (UiTM), Malaysia.

Perrotta, C., Featherstone, G., Aston, H. & Houghton, E. (2013).*Game-based Learning: Latest Evidence and Future Directions* (NFER Research Programme: Innovation in Education). Slough: NFER.

Peffers, K., Tuunanen, T., Rothenberger, M. a., & Chatterjee, S. (2007). *A Design Science Research Methodology for Information Systems Research.* Journal of Management Information Systems, 24(3), 45–77. doi:10.2753/MIS0742-1222240302

ISBN: 978-1-387-00704-2

Article 29

Web-Based Application of the Internship Management System

FazeeraSyuhada Abdullah, Azmi Abu Seman, Dr. Norfiza Ibrahim, Noor Aishatun Majid, Nor Mazlina Abdul Wahab, MohdSyamaizar Mustafa
UniversitiTeknologi MARA Perlis Branch, Malaysia

Noor FaezahMohd Sani
Faculty of Applied Sciences
UniversitiTeknologi MARA Perak Branch, Malaysia

Abstract
Placement of students in the industry or organization related to their study field is compulsory in order to fulfill the requirement of Ministry of Higher Education policy. It became one of the courses that must be fulfilled by students in order to finish their study at university or other institutions. Increment on the number of students in universities caused the management of internship program become uncontrolled. At UiTM Perlis, students who have been using the manual system in conducting internship have caused many problems. The main problem exists in UiTM Perlis is the manual management in internship program which involves a lot of paper, time-consuming and poor management between academician and industry as well as students. Thus, an internship management system using case-based in web environment is developed to solve the problem that occurred among students, coordinator and employer. The system will help in reducing the workload to the three users mentioned previously. Based on the system, the requirements from the industry will be matched with the qualification from the students. Therefore, the placement for the students will be easily generated by the system. Two methods of testing were conducted namely heuristic evaluation and user acceptance test. The results proved that the systematic online industrial training application system achieved very good level of performance in terms of user interface satisfaction, usefulness and ease of use and its usability by users.

Keywords: Easy-match industrial training system, internship, online application system, systematic management, user-friendlywebsite

Introduction

Internship referred to the placement of students in the industry or organization related to their study field and this is one of the courses that must be fulfilled by students in order to finish their

ISBN: 978-1-387-00704-2

study at university or other institutions.Stirling, Kerr, and Macpherson (2014) defined the internship as a program which student need to go through it within six months or a year. It is a working experience that student needs to work in an organization with supervision from the supervisor for their achievement throughout the internship program. Whereas management is the process of doing thing together that organized informally (Carpenter, Bauer, &Berrin, 2012).

During recent years, the number of students in universities increased and caused the management of internship program become uncontrolled. In UiTM Perlis, the students that involved in internship need to manage their documents and search the organization manually. They had to create their resume and submit to the organization in conventional way such as through email, post or by hand. They have to wait for the feedback from the organization either the application is accepted or not. Then after receiving an offer letter, the coordinator needs to be notified by the student and proceed with the acceptance letter to the organization. The process consumes ample of time just to ensure the students secure their placement in an organization for the internship. Besides, the coordinator had to face the problem in dealing with the documentation since a student needs several files that contain important information to be kept by the coordinator.As for the employer, they got affected by the manual system use in managing internship because do not have precise information about UiTM Perlis' internship program, and also do not know much about student's qualification that had applied to their organization (FazeeraSyuhada, 2017).

In this paper, a systematic online industrial training application system was developed to facilitate student, coordinator and employer in the industry or organization. The manual system used in universities had been transformed into the automation system. The system able to list out all the organization that registered in the system which offered an internship in their

ISBN: 978-1-387-00704-2

organization. A suitable searching technique used in this system search and recommend the best organization to the user. The system eased the students to find the organization easily by giving a recommendation which organization suitable for them based on their qualifications. This system had already been implemented at other universities and the majority agreed that the system succeeds to overcome the problem. Prospective employers need to register with the application system and provide with the required information regarding the background of organization. The students also need to register with the system and provide qualification details and achievement. As registered employers, they can select qualified students to undergo internship at their respective organization after the student submits an application letter to their organization.

Related Works

v. *Industrial Training System- UniversitiTeknologi Malaysia (UTM)*

In UTM, the internship management system is used by the entire faculty in UTM. UTM uses an online system in managing the industrial training courses (ITS-UTM, 2017). The system consists of for registered users, which are the system administrator, industrial training committee, lecturer and also students.

vi. *Industrial Training System University Malaysia Sarawak*

The Industrial Training System is developed for the Faculty of Resource Science and Technology in UNIMAS in handling the internship courses. The purpose of developing this system is to solve the problem where when the number of students applied to this courses increase, but the number of organizations that open for internship in this course is less due to the difficulty of registering (UNIMAS, 2017). This system focuses on management and works especially for the coordinator. The target user of this system also targeted to the students, coordinator and also for the employer.

ISBN: 978-1-387-00704-2

vii. FTK Industrial Training System UniversitiTeknikal Malaysia Melaka

The FTK industrial training system is a system that developed by UniversitiTeknikal Malaysia (UTeM) and it is based on latest technology where the goal is making the management becomes easier, quicker and efficient. The system is designed for an administrator, students and industry to help student in Faculty of Engineering Technology to a better management in a work placement for industrial training (UTeM, 2017). This system will provide four processes which are registration process, confirmation and announcement. However, this system is not a standalone website, but the system is attached to the official portal of their university.

Application System Development

The construction process of the system has applied System Development Life Cycle (SDLC) methodology. Internship Management System (IMS) development is continued with the third phase of methodology which is system design. Adobe Dreamweaver CC 2014 and XAMPP are the software used in the development. The interface of the system that shows the was clearly shown in this chapter by the screenshot of the entire interface.Figure 1 shows the interface of coordinator view for student and her placement details.

ISBN: 978-1-387-00704-2

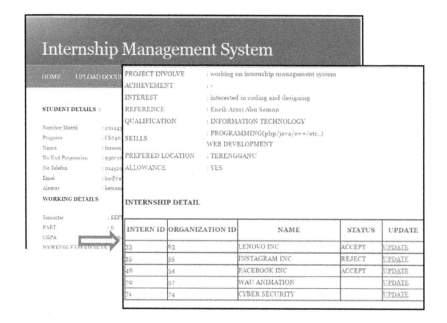

Figure 1: Coordinator view for student and placement details

Testing and Finding

There were two different testing was conducted which are usability testing and heuristics evaluation in order to determine the effectiveness of the system and to study the interaction of users and their responses towards the IMS.

Before conducting the test, the target users were identified. For this study, final year students from Information Technology, Data Communication and Networking and Netcentric program as well as a few selected organizations were involved. All the students will have their internship for the following semester.

Usability test

All the respondents need to complete ten tasks and interact with the system based on the given instruction. IMS system is tested on the design, content, recommender features and interactivity. A questionnaire is provided to the respondents to let them to rate

ISBN: 978-1-387-00704-2

and comments the system after they have completed all the tasks. The questionnaire is used for future enhancement of the system. Table 1 and Table 2 exhibit the tasks given to the students and organizations.

Table 1: Usability testing task for student

Task	Instruction
Task 1	Register for the first user
Task 2	Log in to the system
Task 3	Fill the resume form
Task 4	View the profile
Task 5	Update user profile
Task 6	View the recommendation of the organization
Task 7	Choose the organization
Task 8	Update student placement
Task 9	Print complete resume
Task 10	Download any document

Table 2: Usability testing task for organization

Task	Instruction
Task 1	Register organization
Task 2	View organization detail

Based on the analysis, the majority of the respondents successfully accomplished the tasks. They managed to understand the flow of the system without any guideline given to the respondents. However, there are some parts of the system that need to be improved so the system will be more usable and efficient. For example, the system do not have back button for certain parts of the system that has caused difficulty for the user.

As for the organizations, all the respondents accomplished the task successfully. They managed to understand the flow of the system without any guidelines. Their tasks are only to register and view the organization, and no other complicated process. Therefore, the respondents were satisfied towards the system. From the analysis, it can be concluded that the users are able to complete the task given successfully. The system is easy to navigate, fast loading and easy to understand.

ISBN: 978-1-387-00704-2

Heuristic evaluation

Expert Reviews is conducted by the three internship coordinators. During the testing, the experts are given a questionnaire after they have completed reviewing the system. The questionnaire is on the usability of the system and is divided into three different parts which are user interface satisfaction, usefulness and ease of use and in terms of the system usability. The result of the testing is analyzed and evaluated.

Based on the observation, the experts are satisfied with the system with some suggestions to the system to be more effective to the user. As for the user interface, all the experts were satisfied rated the interface as 'very good'. However, the login interface for coordinatordoes not meettheir expectation. The interface said to be cluttered and confused them to click the log in button. On the other hand, all ofthe experts rate for 'very good' and 'excellent'for the usefulness and ease of use the system. They were able to complete the entire tasks in a few minutes and satisfied with the functions exist in the system. Besides, the experts agreed that the system ismuch related to the internship management system.

Figure 2 exhibits the findings from the expert review in the graph. Overall, the system is good but there were a few processes that need to be added to the system in order to have a complete process of internship management system.From the results, the refinement of the system has been done in order to achieve user satisfaction.

ISBN: 978-1-387-00704-2

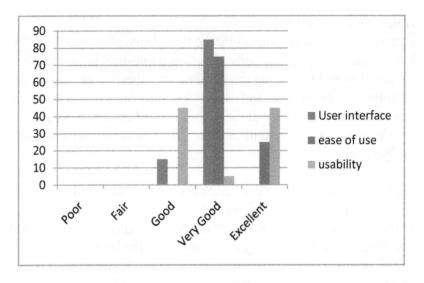

Figure 2: Results from expert review

Conclusion

The web based application of the Internship Management System (IMS) is a recommender system which can guide students to find the best organization that suits their qualification. The recommender is developed by using case based approach which is the best approach to obtain the result of the best recommended organization. The website had been successfully developed and has received many positive feedbacks from the user during the testing phase. It can be concluded that the system is user friendly because most of the users are able to use the system smoothly in a short time. Besides, the interface design included the buttons and the forms are very simple that make the user feel connected to the system. Apart from that, all the criteria that have been included in this recommender system are based on the provided criteria by the students into the system. The placement for the student is recommended based on allowance, qualification and also preferred location. This system can give a lot of benefits to the coordinator, organization and student in handling the internship program.

ISBN: 978-1-387-00704-2

References

Carpenter, M., Bauer, T., &Berrin, E. (2012). *Management Principles v. 1.0.Creative Commons.* Retrieved from http://2012books.lardbucket.org/pdfs/management-principles-v1.0.pdf

FazeeraSyuhada Abdullah. (2017). Developing Online Internship Management System Using Web Based for UiTM Perlis.Bachelor of Information Technology Thesis.UniversitiTeknologi MARA (UiTM), Malaysia.

ITS-UTM.(2017).*UTM Industrial Training System.*Retrieved from http://its.utm.my/itsv4/index.php

Stirling, A., Kerr, G., & Macpherson, E. (2014).*What is an Internship ? An Inventory and Analysis of " Internship " Opportunities Available to Ontario Postsecondary Students.* The Higher Education Quality Council of Ontario, 10–50. Retrieved from http://www.heqco.ca/SiteCollectionDocuments/Internship ENG.pdf

UNIMAS.(2017). *Faculty of Resource Science and Technology.Industrial training.* Retrieved from http://www.frst.unimas.my/student/industrial-training-2

UTeM.(2017). *FTK industrial training system.* Retrieved from http://www.ftk.li/

ISBN: 978-1-387-00704-2

Article 30

Applying Green Gamification to Support Green Campus Initiatives in Reducing Carbon Emissions

Romiza Md Nor, Nur Alyaa Azhar
Faculty of Computer and Mathematical Sciences
Universiti Teknologi MARA Perlis Branch, Malaysia

Abstract
Green gamification is a technique with the purpose of using game elements in non-game context to encourage positive environmental behaviours. It is believe to be able to support behaviour change with the help of persuasive technology which is the Go Green Campus web application. The objective of this project is to create awareness on environment sustainability by applying green gamification technique to encourage behaviour change in reducing carbon emissions which is believed to be more fun and enjoyable. This research focuses on the college students in UiTM Perlis as an initiative to Green Campus concept. The research significance is to motivate people to change their behaviour in order to reduce carbon emission. Evaluation of the web application has been conducted using heuristic evaluation which consists of three elements: perceived, structural and perceptual elements. Questionnaires were distributed among ten college students where they had been closely monitored by researchers for two weeks. The results show that besides feeling motivated to realize that each activity can contribute to reducing carbon emission, almost all participants enjoyed the green gamification elements since they are enjoyable and fun.

Keywords: Green gamification, carbon emission, Green Campus Initiatives

Introduction

Nowadays, carbon emission issues have become a highly concerned topic. The atmosphere's concentration of carbon dioxide (CO_2) has increased by more than 30 percent over the last 250 years, mainly due to human activities and most of it has occurred for past 50 years (Socolow, R., et al, 2004). There are many initiatives that have been made in order to overcome the carbon emission issues. One of them is the "Green Campus" initiative. Green campus is a place where environmentally responsible practice and education go hand in hand and where

ISBN: 978-1-387-00704-2

environmentally responsible views are borne out by example (Emmanuelle M., et al, 2010). This concept offers higher institutions a chance to take the lead in rethinking its environmental culture and developing new paradigms for solving problems regarding nature. By applying the same green campus concept, this research will enable the students to see the amount of carbon emission that they have contributed to the environment if solid waste is not managed by them in the right way. The technique that will be used is called green gamification. Gamification itself refers to the use of game design components in a non-game context (Deterding et al., 2011). Meanwhile, green gamification is the technology-incorporated game mechanics in the context of "green" behaviours (Froehlich et al. 2012, 2009).

It is a type of persuasive approach wherebya computing system is interactively designed to change people's behaviours (Fogg 2003, 6). There are many factors that lead to behaviour change. Many researchers before this had implemented persuasive technology. Most of them are to create people who are conscious about a healthy lifestyle. This project will incorporate green gamification which is an extension of persuasive technology itself, primarily to keep people concious towards the environment that as illustrated in Figure 1.

Figure 1: Research model

ISBN: 978-1-387-00704-2

Related Works

i. Green Gamification

Green Gamification is the use of game elements to make sustainability fun and rewarding. This technique has been used widely these days as an initiative to make the world "greener". The use of game elements like collecting points, goals to achieve, leaderboard, feedback, customization and playfulness has made the gamification of the environment much more enjoyable. Froenlich has enumerated green gamification and eco-feedback examples in the context of three environmentally significant domains namely, home resource consumption, personal transportation, and waste disposal behaviours (e.g., littering and recycling) (Froenlich J., 2015). With the growth of ubiquitous Internet connectivity, mobile and in-home displays, and smart meters, there is an increase of promotion and support towards pro-environmental behaviours at home using this technology. In the last few years, there are inventions for almost everything we use in our daily life, ranging from cars, buses and even motorcycles that rank and reward fuel-efficient driving performance. For example, in Figure 2, the Nissan Leaf Carwings system gives virtual rewards to efficient driver and to services that monitor and reward home recycling behaviours asshown in Figure 3.

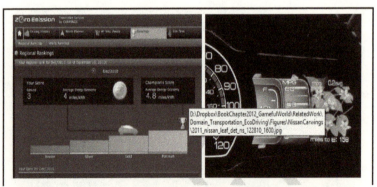

Figure 2: Nissan Leaf Gamification Interface (O'Dell, 2009)

ISBN: 978-1-387-00704-2

Figure 3: How RecycleBank works. (RecycleBank, 2011)

This concept of gamification which is uses game design elements in traditionally non-game contexts (Deterding et al. 2011) technique is related to persuasive technology, mainly to sustain and encourage a better behaviourtowards the environment.

ii. Carbon Emission

Carbon emission is the release of carbon into the atmosphere. To talk about carbon emissions is simply to talk about greenhouse gas emissions which are the main contributor to climate change. Since greenhouse gas emissions are often calculated as carbon dioxide equivalents, they are often referred to as "carbon emissions" when discussing global warming or the greenhouse effect (Ecolife, 2013). Since industrial revolution has increased, it directly correlates to the increase of carbon dioxide levels in our atmosphere and thus causing the rapid increase of global warming. It can also be caused by an organization, event, products or individual. The amount of carbon emissions calculated is called carbon footprint. Nowadays, the carbon emission issues is a topic of great concern. Although many actions have been taken to raise awareness, there is no sign of real solution to these problems. Thus, by developing this application, the amount of carbon emission can be reduced if the

ISBN: 978-1-387-00704-2

community knows how much they have contributed to carbon emission to the atmosphere.

iii. Effect of Behaviour Change in Reducing Carbon Emission

Behaviour change has been an important starting point for people to overcome many issues. Previous researches had used persuasive technology to promote behaviour change in order to solve problems. Gasser (2006) has proposed a mobile lifestyle coaching application, which was intended to improve the users' healthy behaviour as well as their health. It also highlighted the importance of behaviour change in humans' live. Other than that, UbiFit Garden (Consolvo et al., 2009) is another application that also applies persuasive technique to inspire users to maintain the desired level of their physical activities in everyday life. Both applicationsdemonstrate attractive elements as a display when the user reaches a certain goal. The use of attractive elements motivates users to use the application frequently since it is fun and in a way it encourages users to do more physical activities voluntarily. This will then promote behaviour change among users to be more fit and concerned about their physical well-being. Hence, this shows how changing of people's behaviour will help in achieving something. Thus, behaviour change will be promoted in this project in order to reduce carbon emission.

iv. Green Campus Initiative

A green campus initiative carries out functions according to a system-wide culture of environmental sustainability, balancing function and design with existing and foreseen resources (Allen, A. S., 1999). This initiative is being made in order to sustain pro-environmental behaviours in a student's daily life. Colleges and universities develop green campus' best practices through research, implementation and the willingness to revise and adapt. These best practices should be shared with colleagues to ensure that effective strategies and successful initiatives can be easily adapted and replicated (Emmanuelle M. &Humblet, R. O., 2010) (Allen, 1999)). In this project, green campus initiative is

ISBN: 978-1-387-00704-2

implemented through web application by using both green gamification and persuasive technology in order to change behaviours into the ones that will help in reducing carbon emission.

Conclusion

This project enhances the use of web application in reducing carbon emission through changing people's behaviours using a proposed technique, green gamification. Rewards are given to students that contributed to more reducing carbon emission activities and through this Go Green College web application, they can view the rewards collected by students of each floor in Block A, Dahlia 3 and hence making them feel motivated to do better in collecting points.

The web application user interface is designed based on persuasive technology tools strategies and green gamification elements such as reduction, tunneling, points, scoring and leaderboard. In the testing phase, two types of questionnaires weredistributed, pre-questionnaire and post-questionnaire. The pre-questionnaire set was distributed to look intousers' familiarity towards Go Green College initiatives via web application. Meanwhile, for post-questionnaire phase, ten questionnaires were distributed. The students had been closely monitored by researchers for two weeks to update their activities via the web application. This is important it is to find out the impact of the design and content of the developed web application which adopts the green gamification techniques, on the college students' behaviour change. Thus, the post-questionnaires were evaluated using heuristic evaluation which consists of perceived, structural and perceptual elements and is suitable for green gamification techniques.

From this result, it can be concluded that the perceived elements which convey the enjoyable and attractive elementshave been well received by the participants. It is because by viewing the

ISBN: 978-1-387-00704-2

web application, there are various green gamification elements that can be found which are point scoring, star rating, leaderboard and many others (Figure 4). Other than that, the animated virtual aquarium that represents the reward also attracted users' attention. For structural evaluation that focuses on interactivity, each of the structure of the website has to be interactive and easy to be used. The web application is an easily navigated web application with various interactive animations to attract and motivate students at the same time. Lastly, perceptual elements which are about the narrative persuasion or reward-related elements are well received by the participants. It is because the reward-related elements are fun and enjoyable. Other than that, it may motivate them indirectly.

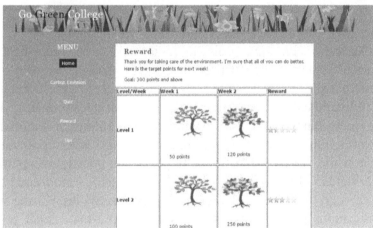

Figure 4: Rewards page

Therefore, the initiative taken towards achieving the "Green Campus" concept by starting at the place where students spend time the most which is the college, is only the beginning. Many more intervention techniques could be introduced in order to achieve the concept. The development of Go Green College web application is to request students to take the complex issues such as environment seriously. Thus, by using this web application, students will understand betterthat each activity in their daily-life

ISBN: 978-1-387-00704-2

can contribute to carbon emission. Other than that, the separate-your-waste initiative allowed users to obey the new law that has been enforced, which requires each and every household to separate their solid wastesaccordingly. Students also will get rewards and points if they participate in an activity that reduces carbon emission which motivates them to do more activities that could help the environment to get higher points. Other than that, the use of green gamification elements like points scoring, star rating, quiz and leaderboard makes the web application fun and enjoyable; hence, persuaded students to use it often.

References

Pacala, S., & Socolow, R. (2004). Stabilization wedges: solving the climate problem for the next 50 years with current technologies. *Science*, 305(5686), 968-972.

Humblet, E. M., Owens, R., Roy, L. P., McIntyre, D., Meehan, P., & Sharp, L. (2010).Roadmap to a green campus.*Washington, DC: US Green Building Council.*

Deterding, S., Dixon, D., Khaled, R., &Nacke, L. (2011, September). From game design elements to gamefulness: defining gamification. In *Proceedings of the 15th international academic MindTrek conference: Envisioning future media environments* (pp. 9-15). ACM.

Froehlich, J. (2015). Gamifying Green: Gamification and Environmental Sustainability. In Walz, S. &Deterding, S. (Eds.), *The Gameful World*, MIT Press. To Appear.

Jon Froehlich, T. D., PredragKlasnja, Jennifer Mankoff, Sunny Consolvo, Beverly Harrison, James A. Landay (2009). "UbiGreen: Investigating a Mobile Tool for Tracking and Supporting Green Transportation Habits."

Fogg, B.J., (2002). Persuasive technology: using computers to change what we think and do. *Ubiquity*, p.5.

Fogg, B.J., Soohoo, C., Danielson, D.R., Marable, L., Stanford, J. and Tauber, E.R., 2003, June. How do users evaluate the credibility of Web sites? A study with over 2,500 participants. In *Proceedings of the 2003 conference on Designing for user experiences* (pp. 1-15). ACM.

*Ecolife (2013), Retrieved from*https://www.ecolifeconservation.org

Gasser, R., Brodbeck, D., Degen, M., Luthiger, J., Wyss, R., &Reichlin, S. (2006). Persuasiveness of a mobile lifestyle coaching application using social facilitation.*Persuasive technology*, 27-38.

Consolvo, S., McDonald, D. W., &Landay, J. A. (2009, April). Theory-driven design strategies for technologies that support behavior change in

ISBN: 978-1-387-00704-2

everyday life. In *Proceedings of the SIGCHI conference on human factors in computing systems* (pp. 405-414).ACM.

Allen, M. R., Frame, D. J., Huntingford, C., Jones, C. D., Lowe, J. A., Meinshausen, M., &Meinshausen, N. (2009).Warming caused by cumulative carbon emissions towards the trillionth tonne.*Nature, 458*(7242), 1163-1166.

ISBN: 978-1-387-00704-2

Article 31

Applying Augmented Reality In Teaching And Learning

Umi Hanim Mazlan, Izleen Ibrahim
Faculty of Computer and Mathematical Sciences,
Universiti Teknologi MARA Perlis Branch, Malaysia

Nurulhuda Ghazali
Faculty of Computer and Mathematical Sciences,
Universiti Teknologi MARA Melaka Branch, Malaysia

Zalikha Zulkifli, Samsiah Ahmad
Faculty of Computer and Mathematical Sciences,
Universiti Teknologi MARA Perak Branch, Malaysia

Wan Saiful'Azzam Wan Ismail
Faculty of Computer and Mathematical Sciences,
Universiti Teknologi MARA Kelantan Branch, Malaysia

Abstract
In this era of teaching and learning, most students are fond of interactive learning compared to traditional lectures that uses whiteboard and marker pen. Because of that, educators need to be more creative in preparing their teaching material in order to attract students' attention during teaching and learning process. With the technology advancement, there is variety of software that can help educators to produce a creative material. Augmented reality, AR, is technology where virtual reality is combined with the real world. The main devices for AR are displays, computers, input and tracking devices but recent advances in smartphone technology making them suitable as an AR platforms. This augmentation technique seems relevant to be applied in teaching field because it will help teachers to develop a dynamic material that is capable to capture students' attention, engagement and participation in a classroom. In addition, AR is very helpful in learning process where students can always listen and view the lecture videos anytime they pleased. This is suitable for blended learning purpose where students can learn on their own with less supervision from lecturers. Therefore, this paper reviews the AR technology which can be utilized to enhance the process of teaching and learning.

Keywords: Augmented Reality, Teaching Material, Interactive Learning

ISBN: 978-1-387-00704-2

315

Introduction

Recent advances in technology has been widely adapted by young generations in all aspects of life including in teaching and learning. These youngsters are more comfortable with gadgets rather than facing directly with educators in order to learn about their courses or subjects. The usage of YouTube video tutorial has becoming a trend and a lot of educators gradually have emerged to publish their own lecture videos. This method suits the students learning style and attract their interest to study the subject matter. Hence the existence of Augmented Reality in teaching and learning are being brought up recently to meet the students' preferences. The augmentation approach in academic field is more likely easier to grab the student's attention, engagement and participation during lecture. Besides image, lecture videos also can be used as an overlay action in augmented reality application. Therefore, apart from provide fun learning, the students also can repeatedly watch the videos whenever they scan the trigger image. In addition, it will become a very helpful tool especially during non-face-to-face session or students' self-learning.

Literature Review

i. Augmented Reality

The research of Augmented Reality (AR) started in 1960 by Ivan Sutherland who introduced the Helmet Mounted Display (Utusan Online, 2016). During the time, helmet was used by the U.S army to shot the missiles (Rolland, 2005). In line with the current environment, the AR technology has evolved where it can be used in various field including education. Through AR, information can be displayed viavirtual objects that cannot directly detected by user's senses, which allow them to possibly interact with the real world in ways never before (Gopalan et. al, 2016). In teaching and learning, the use of AR is still deemed new, but the impact of technology is growing as the platforms for AR become more widely reachable.Although AR technology has the power to transform the educational systems while helping a

ISBN: 978-1-387-00704-2

new generation of students learn more effectively, there are still technological and pedagogical challenges such as slow response times, incompatible software and incompatible environmental setting (Garrett et. al, 2015). Therefore, several key ideas about AR implementation in the classroom that have been established by Billighurst and Duanser (2012) can be used as a guideline in preparing teaching material that applies AR. The key ideas are as follows:

- AR technology is robust enough to convey learning experiences, especially in augmented books and mobile AR applications;
- AR experiences should not replace traditional curriculum material but complement it;
- valuable learning occurs during the development of AR content as well as in using the AR application itself; and
- AR provides real advantage for reading comprehension and in understanding spatial data, especially for those with low reading ability.

ii. Augmented Reality Applications for Education
There are about 32 AR applications that is suitable to use in a classroom which have been identified by Mike Lee (2016). Think Mobiles Team (2017) has divided the wide number of AR applications in 3 main categories as follows:
  i) the most serious, heavy and specialized, best suitable for students' needs.
  ii) easy and colourful, created for kids and children to engage them into learning.
  iii) the best for everyone in polishing some knowledge and skills.

ISBN: 978-1-387-00704-2

Table 1: Categories of AR applications

Category	Example	Description
Student	Elements 4D	Application that supports students in exploring fields of chemistry subjects by allowing to combine different elements to see how they react in reality
	Anatomy 4D	Best suitable for medical student's needs as they may customize any part of human body, observe how parts fits, how different are joint moves and how human organs functioning
Children	Math alive	Designed for prekindergarten (3 years old children). Provide practise in basic numeracy and counting skills
	Animal Alphabet AR Flashcard	The application helps children to learn letters using special cards that make the animals become real when scan on it
General	Aurasma and Layar	The two most powerful and popular tools to create AR

ISBN: 978-1-387-00704-2

		content. Both of apps can be used for various field including education. Recommended for AR beginners since both of apps have most user-friendly constructors, also supported with tons of guides and tutorials.

iii. Augmented Reality Implementation in Teaching and Learning
The emergence of various AR apps with the sole purpose for education as discussed earlier ease the educators to embed AR in their teaching material. The AR software works in two stages namely tracking and reconstruction. The AR device will recognize what it looks at during the tracking stage, while in reconstruction stage, it brings up a second tier of information. In the tracking stage, the trigger point is needed and it can be any image. If the trigger image scanned, it will move to reconstruction phase that resulting the overlay displayed (Wagner &Schmalstieg, 2006). In teaching and learning, AR is best applied for the topic that needs additional elaboration such as 3D image or video that elevate student understanding. By using a few simple steps, teachers can embed their teaching material with AR while students can experience the AR. Both teachers and students need to download and launch the chosen AR application in order to create and experience AR. For instance, when the students point their camera on the trigger image provided in the teaching material, they immediately can view the overlay such as the video on how to solve the tutorial question that prepared by their lecturer.

ISBN: 978-1-387-00704-2

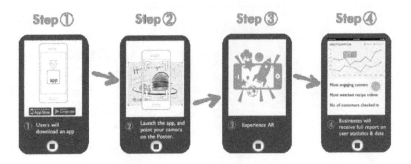

Figure 1: Steps to experience AR
Source: virtualmob.co.uk

On-going Research

For many years, schools and universities had to change the way they work and teach in order to fit in with technology. The approach of AR in teaching programming languages can become a very helpful tool to conduct teaching programming languages subject. Since this subject requires an ability to visualize how to design and code, thus this approach can easily be implemented to help students because AR has the potential of bringing abstract concepts or topics into the physical world. Additionally, AR can make the studying experience more fun since it can provide engaging content and interactions for students. Students can use AR to get explanation on a topic of interest as well as obtaining additional information. For this project,the tutorial questions have been chosen to be embed with AR. For instance, when students scan the trigger image on the page of their tutorial, a video of their teacher helping them solve a problem will be pop out. In order to develop the aura (the page that have been embedded with AR), this project is using Aurasma application which is available for smartphone and computer. The following figure is the example of the developed aura for tutorial of computer programming tutorial subject:

ISBN: 978-1-387-00704-2

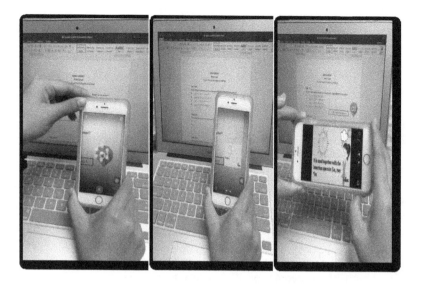

Figure 2: Example of Aura

Conclusion

The research of this article supported the use of augmented reality as an alternative for student in learning computer programming. The use of this technology is beneficial to the educators and the learners where it may help to improve the quality of teaching and learning. Hence, the AR technology provide positive suggestion for future research and innovation in teaching and learning. It is hoped that the aura which being developed can be completed soon so that it can be used widely by other students and teachers who learn and teach computer programming. Also, through this research other teachers may get some knowledge and inspired to apply AR technology later on.

References

Billinghurst, M &Duanser, A. (2012).Augmented Reality in the Classroom, *What's Real About Augmented Reality*, IEEE, 45(7), pp. 56-63

Lee, M. (2016).*32 Augmented Reality Apps For The Classroom From Edshelf*. Retrieved from
http://www.teachthought.com/the-future-of-learning/technology/32-augmented-reality-apps-for-the-classroom-from-edshelf/

ISBN: 978-1-387-00704-2

Garrett, B M, Jackson, C, & Wilson, B. (2015). Augmented reality m-learning to enhance nursing skills acquisition in the clinical skills laboratory. *Interactive Technology and Smart Education,12*(4), 298-314. doi:10.1108/itse-05-2015-0013

Gopalan, V, Zulkifli, A. N, Fasial M, N. F, et. al. (2016). Augmented Reality Books For Science Learning – A Brief Review, *International Journal Of Interactive Digital Media, 4(1)*, pp. 6 -9

Rolland, J & Hua, H. (2005). Head-Mounted Display System, Encyclopedia of Optical Engineering, pp. 1-14

ThinkMobiles Team. (2017). *Augmented Reality in education.*Retrieved from https://thinkmobiles.com/augmented-reality-education/

Utusan Online.(2016). *UTM BangunkanTeknologiAlam Maya KepadaPaparanNyata*. Retrieved from http://www.utusan.com.my/sains-teknologi/teknologi/teknologi-augmentasi-realiti-1.239990#nav-allsections

Wagner, D &Schmalstieg, D.(2006). Handheld Augmented Reality Displays.IEEE Conference on Virtual Reality, pp. 321

ISBN: 978-1-387-00704-2

Article 32

Interactive Android Phonic Reading for Preschool Children

Hawa Mohd Ekhsan, Jiwa Noris Hamid, Muhammad Mohd Sobri
Faculty of Computer and Mathematical Sciences
Universiti Teknologi Mara Perlis Branch, Malaysia

Abstract
The learning process at preschool level becomes more important in early education for children. Suitable learning tools need to be used by teachers in order to enhance the learning process. Due to that reason, this Android phonic reading application has been developed for preschool children since the technology can attract and engage children's attention. This application is known as 'Kenali ABC' and focuses on the phonic reading approach. This application has been tested using the usability test on the targeted users including preschool children, preschool teachers and Universiti Teknologi Mara (UiTM) lecturers as the experts. The results of the usability test indicate that the application has potential to be used as an alternative method in reading using phonic technique.

Keywords:Android application, phonic reading, preschool children

Introduction

Nowadays, children are continually gaining the reading skills and other significant knowledge at the preschool level. Preschool children develop their early reading skills at different paces and different paths. Some of them are excel while others struggle in their learning.

Children's reading development depends on the understanding of the relationships between letters and its sounds. One of the teaching techniques for reading is known as phonic. Phonicemphasizes the association betweenthe sound of spoken languageand printed symbols (Cecil, 2011). It offers interactive approach of learning process and provides an effective method of teaching and learning strategies to develop children's phonics

ISBN: 978-1-387-00704-2

knowledge and skills(Su & Hawkins, 2013). Previous studies demonstrate that phonic technique improved reading skills development (Giti& Hadis, 2015; Shelly et al., 2016; Taylor et al., 2017). By introducing children with effective phonics approach at preschool level, teachers provide children with a solid reading foundation for their lifelong learning.

With the advancement of today's technology, teaching and learning at preschool should also be in line with the emerging technology that offers more attractive and attentive environment (Dina &Pierpaolo, 2016). Definitely, enjoyment plays an important role in engaging children in learning (Andriani et al., 2016).

Using the traditional methods such as using books, flash cards and slides presentations or coursewares,children can have a visual and auditory learning with their teachers. The effectiveness of these materials depends on how teachers inspire the children and how attractive the materials are. Unfortunately, some of these approaches limit the interactivity between children and the learning material itself. Thus, some children are unable to obtain the knowledge due to time constraint in the learning period at preschools.

In order to provide better learning method at preschool, children need to be exposed with an efficient reading method such as the interactive android phonic reading for free and easy learning. Instead of learning it at school, they can also use it at home or any other places (Gao et al., 2011).If preschool childrenrely solely upon what teachers teach at school, they will have difficulties in understanding what they had learned if they do not have time for independent practice at home. Even worse, they can easily forget what they had learned at school.

Thus, this paper focuses on the development of Android-based phonic reading application that provides interactivity elements and suitable design for children. The application can help the

ISBN: 978-1-387-00704-2

children to have a flexible learning process where it can be done at any time and regardless of the place. The target user for this Android phonic reading is preschool children aged 5 to 6 years old.

A research performed byHollands et al.(2013) reveals that Android application can attract children to learn, thus improving self-learning of the children (Rosetto& Dutra, 2016). Therefore, it can meet the demand of personalized learning for preschool children (Gao et al., 2011).On the parent part, they can easily observe the progress of their children and ensure that the reading skill development is right on the track.

The development of Kenali ABC application features the concept of learning through play as the main idea, in line with the nature of children who love to play at their age (Qi &Yonghai, 2015; Andriani et al., 2016). The purpose of implementing the concept is to motivate and encourage the children in learning to read. This application provides basic phonic skills practice, including recognizing the letters, learning upper-case and lower-case letters, and they can explore several activities to test their reading skills as well.

The Development of 'Kenali ABC' Application
To design the interface, there are some functional requirements which need to be followed. The design adopted the criteria presented in the framework created by Andriani et al., (2016)such as engaging, touch-based interface, provide clear instructions, use simple language, and respond with encouraging messages. The flow of the application is done on storyboard and a flowchart form. This section explains the storyboard, flowchart, software specification and interface design.

i. Storyboard
Storyboard design is importantat the beginning level of designing process. It is used to determine the suitable and logical design, and the format for this mobile application. A full illustration of

ISBN: 978-1-387-00704-2

the storyboard can show how the interface will look like and how the application works. The storyboard for this mobile application is developed in sketching design including the visual and auditory elements. The mobile application that has been developed might not fully coincide the storyboard due to some improvement made during the development process.

ii. Flowchart

Flowchart is used to signify the sequences of movements involved in this application. This flowchart explains the process that needs to be done from the beginning to the end of the development. It shows how the interface, button and icon should link to other pages in this mobile application.

iii. Software specification

Table 1 shows the software involved in the development of this mobile application.

Table 1: Software Requirements for the Development

Software	Description
Balsamiq Mockup	This software is used to design the interface after the paper sketching is done. It is a built-in wireframe, icons, labels, texts and buttons that makes the process of designing the interface and linking of each page easier.
Android Studio	This software provides a variety of layouts to be used by developers
Adobe Photoshop	Adobe Photoshop has many functions that are useful to edit or create images

iv. Interface design

The interface design involves several steps as shown in Figure 1. The steps start with sketching the interface on paper, followed by transferring the design into Balsamiq Mockup software. The background image, buttons and icons are created using Adobe Photoshop. Then, the development in Android Studio involves XML and Java programming language.

ISBN: 978-1-387-00704-2

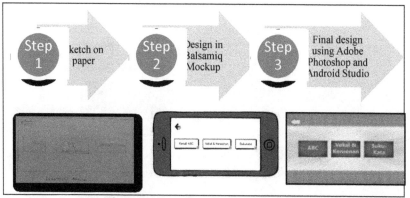

Figure 1: Interface Designing Steps

Figure 2 shows the welcoming interface of the application. The suitable design for children is crucial so that the application is engaging, enjoyable and usable for children. The chosen colour, icons, buttons, sounds and interactivity are among of the important criteria that should be taken into consideration when developing mobile application for children.

Figure 2: Welcoming Interface of Kenali ABC

Table 2 depicts some of the modules in 'Kenali ABC' application. The application is divided into 2 submodules; learning module and exercise module.

ISBN: 978-1-387-00704-2

Table 2: Interface Design of the Modules

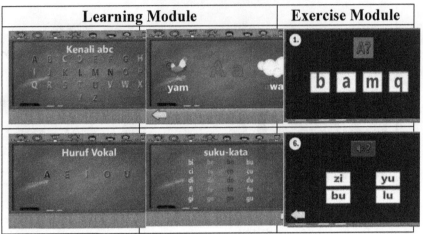

Learning Module		Exercise Module

Results and Findings

Once the application has been completely developed, the next step is to test the application in terms of its effectiveness and usability. A total of 20 respondents involved preschool children, preschool teachers and UiTM lecturers as the experts in Information Technology (IT) have taken part in this testing.

Thisusability testing is very important to the developer so that the strengths and weaknesses of the mobile application can be identified. The scale used for the testing is from 1 to 5. Table 3 shows the scale and its equivalent value.

Table 3: Scale of the Respondent Answer

Scale	Value
Strongly Agree	5
Agree	4
Neutral	3
Disagree	2
Strongly Disagree	1

ISBN: 978-1-387-00704-2

The testing results in Figure 3 show that preschool children prefer simple but attractive interface for their mobile application. Each criterion that has been tested produces more than 4.4 mean scores out of 5. These scores indicate that the user is satisfied and enjoy the application.

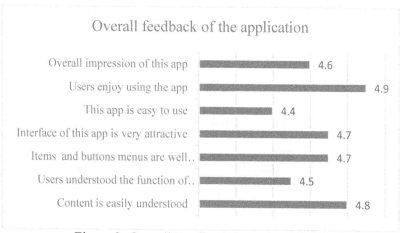

Figure 3: Overall Feedback from the Testing

Conclusion

This project is very significant since we can improve the early learning process especially in reading among preschool children. It may help teachers and parents in guiding the children to strengthen reading skills regardless of the time and place. It is also beneficial to preschool children as a preparation for the next level of education in primary schools. Other than that, preschool children will get interactive experience and have fun while using the application.

References

Adriani, P., Markos, M. & Anna, V. (2016). Learning Through Play: the Role of Learning and Engagement Theory in the Development of Educational Games for Intellectually Challenged Children. *International Conference on Interactive Technologies and Games.*

Cecil, N. L. (2011). *Striking a balance: A comprehensive approach to early literacy.* Scottsdale, AZ: Holcomb Hathaway.

ISBN: 978-1-387-00704-2

Dina, D. G. & Pierpaolo, V. (2016). The silent reading supported by adaptive learning technology: Influence in the children outcomes. *Computers in Human Behavior, Vol. 55, pp. 1125 – 1130.*

Gao, Z., Lee, A. M., Xiang, P., & Kosma, M. (2011). Effect of Learning Activity on Students' Motivation, Physical Activity Levels and Effort/Persistence. *ICHPER-SD Journal of Research, 6(1), 27-33.*

Giti, K., &Hadis, S. (2015). Teaching Alphabet, Reading and Writing for Kids between 3-6 Years Old as a Second Language. *In Procedia - Social and Behavioral Sciences, Vol. 192, pp. 769-777.*

Hollands, F. M., Pan, Y., Shand, R., Cheng, H., Levin, H. M., Belfield, C. R. & Hanisch-Cerda, B. (2013). Improving early literacy: cost-effectiveness analysis of effective reading programs. *New York: Center for Benefit-Cost Studies of Education, Teachers College, Columbia University.*

Qi, N. & Yonghai, Y. (2015). Research on educational mobile games and the effect it has on the cognitive development of preschool children. *Third International Conference on Digital Information, Networking and Wireless Communication (DINWC 2015).*

Rosetto, A. D. F. & Dutra, A. (2016). The analysis of the use mobile technology in 6 – 8 years old children's literacy process. *International Sysmposium on Computers in Education (SIIE 2016).*

Shelley, S. A., Belinda, B., Genevieve, M., Kathryn, N. N., & Jonathan, M. P. (2016). Phonics Training Improves Reading in Children with Neorofibromatosis Type 1: A Prospective Intervention Trial. *The Journal of Pediatrics. Vol. 177, pp. 219 – 226.*

Su, S., & Hawkins, J. (2013). THRASS Phonics: A case stsudy of Thomas as an emerging reader in English. *The English Teacher, XLII(April), 52–73.*

Taylor, J., Davis, M., & Rastle, K. (2017). Comparing and validating methods of reading instruction using behavioural and neural findings in an artificial orthography. *Journal of Experimental Psychology: General, 1-34.*

ISBN: 978-1-387-00704-2

Article 33

Analysing Driver Behaviour within Dilemma Zone at Signalised Intersection: The Observational and Survey Methods

Haryati Fauzi, Aznoora Osman
Faculty of Computer and Mathematical Sciences
Universiti Teknologi Mara Perlis Branch, Malaysia

Abstract
Signalised intersections is deemed amongst complex issues in road safety control system. Due to the growing number of crashes at signalised intersection every year in Malaysia, this research aims at understanding driver behaviour at signalised intersection. This paper discusses the methods to analyse driver behaviour at signalised intersection, which consist of field data collection using video recording technique and administration of a survey pertaining to driving behaviour within dilemma zones with selected participants (car driver).The methods are designed to gain a better understanding of driver behavioursthat influence their decision-making of non-compliance at signalised intersection, within the dilemma zones.The main goal is to reveal driver responses at dilemma zone during amber signal light, with respect to the vehicle distance from stop line, signal timing and approaching speed.

Keywords:driver behaviour, signalised intersection, dilemma zone, observational methods, survey methods

Introduction

MIROS (2016) reported that 1.24 million road traffic deaths are recorded worldwide every year and the death toll in 2015 in Malaysia is 6 706, causing a loss to national economy up to RM 8.7 billion. The high rate of severity and the incurring cost after crashes at signalised intersection can negatively impact the country since the outcome of the result are damages of infrastructure, property and loss of lives. In order to maintain traffic safety, it is important to identify driver behaviours that lead to unsafe traffic conduct.

ISBN: 978-1-387-00704-2

In the aspect of driving, the two terms that are commonly used and related to each other, but can cause confusion, are driver behaviour and driver performance. Driver performance can be defined as a condition of what the driver can do, as driver's knowledge, perceptual skills and cognitive abilities(Evans, 2004). In contrast, driver behaviour explains the driver choices on how to react with all attributes that has been mentioned before (Evans, 2004). For instance, the capability to control the vehicle speed and the ability to judge the speed, are driver performance aspects, while the speed chosen falls under driver behaviour aspect. According to Cacciabue & Carsten (2010), there are factors that influence the driver performance and behaviour which are attitudes/personality, experience, driver state (impairment level), task demand (workload) and situation awareness.

Traffic signal compliance is a main indicator in determining driver behaviour at signalised intersections, which in any case is not free of the whole condition at the intersection. Non-complying with traffic signal regulation leads to violations and eventually to near accidents or accidents. Drivers' behaviour can be influenced by other factors such as the intersection layout, trip purpose, flow conditions, weather conditions, and signal settings. It is stated that the driver generally face difficulty to decide whether they have to stop or proceed, when approaching the onset of amber light;which is known as dilemma zone (Jamil, Shahabadin, & Ho, 2012).

Dilemma Zone

Dilemma zone can be categorised into Type I and Type II, controlled and affected by different factors (Lavrens, Pyrialakou, & Gkritza, 2014; Machiani, 2014). A Type I dilemma zone, is a condition where the driver does not comply to clear the intersection during the onset of amber, which is a result from the physical parameters, such as the short of time of yellow phase, geometric characteristics of the road and vehicle speed limit

ISBN: 978-1-387-00704-2

(Machiani, 2014). On the other hand, Type II dilemma zone, involving difficult interpretation and prediction of driver behaviour, depends essentially on driver characteristics, impairment, and distraction level. In other words, a hard decision need to be made by driver in a short amount of time either to stop at the stop line of signalised intersection or vice versa. This research focuses on Type II dilemma zone.

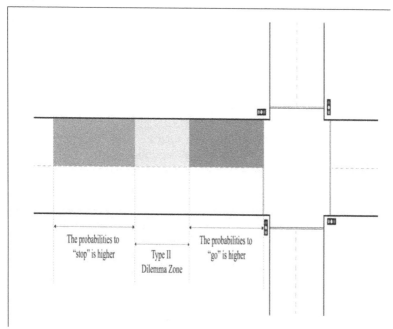

Figure 1: Type II Dilemma zone, adapted from
Urbanik&Koonce(2007)

Driver behaviour and responses at dilemma zone during amber light and compliance to red signal light is important because the results will contribute to the rate of accident at signalised intersection. Therefore, it is important to develop a driver behaviour models based on localised subjects and scenarios, such as the traffic conditions, driver habits, and vehicles characteristics. Accordingly, the primary goal of this study is to develop knowledge of the characteristics of driver behaviour and

ISBN: 978-1-387-00704-2

compliance at signalised intersection and establish the driver behaviour models. In order to maintain traffic safety, it is important to identify driver behaviours that lead to unsafe traffic conducts.

The Methods to Study Driver Behaviour within Dilemma Zone

To study the driver behaviour at signalised intersection within the dilemma zone, anobservational method and survey method is designed, as shown in Figure 2,which will fulfil the research objectives and to ensure the correct value of data is collected.

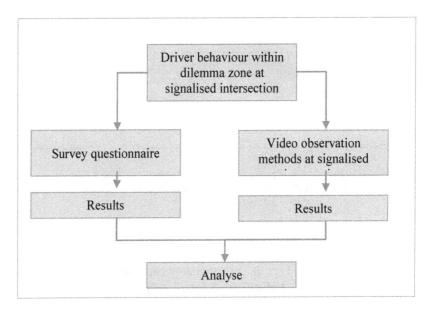

Figure 2: Flow of the methods to study driver behaviour within dilemma zone

Data of driver responses to amber light are collected viaobservation and survey. Observationuses field video recording at signalised intersections, while survey will be carried out with any car driver who volunteers to participate in the study. The video data collected in the field will be used to analyse driver

ISBN: 978-1-387-00704-2

behaviours during amber light at signalised intersections on actual road, while the survey would be able to personally inquire participants' likely driving response during amber light.

i.   Survey through questionnaire
This method focuses on the car's driver experiences and responses while approaching the signalised intersection during the amber signal light. A survey is developed and will be administered to a selected group of drivers through Google Form, a free online tool offered by Google to create and manage documents such as surveys. This survey responses will be stored online.

The main criteria of the survey's participant is they must be more than 18 years old, own a driving licence and have an experience of driving a car. All participants will be informed that their participation in the survey is voluntary and their responses and information will be discreet.

The questionnaire will be delivered in two ways; (1) via email link, or (2) the researcher will approach the selected participants and they will answer the questionnaire online, with the presence of researcher, so the researcher can explain in details if there is any inquiry regarding the question in the survey. In the former delivery, the questionnaire will be sent to selected participants via e-mail, which can be accessed and answered instantaneously. A user guide will also be given before the participant access the questionnaire. It is to ensure the participant get a brief idea on what this survey is all about and how to answer the survey.
Before using the questionnaire for actual study, a reliability test will be conducted with 40 participants to compute the questionnaire's alpha value.

The outline of survey's question
The survey questionnaire will be divided into two sections. The first section of the survey will be inquiries of the basic personal information, such as participant's gender, age, years of driving

ISBN: 978-1-387-00704-2

experience and how often they drive. The second section will deliver questions regarding participants' response that could influence their decision during amber signal light at signalised intersection. The questions will include images of on-road situation at signalised intersection, along with short brief that will help them to answer the questions. Questions involving their driving response while in dilemma zones will also be designed, which include their prediction of the duration of the amber signal light, and an open-ended question regarding the factors that influence their decision-making. Participants will be advised to answer based on their actual behaviour while encountering the same traffic situation.

ii. Observation methodusing video recording
This method focuses on getting the quantitative data of driver behaviour within dilemma zone at signalised intersection. The recordings may help transpires the driver behaviour so that an understanding of driver's behaviourcan be achieved. Moreover, the video recording allows an opportunity to transcribe all the data needed and plays the video recording repeatedly, which is very useful in the analysis process.

The data collections
The data of driver behaviour from observation area will be collected via video recording, which includes (1) layout of the observation site, (2) particulars of the site as date, time, and weather conditions, (3) signal timing, and (4) traffic volume and violations. The observation location will be a signalised intersection nearby the university area, and consists two lanes for each directions. A video camera attached to a tripod will be installed 120 meters from stop line of signalised intersection, to get a clear view of video recording starts from 100 meters until stop line. The video recording will last for two hours during peak-off hours (10AM to 12PM) and peak hours (4PM to 6PM), considering different numbers of traffic congestion on a randomly selected weekday and weekend.

ISBN: 978-1-387-00704-2

Conclusion

This paper discusses the design of observational and survey methods to study driver behaviourwithin the dilemma zone at signalised intersection. The decision-making process within the dilemma zone is critical because wrong decision could lead to a crash at signalised intersection during the amber light intervals. The questionnaire's purpose is to reveal specific factors that influence the driver's perception and decision-making during the amber light intervals. On the other hand, observational method using video recording technique is administered to get a quantitative result of driver behaviour within the dilemma zones during the amber light intervals. The quantitative data includes distance of non-compliant car from the traffic light, acceleration and deceleration rate of vehicle during the yellow light intervals, and brake perception-reaction time which impacted by the vehicle's time to stop line at intersection. The result of this study will provide necessary guidance for future study and could be used to develop scenarios in driving simulator.The new knowledge of local driver behaviour patterns from this research will allow us to make our road safer, which is in line with NKRA vision to improve transportation.

Acknowledgements

This work is funded by the Ministry of Higher Education Malaysia through research grant RAGS/1/2014/ICT02/UITM//3.

References

Cacciabue, P. C., & Carsten, O. (2010). A simple model of driver behaviour to sustain design and safety assessment of automated systems in automotive environments. *Applied Ergonomics*, *41*, 187–197.

Evans, L. (2004). Chapter 1: Introduction. In *Traffic Safety* (pp. 1–18).

Jamil, H. M., Shahabadin, A., & Ho, J. S. (2012). A case study of the Prevalence and characteristics of red light runners in Malaysia. *Injury Prevention*, *18*(1), A201–A201.

Lavrens, S. M., Pyrialakou, V. D., & Gkritza, K. (2014). Modelling driver behavior in dilemma zones: A discrete/continuous formulation with selectivity bias corrections. *Analytics Methods in Accident Research*, *3*(4), 44–55.

ISBN: 978-1-387-00704-2

Machiani, S. G. (2014). *Modelling driver behaviour at signalized intersection: Decision dynamics, human learning, and safety measures of real-time control systems.*

MIROS. (2016). *MIROS and its Roles in ASEAN.*

Urbanik, T., & Koonce, P. (2007). The dilemma with dilemma zones. *Proceedings of ITE District, 6.*

ISBN: 978-1-387-00704-2

Article 34

Developing Cyber-bullying Knowledge and Awareness Instrument (CBKAi) to Measure Knowledge and Perceived Awareness Towards Cyber-bullying among Adolescents

Nadia Abdul Wahab
Faculty of Computer and Mathematical Sciences
Universiti Teknologi MARA Perlis Branch, Malaysia

Wan Ahmad Jaafar Wan Yahaya
Centre For Instructional Technology & Multimedia
Universiti Sains Malaysia, Penang, Malaysia

Abstract

In this study, the researcher developed an instrument to measure the level of adolescents'knowledge and perceived awareness on cyber-bullying. This instrument is known as the Cyber-bullying Knowledge and Awareness Instrument (CBKAi).Content validity was performed to determine whether the instrument comprises a representative sample of the behaviour domain to be measured. CBKAi was validated by a senior lecturer from a public university who is also an expert in cyber-bullying and also two secondary school counsellors.Apart from that, CBKAi was also tested for its reliability with 30 respondents. The Cronbach's alpha internal consistency reliability coefficient for the instrument is 0.919 for items that are related to knowledge and 0.810 for items that are related for perceived awareness. The statistics show that CBKAi is a reliable instrument to be utilized to measure knowledge and perceived awareness towards cyber-bullying among adolescents.

Keywords:validity, reliability, cyber-bullying

Introduction

The issue of bullying has long been a topic of discussion amongst educationists, academicians and researchers. Smith and Thompson (1991) defined bullying as a set of conduct that is done intentionally and causes physical and psychological harm to the receiver. According to Kowalski and Limber (2007), as technology evolves, bullying has also evolved to include

ISBN: 978-1-387-00704-2

electronically based forms of aggression. Now, there is a new channel through which someone is bullied, and that is through the Internet and other telecommunication devices like cell phones. This form of bullying is known as cyber-bullying(Kowalski and Limber, 2007). Like traditional bullying, cyber-bullying victims are also exposed to the negative consequences of this phenomenon. They might isolate themselves especially from school activities, become stressed as well as ill and possibly contemplate suicide (Willard, 2007).

Knowledge and awareness of cyber-bullying is still looked upon lightly by the society (Nadia and Wan Ahmad Jaafar, 2012). What the public are not aware of is the threat of cyber-bullying that can be compared to an illness that will destroy the society especially, adolescents. A national survey in 2013 also showed that adolescents' awareness of cyber-bullying were still low (CyberSAFE in Schools 2013 Survey, 2013).

Even though laws such as the Computer Crimes Act 1997 and the Communications and Multimedia Act 1998 have been enacted in Malaysia, knowledge and awareness of the public with regards to cyber-bullying remain low. There are many in the society who do not know or do not consider cyber-bullying to be a serious matter. This is evident as very few cases have been reported to the authorities (Topçu, Erdur-Baker and Capa-Aydin, 2008).

In this study, the researcher developed an instrument to measure the level of adolescents'knowledge and perceived awareness on cyber-bullying. This instrument is known as the Cyber-bullying Knowledge and Awareness Instrument (CBKAi). The instrument could be utilized to measure the level of knowledge and perceived awareness towards cyber-bullying among adolescents. Berne, et.al (2012) who had conducted a systematic review on forty-four (44) cyber-bullying instruments found that there were no instrument that had been specifically developed to measure the

ISBN: 978-1-387-00704-2

level of adolescents' knowledge and awareness on cyber-bullying.

From literature review, it was found that most instruments that had been developed were more structured towards exploring how far adolescents were involved in cyber-bullying activities, either as victims, bullies or bystanders; for instance, the instrument developed by Erdur-Baker (2010). Additionally, there were several instruments that studied about the coping strategies of cyber-bullying, such as that developed by Li (2008) and the emotional or behavioural impact of being cyber-bullied by Beran and Li (2005).

Development of CBKAi
The instrument to be discussed in this paper consists of thirty (30) questionnaires, which intended to measure the level of adolescents'knowledge and perceived awareness on cyber-bullying.CBKAi was divided into three different sections. Section 1 of the instrument consisted of demographic variables, whereas Sections 2 to 3 dealt with knowledge and perceived awareness, respectively. The demographic variables included age, gender, race, and also whether the respondent has a smart phone and internet access at home.

In order to construct the items that measure the level of adolescents' knowledge on cyber-bullying,the researcher referred to the findings of Willard (2007), Dilmac (2009) and Kowalski and Limber (2007).In developing the items that measure thelevel of perceived awareness of adolescents on cyber-bullying, the researcher referred to several studies that were conducted by cyber-bullying expert such as Hinduja and Patchin (2006) and Beran and Li (2005). Furthermore, the researcher also referred to several sources such as guidelines on cyber-bullying that were outlined by Willard (2005).

ISBN: 978-1-387-00704-2

In CBKAi, there are 12 items that have been utilized to access the level of knowledge that the adolescents possess in understanding the characteristics, method and the nature of cyber-bullying. The respondents need to determine whether each action could lead to cyber-bullying or resembles cyber-bullying act or not. All questions related to knowledge had two possible options i.e., "Yes" and "No". Below are some examples of questions for knowledge of cyber-bullying:

i.   Sending or posting untrue statements about a person to other people,

ii.   Sending or posting material about a person that contains sensitive, private, or embarrassing information (e.g. private messages or images),

iii.   Creating a fake account in social media just for fun,

iv.   Intentionally exclude a person from an online group (e.g. Whatsapp group) and

v.   Sharing social media password with a best friend.

vi.   Pretending to be someone else online in order to solicit or post personal or false information about someone else.

Another 18 items has been used to measure the level of perceived awareness that the students have on the consequences of cyber-bullying, coping strategy of cyber-bullying and steps to prevent the growth of cyber-bullying among adolescents.All questions related to perceived awarenesshad five possible options i.e., "Strongly Unaware", "Unaware", "I am not sure", "Aware" and"Strongly Aware". Examples of questions for perceived awareness of cyber-bullying are as below:

i.   Do you aware that you should keep evidence of cyber-bullying (e.g screen shot) and you could use this evidence to report cyber-bullying incidents?

ii.   Do you aware cyber-bullying often stop if you do not respond to the cyber-bully?

iii.   Do you aware that you could block the person who is cyber-bullying?

ISBN: 978-1-387-00704-2

iv. Do you aware that most victims of cyber-bullying have the tendency to commit suicide?

v. Do you aware that if you have been a witness to cyber-bullying incidents, you should report the cyber-bullying to someone who can help the victim?

Validity of CBKAi

As suggested by Anastasi and Urbina (1997), content validity is performed to determine whether it comprises a representative sample of the behaviour domain to be measured. Foxcroft, Paterson, Le Roux and Herbst (2004), stated that the content validity could be improved by using a panel of experts to review the test specifications and the selection of items.CBKAi was developed by the researcher and then validated by a senior lecturer from a public university who is also an expert in cyber-bullying. It was also validated by two secondary school counsellors. These experts reviewed the items from the instrument and commented whether the items comprise of a representative sample of the domain.

The first draft of the instrument was presented to the experts, who judged on the redundancy, content validity, clarity, and readability. The experts evaluated the instrument providing several useful comments. Modifications made to the first draft of the instrument based on the experts' comments. These comments involved rewording, rearranging, deleting, as well as adding items, examples, definitions, and/or easier terms.

Reliability of CBKAi

Reliability is defined as "the consistency with which a measuring instrument yields a certain results when the entity being measured has not changed" (Leedy and Ormrod, 2005). Reliability can be established in four different ways: equivalency, stability, inter-rater, and internal consistency (Carmines and Zeller, 1979). Cronbach's alpha is the ideal statistic for estimating the internal consistency reliability of a measure (Cohen and Swerdlik, 2005).

ISBN: 978-1-387-00704-2

CBKAi was tested for its reliability with 30 respondents. The analysis was done using SPSS ver. 22. The Cronbach's alpha internal consistency reliability coefficient for the instrument is 0.919 (Table 1) for items that are related to knowledge.

Table 1 Reliability Statistics for Items Related to Knowledge

Cronbach's Alpha	Cronbach's Alpha Based on Standardized Items	N of Items
.919	.912	12

The Cronbach's alpha internal consistency reliability coefficient for the instrument is 0.810 (Table 2) for items that are related for perceived awareness.

Table 2 Reliability Statistics for Items Related to Perceived Awareness

Cronbach's Alpha	Cronbach's Alpha Based on Standardized Items	N of Items
.810	.810	18

The Cronbach's alpha internal consistency reliability coefficient values in Table 1 and Table 2 show that CBKAi is a reliable instrument to be utilized in order to measure the level of adolescents'knowledge and perceived awareness on cyber-bullying.

Conclusion
In this study the researcher developed and validated an instrument, CBKAi, which consists of thirty (30) questionnaires, to measure the level of knowledge and perceived awareness on cyber-bullying among adolescents. The instrument was validated by a panel who are experts in cyber-bullying. This instrument was also tested for its reliability with 30 respondents. The Cronbach's alpha internal consistency reliability coefficient values from the reliability test show that CBKAi is a reliable instrument to be

ISBN: 978-1-387-00704-2

utilized to measure knowledge and perceived awareness towards cyber-bullying among adolescents.

References

Anastasi, A., & Urbina, S. (1997). Validity. Psychological Testing: Upper Saddle River (NJ): Prentice Hall.

Beran, T., & Li, Q. (2005). Cyber-harassment: A study of a new method for an old behavior. *journal of educational Computing Research, 32*(3), 265-277.

Berne, S., Frisén, A., Schultze-Krumbholz, A., Scheithauer, H., Naruskov, K., Luik, P., et al. (2013). Cyberbullying assessment instruments: A systematic review. *Aggression and violent behavior, 18*(2), 320-334.

Carmines, E. G., & Zeller, R. A. (1979).*Reliability and validity assessment* (Vol. 17): Sage.

Cohen, R., &Swerdlik, M. (2005). Psychological testing and measurement: An introduction to tests and measurement. *McGraw-Hill, Boston, MA.*

CyberSAFE in Schools 2013 Survey. (2013).

Dılmaç, B. (2009). Psychological Needs as a Predictor of Cyber bullying: a Preliminary Report on College Students. *Educational Sciences: Theory & Practice, 9*(3).

Foxcroft, C., Paterson, H., Le Roux, N., &Herbst, D. (2004). Psychological assessment in South Africa: A needs analysis. *The test usage patterns and needs of psychological assessment practitioners.*

Kowalski, R. M., & Limber, S. P. (2007).Electronic bullying among middle school students.*Journal of Adolescent Health, 41*(6), S22-S30.

Leedy, P. D., &Ormrod, J. E. (2005).*Practical research*: Pearson Merrill Prentice Hall Columbus, OH.

Li, Q. (2008). A cross-cultural comparison of adolescents' experience related to cyberbullying. *Educational Research, 50*(3), 223-234.

Patchin, J. W., &Hinduja, S. (2006). Bullies move beyond the schoolyard a preliminary look at cyberbullying. *Youth violence and juvenile justice, 4*(2), 148-169.

Smith, & Thompson, D. (1991).*Practical approaches to bullying*: David Fulton Publish.

Topcu, Ç.,&Erdur-Baker, Ö. (2010). The revised cyber bullying inventory (RCBI): Validity and reliability studies. *Procedia-Social and Behavioral Sciences, 5*, 660-664.

Topçu, C., Erdur-Baker, Ö.,&Capa-Aydin, Y. (2008). Examination of cyberbullying experiences among Turkish students from different school types. *CyberPsychology& Behavior, 11*(6), 643-648.

Wahab, N. A., &Yahaya, W. A. J. W. (2012).*A Preliminary Investigation: Feasibility of Web-Based Multimedia Learning (WBML) in Raising Awareness of Cyber Bullying.* Paper presented at the Proceeding of the Post Graduate National Mini Conference, Sungai Petani, Kedah.

ISBN: 978-1-387-00704-2

Willard, N. (2005). Educator's Guide to Cyberbullying Addressing the Harm Caused by Online Social Cruelty. Retrieved July, 26, 2012, from http://www.asdk12.org/middlelink/avb/bully_topics/educatorsguide_cyber bullying.pdf

Willard, N. E. (2007). *Cyber-safe kids, cyber-savvy teens : helping young people learn to use the internet safely and responsibly*: San Francisco, Calif. : Jossey-Bass, c2007 (Norwood, Mass. : Books24x7.com [generator]).

ISBN: 978-1-387-00704-2

Article 35

Evaluating the Usability of Emergency Fund Target Web System among Young Adults

Izzatie Zakaria,
Faculty of Computer and Mathematical Sciences
Universiti Teknologi MARA Perlis Branch, Malaysia

Nor Azzyati Hashim
Faculty of Computer and Mathematical Sciences
Universiti Teknologi MARA Perak Branch, Tapah Campus, Malaysia

Abstract

Young adults need to know the importance of having a good financial management to prevent the engagement in extensive debt. One of the ways is by having saving for emergency fund. Emergency fund is vital as it can be used during any unwanted events such as job loss, health emergency and other unexpected expenses. Most existing web systems for personal financial management are more towards budgeting and tracking expenditures. Thus, to encourage people especially young adults to build emergency fund, a web system called Emergency Fund Target (EFT) was developed. This paper investigates the ease-of-use and benefits of EFT web system among young adults. Evaluation for this web system using usability testing involved 15 young adults who already being employed. From the findings, it is discovered that EFT system is easy to use and enables users to learn about emergency fund in order to use the system to keep track their saving for emergency fund. For the future works of EFT, the web system will enhance to advice users who has completed the emergency fund saving on moving into investment for short, medium and long term financial goals.

Keywords: Financial Management, Emergency Fund, Usability Testing

Introduction

Young adults are people from 18 to 35 years of age (Arnett, 2000). Upon starting working, they enter the phase from financial dependence to financial independence (Soyeon et. al., 2009) as they should no longer rely on their parents. Those who graduated from colleges and universities face a bigger challenge as they need to manage financial independently not only for

ISBN: 978-1-387-00704-2

accommodation and transportation but also burdened by education loan. If financial management is not done wisely, it could lead to overspending, deficit and eventually extensive debt. Hilgert, Hogarth and Beverly (2003) stated that the task of managing financial independently is more complex as it involves money management, credit management, saving and investing management.

Generally, a good money management involves controllable credit management to achieve saving for future needs. One of the important savings that young adults must have is emergency fund. Using savings for establishing emergency fund should be done before investing for other short, medium and long term financial goals (Begin Young, 2016). The term emergency fund refers to the fund that can be used to respond to emergent events and financial emergency such as loss of job, reduction of income, health emergency, automobile repair, and house repair (Money Management International, 2016).

Currently, there are many web systems for personal financial management. Nonetheless, these web systems emphasize on financial budgeting and expenditures tracking but lack on establishing emergency fund. Accordingly, a web system called Emergency Fund Target (EFT) was developed to inform young adults about emergency fund and to enable them to use the system for emergency fund saving. Usability testing was conducted to evaluate the ease-of-use and benefits of EFT web system amongyoung adults.Nielsen Usability Model (Nielsen, 2012) was adapted in the usability testing.

Research Model

Figure 1 shows the research model that has been applied in the development of EFT web system.

ISBN: 978-1-387-00704-2

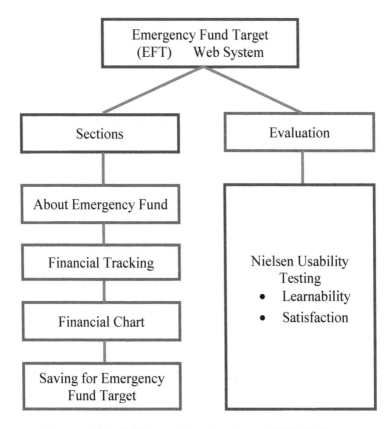

Figure 1: Research Model for the Development of EFT Web System.

Methodology

The usability testing involved15 young adults aged between 24 to 30 years old. The young adults are users that have at least a bachelor degree and come from various education disciplines such as Computer Science, Chemistry, Physics, Accounting and Quantity Surveyor.

The type of usability method used is questionnaire. The questionnaire questions were classified according to usability quality components that is adapted from Nielsen Usability Model as summarized in Table 1.

ISBN: 978-1-387-00704-2

Table 1: Quality Components of Usability (Adapted from Nielsen, 2012)

Classification	Explanation
Learnability	*Refer to the ease-of-use of the users to accomplish the tasks the first time they use the system.*
Satisfaction	*Refer to pleasant experience of the users in using the system.*

Questionnaire regarding learnability component evaluate the ease-of-use of the user to effectively accomplish the tasks of the system from learning 'About Emergency Fund' section, to key-in income and expenses in 'Financial Tracking' section, to view the 'Financial Chart' section that displays expenditures breakdown and to monitor 'Saving for Emergency Fund Target' section. Questions on satisfaction component evaluate the user pleasant experience in using the EFT web system.

Results and Findings

Respondents answered 12 questions to evaluate EFT web systemlearnability and users' satisfaction. The range response for each questionnaire question is measured between 1 (*Strongly Disagree*), 2 (*Somewhat Disagree*), 3 (*Neutral*), 4 (*Somewhat Agree*) and 5 (*Strongly Agree*) as shown in Table 2.

Table 2: Measurement Criteria

Rank	Value
Strongly Agree	5
Somewhat Agree	4
Neutral	3
Somewhat Disagree	2
Strongly Disagree	1

The result of the questionnaire for learnability and satisfaction is as tabulated in Table 3.

ISBN: 978-1-387-00704-2

Table 3: Result ofEFT Web System Learnability & Satisfaction

No.	Learnability	Mean Score
1	I understand the sentences, words, buttons and symbols that are used in EFT system.	4.1
2	I find that the pages (About Emergency Fund, Financial Tracking, Financial Chart and Saving for Emergency Fund Target) are easy to understand.	4.0
3	I find that the pages in EFT system (About Emergency Fund, Financial Tracking, Financial Chart and Saving for Emergency Fund Target) are easy to navigate step-by-step.	4.3
4	I understand to fill the form in the 'Financial Tracking' section.	4.1
5	I am able to complete all the tasks in the EFT web system towards understanding about emergency fund savings.	4.1
6	Overall, I find that this EFT web system is easy to use.	3.7
	Satisfaction	
7	I am satisfied with all the pages (About Emergency Fund, Financial Tracking, Financial Chart and Savings for Emergency Fund) in helping to understand about emergency fund saving.	4.1
8	The EFT system makes me easy to learn about savings for emergency fund.	3.9
9	With EFT system, I understand how emergency fund is calculated.	3.8
10	I find that the EFT system enables me to self-monitor my savings.	3.9
11	I find that the EFT system encourages me to keep engage in savings for emergency fund.	4.1
12	I will use this application to keep track on my emergency fund saving.	3.9

Usability testing on learnability refers to the ability of users to easily learn to use the EFT system to accomplish tasks. Testing on learnability quality component is important to evaluate

ISBN: 978-1-387-00704-2

whether users are able to understand the system. Result of EFT web system learnability shows that from question number 1 to 5, majority of the users choose *moderately agree* and *strongly agree*. In spite of that, one user answered *moderately disagree* and four users choose *neutral* making question 6 result slightly below mean score of 4.

The next usability testing is on users' satisfaction. This testing evaluates the pleasant experience of users upon using the EFT system. Evaluation on users' satisfaction is crucial to enable young adults to know about emergency fund thus, empower them to use the system to save money for emergency fund. The data collected shows that for question number 7 and 11, majority of the users choose *moderately agree* and *strongly agree*. For question number 8, 9, 10 and 12, the result is slightly below mean score of 4 because one user answered *moderately disagree*for the questions with a few users choose *neutral*.

From the users' feedback, users who answered *moderately disagree* or *neutral* neither has knowledge about financial management nor tracks their monthly expenses making them less understand the system. Nevertheless, the majority of the users found that it is easy to learn to use the EFT system and most of the users are satisfied with the benefits of the system. Although for some questions the score is below mean score of 4, the score is not too low. Out of 15 users, 10 users agree that the EFT system is easy to use. In addition to that, 11 users agree that they will use EFT system to keep track of emergency fund saving.

Conclusion and Future Works

EFT is a web system that can inform young adults about emergency fund and enable them to use the system to monitor savings for emergency fund. These can be achieved through the four sections of the system that consist of About Emergency Fund, Financial Tracking, Financial Chart and Saving for Emergency Fund Target.

From the findings, it can be concluded that theEFT web system is easy to use. The system can help young adults to know about emergency fund. Majority of the young adults agree that they

ISBN: 978-1-387-00704-2

will use the system to save money for establishing emergency fund.

For future works, the EFT system can be enhanced by providing quiz section to improve the young adults' knowledge about emergency fund especially for those who do not have financial background studies.In addition to that, the web system can be extended to include other functions of investment to manage saving for short, medium and long term financial goals, once a dependable emergency fund target has been achieved by users of the system.

References

Arnett, J. J. (2000). Emerging adulthood: A theory of development from the late teens through the twenties. American Psychologist, 55(5), pp. 469-480.

Begin Young. (2016). *Emergency Fund*. Retrieved from https://beginyoung.com/emergency-fund/

Hilgert, M. A., Hogarth, J. M. & Beverly, S. G. (2003). Household financial management: The connection between knowledge and behavior. Federal Reserve Bulletin, pp. 309-322.

Money Management International. (2016). *Establish an Emergency Savings Account*. Retrieved from http://www.moneymanagement.org/Budgeting-Tools/Credit-Articles/Savings/Building-Personal-Financial-Security-Establish-an-Emergency-Savings-Account.aspx

Nielsen, J. (2012). *Usability 101: Introduction to Usability*. Retrieved from https://www.nngroup.com/articles/usability-101-introduction-to-usability/

Soyeon, S., Jing, J. X., Bonnie, L. B. & Angela, C. L. (2009).Pathways to life success: A conceptual model of financial well-being for young adults, Journal of Applied Developmental Psychology, 30 (6), pp. 708-723.

ISBN: 978-1-387-00704-2

Article 36

A Theoretical Framework for Designing a Multimedia App in Increasing Knowledge and Perceived Awareness towards Cyber-bullying among Adolescents

Nadia Abdul Wahab
Faculty of Computer and Mathematical Sciences
Universiti Teknologi MARA Perlis Branch, Malaysia

Wan Ahmad Jaafar Wan Yahaya
Centre For Instructional Technology & Multimedia
Universiti Sains Malaysia, Penang, Malaysia

Abstract
This paper discusses the theoretical framework in designing and developing a multimedia app intended to increase knowledge and perceived awareness towards cyber-bullying among adolescents. Given that cyber-bullying has become more serious lately, steps should be taken to ensure that this threat is curtailed (Willard, 2007). Other than the conventional methods and the involvement of parents, schools and the society in curtailing this problem, other initiatives that could be taken include developing a Multimedia App on tablets that would be able to assist adolescents in increasing their knowledge and awareness on cyber-bullying. Development of an interactive Multimedia App that comes with attractive graphics, audio and animation have great potential in attracting the interest of adolescents in gaining a deeper understanding of this issue. Therefore, the theoretical framework maps and integrates all relevant theories, principles and guidelines to form a concrete pathway for the design and development of the multimedia app.

Keywords:Cognitive Theory of Multimedia Learning, Principle of Multimedia Learning, Personalization Principle, Persuasive Technology, Constructivist Learning Environment, Cyber-bullying

Introduction
Wolak, Mitchell, and Finkelhor (2007) defined cyber-bullying as sending or posting text messages or images intended to hurt or embarrass another person by using the Internet, cell phones, or other technology. Other researchers define cyber-bullying as a

ISBN: 978-1-387-00704-2

destructive and intentional act carried out by a group or individual, using electronic forms, repeatedly, and over time against a victim who cannot easily defend him or herself (Smith, et. al, 2008).

Generally, based on research carried out between the 2006 and 2012 by Patchin and Hinduja (2012), the highest number of victims of cyber-bullying in those six years was adolescents. The problem of cyber-bullying has become more widespread, not only because of the ease with which an adolescent is able to access the Internet, but also because the Internet makes it easier for a person to interact with another person without revealing her or his true identity, or in other words, anonymity (Patchin and Hinduja, 2006). However, knowledge and awareness of cyber-bullying is still looked upon lightly by the society (Nadia and Wan Ahmad Jaafar, 2012). What the public are not aware of is the threat of cyber-bullying that can be compared to an illness that will destroy the society especially, adolescents. A national survey in 2013 also showed that adolescents' awareness of cyber-bullying were still low (*CyberSAFE in Schools 2013 Survey*, 2013).

Given that cyber-bullying has become more serious lately, steps should be taken to ensure that this threat is curtailed (Willard, 2007). Some schools currently use small group discussions, large school assemblies, or lecture workshops to address the problem of cyber-bullying with students and these methods are often ineffective (Beale and Hall, 2007; Diamanduros et. al, 2008; Keith and Martin, 2005). Other than the conventional methods and the involvement of parents, schools and the society in curtailing this problem, other initiatives that could be taken include developing a Multimedia App on tablets that would be able to assist adolescents in increasing their knowledge and awareness on cyber-bullying.

Development of an interactive Multimedia App that comes with attractive graphics, audio and animation have great potential in

ISBN: 978-1-387-00704-2

attracting the interest of adolescents in gaining a deeper understanding of this issue. Moreover, advanced Internet technology and the existence of gadgets like tablets and smart phones make it easier for adolescents from all walks of life to access these applications (Upadhyay, Jesudass, and Chitale, 2014). Therefore, the researcher needs to construct a theoretical framework to map and integrate all relevant theories, principles and guidelines to form a concrete pathway for the development of the multimedia app.

Theoretical Framework Development
As suggested by Reigeluth and Merill (1978) in Van Patten, Chao, and Reigeluth (1986), the development of the theoretical framework will take such an approach by combining the macro and micro strategies. Macro strategies involve the selection, sequence and organization of the subject-matter topics that are to be presented. It is also described as the overall strategic plan (Gibbons and Fairweather, 1998). On the other hand, micro strategies are concerned with the individual displays; including their characteristics, inter-relationship and sequence that are to be presented to the learners. Micro strategies are also known as presentation strategy; as they involve details of each individual presentation to the learner (Chen, Toh, and Wan MohdFauzy, 2005). Persuasive design principles are the macro strategy while Cognitive Theory of Multimedia Learning (CTML) and Design Guidelines for Teenagers serve as the micro strategies for this study. The study also utilizes the Constructivist Learning Environment (CLEs) which was established by Jonassen (1999). The theoretical framework is illustrated in Figure 1.

ISBN: 978-1-387-00704-2

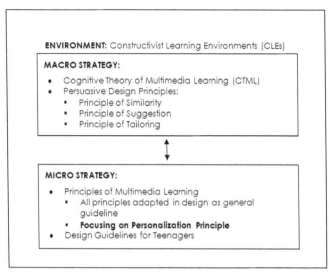

Figure 0: Theoretical Framework of the Study

Although there are a few theories, principles and guidelines supporting this research, the Personalization Principle is the major principle being investigated in this study. This is because the main focus of this study is to investigate the effects of personalization towards knowledge and perceived awareness of cyber-bullying among adolescents.

A. Persuasive Technology

Persuasive Technology is the study related to attitudes and how to change attitudes and behaviour (Fogg, 2003). Persuasive Technology is believed to play an important role in education (Lucero, et. al, 2006). Fogg (2003) outlined many principles of persuasive technology which can be put into use as guidelines while designing and developing a computer technology that is capable of changing the attitude and behaviour of someone. In this study, three principles are applied as the macro strategy in designing the Multimedia App. These principles are:

i.   Principal of Similarity - learners are more readily persuaded by a Multimedia App that is similar to them in some ways.

ISBN: 978-1-387-00704-2

ii.   Principle of Suggestion – the Multimedia App will have greater persuasion power if it offers suggestions at opportune moments.

iii.   Principle of Tailoring – This principle suggests that information that has been prepared by a computer application would be more persuasive if it is constructed and tailored to the needs, interest, personality and usage context relevant to the user.

B. Cognitive Theory of Multimedia Learning (CTML)

Mayer (2009) proposed the *cognitive multimedia learning model* as the human information processing model. This model divides the human memory into three parts, which are (i) sensory memory, (ii) working memory and (iii) long term memory. This model explains that multimedia information is received through sensory memory and the received information is then moved to the working memory. The main process of learning with multimedia takes place in the working memory and the role of the working memory is to actively process the information received through sensory memory (Mayer, 2009). The processing of information which involves the integration of recently received knowledge with existing knowledge in the long-term memory produces new knowledge or coherence mental representation. This new knowledge is stored in the long-term memory in the form of schema (Mayer, 2009).

C. Principles of Multimedia Learning

Focusing on real learning situations, Mayer (2009) conducted several in-depth studies involving the testing of learning theories. From the results of these CTML-related studies, he successfully developed 12 principles of multimedia instruction that have been widely accepted and used by instructional designers and researchers the world over. These 12 principles are as follow:

i.   Multimedia Principle – People learn better from words and pictures than from only words.

ISBN: 978-1-387-00704-2

ii.   Coherence Principle – People learn better when extraneous words, pictures and sounds are excluded rather than included.

iii.   Signalling Principle – People learn better when cues that highlight the organization of the essential material are added.

iv.   Redundancy Principle – People learn better from graphics and narration than from graphics, narration and on-screen text.

v.   Spatial Contiguity Principle – People learn better when corresponding words and pictures are presented near rather than far from each other on the page or screen.

vi.   Temporal Contiguity Principle – People learn better when corresponding words and pictures are presented simultaneously rather than successively.

vii.   Segmenting Principle – People learn better from a multimedia lesson presented in user-paced segments rather than as a continuous unit.

viii. Pre-training Principle – People learn better from a multimedia lesson when they know the names and characteristics of the main concepts.

ix.   Modality Principle – People learn better from graphics and narrations than from animation and on-screen text.

x.   Personalization Principle – People learn better from multimedia lessons when words are in conversational style rather than formal style.

xi.   Voice Principle – People learn better when the narration in multimedia lessons is spoken in a friendly human voice rather than a machine voice.

xii.   Image Principle – People do not necessarily learn better from a multimedia lesson when the speaker's image is added to the screen.

Generally, all the principles suggested by Mayer (2009) are applied during the design and development of the Multimedia App. However, the researcher will emphasize on Personalization

ISBN: 978-1-387-00704-2

Principle developed by Moreno and Mayer (2004), where its effects are investigated in this research.

D. Personalization Principle

The Personalization Principle, developed by Moreno and Mayer (2004), is the main principle underpinning this study and it has been used to investigate the effectiveness of this principle in increasing knowledge and awareness towards cyber-bullying among adolescents. Personalization Principle states that when instructional messages are presented in a conversational rather than formal style, deeper learning will occur. The theory suggests that as a result of a conversational style language being used, feelings of presence are elicited and these feelings facilitate deeper learning (Moreno and Mayer, 2004). This principle also emphasis that learning materials should be written in conversational style that addresses the learner directly as "you" instead of in a formal style that is in the "objective third person" (Moreno and Mayer, 2004). Below are examples on how narration in conversational style has been used in a few screens of the Multimedia App:

i. If you would like to know, all the actions mentioned just now are Cyber-bullying! If you would like to know more about cyber-bullying, please click "Enter"

ii. Guys, say "No!" to cyber-bullying. Let's follow this simple guide to overcome cyber-bullying.

iii. Remember! If you are a victim of cyber-bullying, follow the three most important steps immediately: Stop, Block and Tell!

E. Design Guidelines for Teenagers

Loranger and Nielsen (2005) had conducted empirical usability studies with real adolescents to determine specifics on how websites can be improved to match their abilities and preferences. From the studies, they outlined 61 design guidelines to effectively construct websites for teenagers. Even though these

ISBN: 978-1-387-00704-2

guidelines are developed for constructing websites, they are also suitable to be applied for designing Multimedia App, particularly for adolescents. They are five categories of design guidelines for teenagers applied in this study namely (i) visual design, (ii) interaction design, (iii) multimedia, (iv) navigation and (v) writing.

F. Constructivist Learning Environments (CLEs)

Constructivist Learning Environments (CLEs) was suggested by Jonassen (1999). This environment is based on problem-based learning whereby the learners need to solve the problem by exploring all knowledge components such as related cases, information resources, cognitive tools, conversation as well as collaborative tools and social contextual support. This form of design is the strategy that supports student achievement (Jonassen, 1999). In this study, five out of six components of CLEs have been adapted to ensure that this Multimedia App will foster the problem-solving and conceptual development of the learners.

Conclusion

This paper discusses the theoretical framework in designing and developing a multimedia app intended to increase knowledge and perceived awareness towards cyber-bullying among adolescents. As number of cyber-bullying cases is increasing from day-to-day (Rivers and Noret, 2010), it is crucial for the adolescents to be given ample knowledge and awareness regarding what is cyber-bullying and the method through which cyber-bullying is conducted, the dangers of cyber-bullying, steps to handle cyber-bullying and ways to curb the growth of cyber-bullying. Other than the conventional methods and the involvement of parents, schools and the society in curtailing this problem, the initiatives that could be taken include developing a Multimedia App on tablets that would be able to assist adolescents in increasing their knowledge and awareness on cyber-bullying. Development of an interactive Multimedia App that comes with attractive graphics,

ISBN: 978-1-387-00704-2

audio and animation have great potential in attracting the interest of adolescents in gaining a deeper understanding of this issue.

In order to design and develop the multimedia app, a theoretical framework is needed as it will act as a guideline throughout the process. In this framework, Persuasive Design Principles serve as the macro strategy while Cognitive Theory of Multimedia Learning (CTML) and Design Guidelines for Teenagers act as the micro strategies for this study. The study also utilizes the Constructivist Learning Environment (CLEs) which was established by Jonassen (1999). Personalization Principle is another major principle being integrated in this research. It is hoped that all theories, principles and guidelines integrated in this framework will form a clear pathway for the design and development of the multimedia app that has the ability to increase knowledge and perceived awareness towards cyber-bullying among adolescents.

References

Beale, A. V., & Hall, K. R. (2007). Cyberbullying: What school administrators (and parents) can do.*The Clearing House: A Journal of Educational Strategies, Issues and Ideas, 81*(1), 8-12.

Chen, C. J., Toh, S. C., & Wan, M. F. (2005).*The Design, Development and Evaluation of a Virtual Reality (VR)-Based Learning Environment: Its Efficacy in Novice Car Driver Instruction.* Paper presented at the World Conference on Educational Multimedia, Hypermedia and Telecommunications.

CyberSAFE in Schools 2013 Survey. (2013).

Diamanduros, T., Downs, E., & Jenkins, S. J. (2008).The role of school psychologists in the assessment, prevention, and intervention of cyberbullying.*Psychology in the Schools, 45*(8), 693-704.

Fogg, B. J. (2003). *Persuasive technology [electronic resource] : using computers to change what we think and do / B.J. Fogg*: Amsterdam ; Boston : Morgan Kaufmann Publishers, c2003.

Gibbons, A. S., &Fairweather, P. G. (1998).*Computer-based instruction: Design and development*: Educational Technology.

Ijsselsteijn, W., Kort, Y., Midden, C., Eggen, B., Hoven, E., Lucero, A., et al. (2006). Persuasive Technologies in Education: Improving Motivation to Read and Write for Children (pp. 142).

ISBN: 978-1-387-00704-2

Jonassen, D. (1999). Designing constructivist learning environments.*Instructional design theories and models: A new paradigm of instructional theory, 2*, 215-239.

Keith, S., & Martin, M. E. (2005). Cyber-Bullying: Creating a Culture of Respect in a Cyber world. *Reclaiming Children & Youth, 13*(4).

Loranger, H., & Nielsen, J. (2005).*Teenagers on the Web: Usability Guidelines for Creating Compelling Websites for Teens*: Nielsen Norman Group.

Mayer, R. E. (2009). *Multimedia learning*: Cambridge university press.

Moreno, R., & Mayer, R. E. (2004).Personalized messages that promote science learning in virtual environments.*Journal of Educational Psychology, 96*(1), 165.

Patchin, J. W., &Hinduja, S. (2006). Bullies move beyond the schoolyard a preliminary look at cyberbullying. *Youth violence and juvenile justice, 4*(2), 148-169.

Patchin, J. W., &Hinduja, S. (2012). An Update and Synthesis of the Research.*Cyberbullying prevention and response: Expert perspectives*, 13.

Rivers, I., &Noret, N. (2010). 'I h8 u': findings from a five-year study of text and email bullying. *British Educational Research Journal, 36*(4), 643-671.

Smith, P. K., Mahdavi, J., Carvalho, M., Fisher, S., Russell, S., &Tippett, N. (2008). Cyberbullying: Its nature and impact in secondary school pupils. *Journal of Child Psychology and Psychiatry, 49*(4), 376-385.

Upadhyay, M. A., Jesudass, M. J. J., &Chitale, M. P. (2014).Impact of Electronic Gadgets.*International Journal of Emerging Trends in Science and Technology, 1*(09).

Van Patten, J., Chao, C.-I., &Reigeluth, C. M. (1986).A review of strategies for sequencing and synthesizing instruction.*Review of educational research, 56*(4), 437-471.

Wahab, N. A., &Yahaya, W. A. J. W. (2012).*A Preliminary Investigation: Feasibility of Web-Based Multimedia Learning (WBML) in Raising Awareness of Cyber Bullying*. Paper presented at the Proceeding of the Post Graduate National Mini Conference, Sungai Petani, Kedah.

Willard, N. E. (2007). *Cyber-safe kids, cyber-savvy teens : helping young people learn to use the internet safely and responsibly*: San Francisco, Calif. : Jossey-Bass, c2007 (Norwood, Mass. : Books24x7.com [generator]).

Wolak, J., Mitchell, K. J., &Finkelhor, D. (2007). Does online harassment constitute bullying? An exploration of online harassment by known peers and online-only contacts.*J Adolesc Health, 41*(6 Suppl 1), S51-58.

ISBN: 978-1-387-00704-2

Article 37

Natural Images Contour Segmentation

Khairul Adilah Ahmad, Sharifah Lailee Syed Abdullah
Faculty of Computer and Mathematical Sciences
Universiti Teknologi MARA

Mahmod Othman
Department of Fundamental and Applied Sciences
Universiti Teknologi PETRONAS

Abstract

This paper, a combination of edge detection and contour based segmentation approach for object contour delineation is proposed. The proposed approach employs a new methodology for segmenting the fruit contour from the indoor and outdoor natural images more effectively. The overall process is carried out in five steps. The first step is to pre-process the image in order to convert the colour image to grayscale image. Second step is the adoption of Laplacian of Gaussian edge detection and a new corner template detection algorithm for adjustment of the pixels along the edge map in the interpolation process. Third step is the reconstruction process by implementing two morphology operators with embedded of inversion condition and dynamic threshold to preserve and reconstruct object contour. Fifth step is ground mask process in which the outputs of the inference obtained for each pixel is combined to a final segmented output, which provides a segmented foreground against the black background. This proposed algorithm is tested over 150 indoor and 40 outdoor fruit images in order to analyse its efficiency. From the experimental results, it has been observed that the proposed segmentation approach provides better segmentation accuracy of 100 % in segmenting indoor and outdoor natural images. This algorithm also present a fully automatic model based system for segmenting fruit images of the natural environment.

Keywords: Edge detection, Contour Segmentation, Dynamic Threshold, Fruit, Natural Images,

Introduction

Segmentation is an extremely important phase in many applications of computer vision, which is characteristically related with pattern recognition problems. The essential goal of segmentation is to identify the object of interest in an image or to delineate the object, which are meaningful for a given

ISBN: 978-1-387-00704-2

application. False segmentation will cause degradation of the subsequent image analysis steps such as feature extraction and classification. Generally, segmentation is one the most difficult tasks in image processing where the goal is to detect the presence of object, to separate object from the scene background and to localise the object is space. It can be difficult for many reasons containing ambiguous illumination, ambivalent background and assorted appearance.

The purpose of this paper is to investigate and analyse an efficient method that can be employed to separate the fruit image into two different areas namely, the foreground area and the background area. The foreground area is the part of the image that contains the fruit and hence, provides the information about the fruit. The background area meanwhile contains the noises. The process of separating the image's foreground from the background areas is known as image segmentation.

Related Works
The initial goal in almost all image processing fruit detection and segmentation approaches is to segment the different pixels which appear in image into two classes: fruits and background (soil leaves, stem and grass). Background removal is an essential stage, and it has to be done in an appropriate way to avoid any misclassification. Several methods have been developed for segmenting fruit images. The common segmentation technologies used for this purpose are: threshold-based segmentation, region-based and edge-based segmentation.

i. Threshold
The thresholding approach is a simple and easiest segmentation technique because it classifies pixels into two categories. Basically, there are three types of thresholding: Global thresholding, local thresholding and dynamic thresholding. Global threshold methods such as the one proposed by Otsu (Otsu, 1979) produced an optimal threshold value in order to split

ISBN: 978-1-387-00704-2

the image into two different areas. The critical problem of a single global thresholding is the choice of the threshold value to obtain robust segmentation result (Mahdi & Alzubaidi, 2013). To overcome these drawbacks, local thresholding techniques have been proposed for segmentation which used different thresholds in input image (Huang, Gao, & Cai, 2005). These techniques estimate or compute a different threshold for each pixel according to the greyscale information from the local neighbourhood of the pixel. The ability of the local thresholding therefore has the potential to resolve the problem due to ambiguous illumination conditions and ambivalent background. Then, in dynamic thresholding, each pixel was compared with each dynamic threshold computed from sliding a kernel over the input image. Global thresholding in general has the lowest adaptability to segment objects in natural environment followed by local thresholding and dynamic thresholding.

ii. Region-based

The region-based approach is a commonly used method for the region of interest extraction. Region-based technique is divided into two categories; region growing and merging and region splitting and merging (Du & Sun, 2004). The main idea of region growing-and-merging was to start from a seed point and expand according to the growth rule around a pre-defined seed until it met the growth conditions. The key problems and difficulties of this method was in selecting the seed points. This technique that attempted to model regions using global information was usually not ideal for segmenting intensity inhomogeneity. The region-based technique was unpopular due to numerous limitations (Lin, Wang, Kang, & Wang, 2012). The main challenge in using region-based for fruit contour segmentation was local minima due to the shading effects and presence of strong edges due to the ambivalent background. The algorithm was also computationally more complex thus increasing the computational time.

ISBN: 978-1-387-00704-2

iii. Edge-based

The edge-based approach is the process to mark the points in an image at which the brightness intensity or texture changes sharply. The edges provided important visual information since they corresponded to major physical, photometrical or geometrical variations in images (Ferreira, Kiranyaz, & Gabbouj, 2006; Sharma, Singh, & Kaur, 2013) and was very efficient. Edges characterize object boundaries and were therefore useful for next process of objects in an image. It is a critically low-level operation of image processing because edges represent important information. Applying an edge detector to an image significantly reduces the amount of the data to be processed. The contour of the edges depended on many parameters in the image such as illumination condition (Setayesh, Zhang, & Johnston, 2013), background characteristic (Gongal, Amatya, Karkee, Zhang, & Lewis, 2015) and object properties or large-scale shape phenotype (Karaletsos, Stegle, Dreyer, Winn, & Borgwardt, 2012). . The edge map includes explicit information about the position, orientation and strength of each pixel of the image (Mahmod, Sharifah Lailee, Khairul Adilah, Mohd Nazari, & Ab Razak, 2016).

Material and method

Computer vision process consists of image acquisition, image preprocessing, segmentation. However, the focus of this paper is on the segmentation technique which consists improved edge-based method and contour segmentation. Segmentation process is crucial because the quality of segmented image affects the results of feature extraction and classification task. In order to test the applicability of the proposed method, the Harumanis mango fruit images are chosen to further illustrate the contour segmentation. The Harumanis is chosen because its have similar or identical colour tones for young and ripe mangoes which is a challeng in terms of the similarity of the background to the object of interest (e.g. green fruit against green flora) and foreground

ISBN: 978-1-387-00704-2

complications (e.g. leaves and wrap paper that cross in front of the fruit, breaking its object contour).

Image Acquisition

For this study, 190 images of the Harumanis fruit were captured in natural environment including images taken from the grading house (indoor images) and images taken from the field (outdoor images) as reported in Table 1. A total 105 images were randomly selected from 150 indoor images which were used for the training data set. The other 45 indoor and 40 outdoor images were used as a testing data set.

Table 1: Acquired image

	Indoor image	Outdoor image
Training	105	0
Testing	45	40
Total	150	40

All the images were captured using a digital camera equipped on smart phones. The captured Harumanis images were saved in joint photographic expert group (JPEG) format with a resolution of 1624 X 2448 pixels and maintained in the native RGB (Red, Green and Blue) colour format. Then, image preprocessing involves conversion of RGB image into greyscale image. Greyscale images is a prerequisite because it makes further exploitation of the images more efficient and easy. This ensures less processing time and effectiveness of the algorithm to find edges.

Image Segmentation

The critical task of the computer vision system (CVS) is the recognition of the region of interest through segmentation process of Harumanis mango natural image. Image segmentation was conducted to remove the background area. This process was important to ensure that only the desired object was processed.

ISBN: 978-1-387-00704-2

The two major difficulties faced by the CVS were, non-uniform illumination condition and, the uncertain background which includes different background colors, leaves, stems and other fruits. The conducted segmentation process was intelligent enough to separate the region of interest from the natural images automatically. This was done by integrating improved edge-based algorithm with coner-template and new contour-based delineation (etCD). The diagram of the Edge-template and Contour Delineation (etCD) method for delineating object candidates is shown in Figure 1.

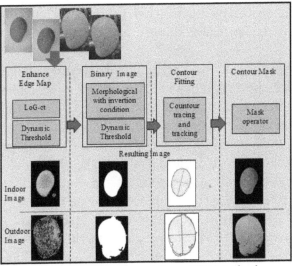

Figure 1: Diagram of the etCD Method

The etCD procedure consisted of four stages, enhances edge map, binary image, contour fitting and contour mask. The first part deals with improved edge detection by integrating Laplacian of Gaussian edge detector and new coner template to identify the fruit object candidate pixels. This improved the quality of edge map by enhancing the image and correcting the effect of non-uniform illumination. A dynamic blob area analysis thresholding algorithm is introduced to extract the mango images from an uncertain background. The algorithm eliminated the unwanted

ISBN: 978-1-387-00704-2

structure, hence preserving edge in uncontrolled acquisition conditions. In the degree of uncertainty in data points is high, then the amount of ambivalent in gradient image data will also be high, which will make the threshold identification is difficult. To solve the problem of ambivalent image this research proposes an algorithm using dynamic blob area analysis threshold to handle uncertainties that automatically selects the threshold value. A thresholding value based on the statistical principles was used to estimate the eligibility of edges to be an object in the image. The flowchart for dynamic blob area analysis threshold is shown in Figure 2. Finding the blobs are usually referred to as connected component analysis or connected component labelling (Grana, Borghesani, & Cucchiara, 2009).

In the second stage, two morphology operators with embedded inversion condition and dynamic thresholds were implemented to preserve and reconstruct the robust fruit contour from various physical appearances. In this operation, a closing operator was used for fruit boundary smoothing and cleaning process by closing the holes in the contours of an object. Inversion condition was applied to identify the centre of the object candidate pixel. Inversion refers to the reverse process on each pixel of the binary image. If the pixel in the centre of the image pixel was black ('0'), an inverse process was executed to change the pixel value from '0' to '1', and vice versa. Next, a region filling operator was employed to fill in the holes within the fruit region. Finally, dynamic threshold was used to select the single object in the binary image. In the third stage, the single binary image was used to fit the appropriate ellipse into the labeled region. Since the shape of mangoes was ovoid, a direct least-squares ellipse fitting algorithm was used (Fitzgibbon, Pilu, & Fisher, 1999) for the shape estimation. In the last stage, the grid of pixels was superimposed together with the initial segmentation map over the processed binary image. This image was processed using the contour-ground mask algorithm adapted from Sharifah Lailee, Hamirul'Aini, Khudzir, & Nursuriati (2010).

ISBN: 978-1-387-00704-2

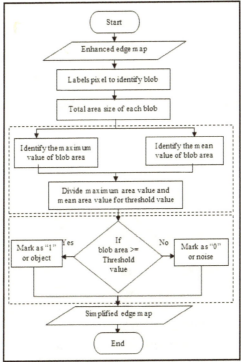

Figure 2: Flowchart of Dynamic Blob Area Analysis Threshold

Results and Discussion

In this research, a visual evaluation and quantitative evaluation method was used to show the performance of etCD algorithm. Visual evaluation was made based on human perception on the shape of the segmented image. For the quantitative evaluation method, a set of reference images called ground truth was created. The performance of etCD segmentations technique was evaluated by measuring the similarity and dissimilarity of the segmented images against the ground truth. The ground truth binary image dataset is a set of segmented images manually sketched by human and a quantitative performance measure was defined. In this research, a cropping technique was used to produce the ground truth dataset. Samples of the ground truth images are shown in Figure 3.

ISBN: 978-1-387-00704-2

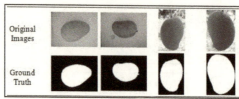

Figure 3: Original Images with Corresponding Ground Truth

For quantitative evaluation, two measurements were used in this research. The measurements were similarity index, Tanimoto Coefficient (TC) (Alaniz et al., 2006; Zijdenbos et al., 1994) and dissimilarity index, false positive rate (FPR) (Fawcett, 2006). The values of TC are between 0 and 1 in which 1 reflects a perfect similarity which indicates high quality of the segmented images.

The TC values measure the number of common pixels in the foreground and background areas shared by both segmented and ground truth images. Otherwise, the FPR known as over-segmentation was calculated when the pixels of the background were misclassified as foreground. The value of FPR also varies between 0 and 1 where the quality of segmented images is better when FPR values are lower.

The segmented results along with indoor ant outdoor images, Enhanced edge map, binary image, contour fitting, contour mask and its accuracy is given in Figure 4 and Figure 5 respectively.

ISBN: 978-1-387-00704-2

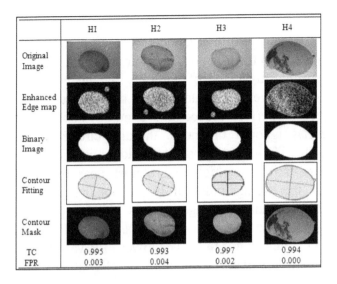

	HI	H2	H3	H4
Original Image				
Enhanced Edge map				
Binary Image				
Contour Fitting				
Contour Mask				
TC	0.995	0.993	0.997	0.994
FPR	0.003	0.004	0.002	0.000

Figure 4: Segmentation of Indoor Images using etCD

For indoor images visual observation, the etCD algorithm has the ability to correctly segment the object contour with either strong or weak illumination exposure also fruit which contained foreground structure noise. In addition, the background areas of the segmented images were perfectly removed. Obviously, the segmentation visual results from the etCD algorithm were very accurate in segmenting fruit contour from indoor images. The TC values for all indoor images were high and almost near to the value of 1, thus indicating that the etCD algorithm is able to produce perfect segmented for indoor images. Then, the evaluation of the algorithm result performed using FPR values were very small and almost near to the value of 1. The smaller FPR values indicated etCD algorithm is able to remove the false positive of background pixels absolutely.

For outdoor images, in binary image, some small parts of the background areas in images F1 and F3 were wrongly classified because the background areas were filled with white pixels. The main factor for this misclassification of the background area was because the background object had similar intensity with the

ISBN: 978-1-387-00704-2

object area. Therefore, contour fitting was used to solve this problem. Contour fitting models was used to trace contour boundaries and to track the object contour using ellipse. Contour fitting has the advantage of naturally handle contour changes such as object over segmentation and therefore able to segment the object properly. Successful contour tracing and ellipse tracking has ignored the noise through circumnavigating the contour. he TC values for all the outdoor images produced by etCD algorithm were high and almost near the value of 1. Moreover, the average value of 40 outdoor images TC is 0.937, thus indicating that the algorithm is able to produce almost perfect segmented for outdoor images. The FPR values were very small which nearer to 0. The lower FPR values also showed that there was less over segmentation of etCD algorithm.

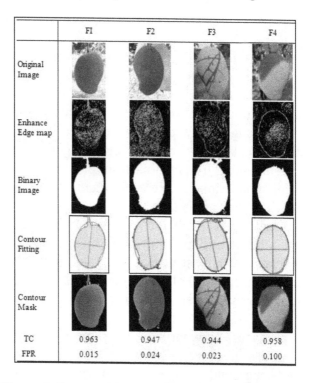

Figure 5: Segmentation of Outdoor Images using etCD

ISBN: 978-1-387-00704-2

Conclusion

In this paper a new method for segmenting fruit contour using the integration improved edge-based algorithm with coner-template and new contour-based delineation (etCD) algorithm had been proposed. The main purpose of this approach is to improve the accuracy of segmentation by reducing the segmentation error. The segmentation through edge detection and area analysis dynamic threshold found to reduce complex calculation which reduces the computation, which is very significant in real time processes. This method has been applied to 45 Harumanis indoor images and 40 Harumanis outdoor images in order to validate the efficiency of the etCD algorithm. In conclusion, the etCD algorithm has the ability to properly segment the contour of the object. Overall, all the segmented images produced by etCD have accurate object contour where all the pixels in the object were correctly filled with white pixels. In addition, the background area of the segmented images was mostly removed. Moreover, it proved to be robust in extracting object contour in the image in natural environment.

References

Ferreira, M., Kiranyaz, S., & Gabbouj, M. (2006). A comparative analysis of feature extraction methods for fruit grading classifications. In *IEEE International Conference on Acoustics Speed and Signal Processing Proceedings* (Vol. 2, pp. 381–384).

Fitzgibbon, A., Pilu, M., & Fisher, R. B. (1999). Direct least square fitting of ellipses. *IEEE Transactions on Pattern Analysis and Machine Intelligence, 21*(5), pp. 476–480.

Gongal, A., Amatya, S., Karkee, M., Zhang, Q., & Lewis, K. (2015). Sensors and systems for fruit detection and localization: A review. *Computers and Electronics in Agriculture, 116*, pp. 8–19. h

Grana, C., Borghesani, D., & Cucchiara, R. (2009). Connected component labeling techniques on modern architectures. In *In Image Analysis and Processing–ICIAP*, pp. 816–824. Springer Berlin Heidelberg.

Huang, Q., Gao, W., & Cai, W. (2005). Thresholding technique with adaptive window selection for uneven lighting image. *Pattern Recognition Letters, 26*(6), pp. 801–808.

Karaletsos, T., Stegle, O., Dreyer, C., Winn, J., & Borgwardt, K. M. (2012). ShapePheno: Unsupervised extraction of shape phenotypes from biological image collections. *Bioinformatics, 28*(7), pp. 1001–1008.

Lin, G.-C., Wang, W.-J., Kang, C.-C., & Wang, C.-M. (2012). Multispectral MR images segmentation based on fuzzy knowledge and modified seeded region growing. *Magnetic Resonance Imaging, 30*(2), pp. 230–46.

Mahdi, A., & Alzubaidi, N. (2013). Hybrid image segmentation method based on global thresholding method and edge detection using canny operator. *Journal of Kerbala University, 11*(3), pp. 63–74.

Mahmod, O., Sharifah Lailee, S. A., Khairul Adilah, A., Mohd Nazari, A. B., & Ab Razak, M. (2016). The fusion of edge detection and mathematical morphology algorithm for shape boundary recognition. *Journal of Information and Communication Technology (JICT), 15*(1), pp. 133–144.

Otsu, N. (1979). A threshold selection method from gray-level histograms. *IEEE Transactions on Systems, Man, and Cybernetics, 9*(1), pp. 62–66.

Setayesh, M., Zhang, M., & Johnston, M. (2013). A novel particle swarm optimisation approach to detecting continuous, thin and smooth edges in noisy images. *Information Sciences, 246*, pp. 28–51.

Sharifah Lailee, S. A., Hamirul'Aini, H., Khudzir, I., & Nursuriati, J. (2010). Improved technique for segmenting images under natural environment. *International Conference on Science and Social Research*, pp. 401–405.

Sharma, P., Singh, G., & Kaur, A. (2013). Different techniques of edge detection in digital image processing. *International Journal of Engineering Research and Applications, 3*(3), pp. 458–461.

ISBN: 978-1-387-00704-2

Article 38

Proposed Framework for Combining Gamification Elements with Open Learner Model in a Collaborative e-Learning System for Programming Course

Harizah Jasin, Mahfudzah Othman, Nurzaid Muhd Zain, Mohd Nizam Osman
Faculty of Computer and Mathematical
Universiti Teknologi MARA Perlis Branch, Malaysia

Abstract
The main objective of the proposed framework that combines gamification and open learner model is to increase students' engagement in learning programming via virtual computer environment, thus enabling them to learn cooperatively and helps them to increase awareness of their own performance. The framework proposed the development of an e-Learning system that includes gamification elements such as the users' level and leaderboard to display users' achievements and rewards. Meanwhile, in order to increase students' awareness of their own milestone in the programming course, the framework also included the Open Learnel Model, which shows the students' milestones via the skills meters. This project also proposed the use of Web 2.0 elements such as chat rooms to allow collaboration and group discussions over the Internet.

Keywords: gamification, e-Learning, Open Learner Model, Web-based application

Introduction

Swacha (2013) has defined in his study that gamification is the gaming metaphors that improve motivation, influence behavior and engagement in the real life task. Whenever elements of game mechanics and game dynamics are applied in a non-game environment, it will consider as gamification (Fox, Kim, Kirk &Zinchermann, 2010). Urh (2015) has explained that in the education field, gamification has been seen as a potential alternative to teaching and learning methods that promote students' engagement and motivation.

ISBN: 978-1-387-00704-2

Ideally, open learner models are learner models that can be viewed or accessed in some way by the learner, or by other users (Bull, 2012). The learner model contents can also be of direct use to the user. This is to enable adaptation to the individual according to their current learning need and in addition to the standard purpose of the learner model of maintaining data. According to Kay (2012), if viewing the information in their learner model may be benefits to the user, a learner model that is inferred using any learner modeling techniques could potentially be opened to the learner. Generally, opening the learner model is more than simply showing the learner the representations from the underlying system's model of their knowledge. To create an effective interface to represent the model and support interaction with it is the key challenge in opening a model.

Gamification is one of the popular choices on web-based activities in motivating user participation. It does help aligning the students' interest with the intrinsic motivation when done well as stated by Zichermann (2011) in his study. This kind of concept also can be adapted into the learner. Based on Monterrat, Lavoue, and George (2014), there are two needs to be fulfilled in order to produce or adopt gamification in learning. Moreover, it is a complex process for turning a game from an actual learning environment.

The idea of combining gamification elements in open learner models is not a new thing. Even so, there is still a lack of research regarding this field of study. If these gamification elements are adapted to the open learner model like e-learning system, there are many positive impacts that might be seen in the students' achievement.

Therefore, this study is conducted to implement selected gamification elements for collaborative e-learning. These included small tasks, rewards for accomplishing the tasks and measurable progressive challenge. Other than that, selected game

ISBN: 978-1-387-00704-2

mechanics such as points, levels, challenges, progress bar and leaderboard will also be implemented. Achievements, competition, and rewards are an example of the selected game dynamics that might be implemented in the open learner model. With all those elements, the students will be more encouraged in having active participations.

Related Works

i.   Motivation for Learning: Adaptive Gamification for Web-based Learning Environment

This paper has proposed the architecture of a system to motivate learners by integrating game elements in the existing web-based learning environment. It is not the ultimate goal of this system to turn every learning activity into a game. This is because games need to be played voluntary and in some context, people are already motivated to learn.

Even so, there are still drawbacks exist in this system. One of the drawbacks is it proposed the adaptation of multiplayer features, where existing environments have already proposed the same game elements for all users. Other than that, it also deals with the adaptation of gamification, where the literature deals more with an adaptation of the game. It also proposed the adaptation of game dynamics where existing system adapts the learning path and difficulty level (Khan Academy, 2006).

ii.   Play As You Learn: Gamification as Techniques for Motivating Learners

This research discussed core game concepts that usually used in implementing gamification elements, which are goal-focused activity, reward mechanisms and progress tracking. It also explained that by adding all these gamification elements in the e-learning platform might increase the engagement of unmotivated learners in the learning process and interaction with other learners. The researchers of this study also discussed and came

ISBN: 978-1-387-00704-2

out with things that need to be questioned before implementing gamification in a learning environment.

It is also highlighted in this study that gamification actually have been adapted into some applications like FourSquare and Crowdrise. For both applications, the users will be given badges and earning some points after they have completed their activities or tasks. To be concluded, it does give positive impact in their engagement for the users of the applications that implement gamification elements.

iii.   Quick Quiz: A Gamified Approach for Enhancing Learning
Quick Quiz is a gamified quiz software tools that developed as a mobile web application. The main aim of this developed tool is to motivate students in revising all the course materials throughout the semester. This tool is embedded with several features to make students more enjoyable while doing all the tasks. The features are included providing multiple choice questions so that students did not need too much thinking, limits the time for students in answering questions to put some pressure and the participation is voluntary.

Students will be rewarded with a point for each question they answered correctly within the time limit given. This is an example of the game mechanics that have been applied in this Quick Quiz tool. After completing answered all the questions, students are allowed to see their own individual performance against the other class members' performance as a holistic feedback.

Based on the data collection, students' engagement, enjoyment, learning and experiences are being evaluated. The students are engaged enough to complete the task with this gamified approach tool. This study also recommends that implementing gamification element in the education system, like e-learning should be investigated more.

ISBN: 978-1-387-00704-2

Proposed Framework of Combining Gamification Elements and Open Learner Model in e-Learning Environment

Figure 1 shows all the elements included in combining the gamification elements with the open learner model. This proposed project will be done using the web application development tools such as PHP and MySQL database that mimics the traditional e-learning system. The enhanced factors of e-learning system proposed in this framework is collaboration and gamification, where the pair programming technique was chosen to represent the collaborative concept. For the purpose to encourage collaboration over the Internet, the Web 2.0 tools will be used to support the online chatting, upload or download electronic materials as well as online discussions to answer the quizzes, whether in groups or individually. In order to provide gamification elements in this system, we have identified gamification elements that represent the game mechanics and game dynamics. The elements proposed are the use of levels of difficulty, progress bar and leaderboard. These game mechanics are used to encourage achievements or accomplishments, provides competition among groups and giving out rewards.

Meanwhile, open learner model proposed in this system, will provide users with their individual skill meters and groups' skill meters. This was to encourage students' engagement and monitoring their own milestones in learning introductory programming. The skill meters are the visual representation of the students' achievements each time they or their team members solve particular online quizzes provided in each chapter. The skill meters, like a progress bar will depict the milestones of the students starting from the least difficult questions until the hardest ones. This way, the students will be able to be part of their own progress and becoming increasingly aware of their performance in programming.

ISBN: 978-1-387-00704-2

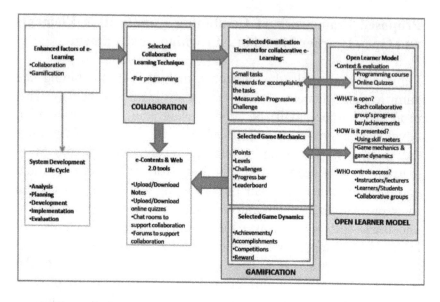

Figure 1: Research Model of Gamification with Open Learner
Model in a Collaborative e-Learning System

In this proposed framework, lecturers were given the access to the
online course and were able to track students' progress,
submissions or achievement in the account management section.
Lecturers can upload online materials, construct online quizzes
that meant to be answered whether individually or by each group
of students registered in the system. Furthermore, online
discussions can also be done among the students and the lecturers
in order to support distance learning.

Conclusion

Combining gamification elements with open learner model in a
web based system environment can be seen as a good initiative to
encourage student participation in learning process. In this paper,
a framework of an enhanced e-learning system for learning
programming was proposed to combine gamification elements
such as leaderboard and levels of difficulty with the concept of
open learner model. Both technologies that include elements of
visual representations will be embedded in the e-learning

ISBN: 978-1-387-00704-2

environment to encourage students' engagements and awareness of their own progress. Besides that, the framework also proposed to include collaborative elements to encourage online discussions and collaborations among students. Through this, students will be able to stay connected and discuss via the Internet from dispersed locations. Lecturers can also participate in the discussions to increase online engagements and provide channel for better online teaching and learning.

References

Swacha, J. (2013). Gamification - based e - learning Platform for Computer Programming Education, (2012).

Urh, M., Vukovic, G., Jereb, E., &Pintar, R. (2015).The model for introduction of gamification into e-learning in higher education.*Procedia - Social and Behavioral Sciences*, *197*(February), 388–397. https://doi.org/10.1016/j.sbspro.2015.07.154

Zichermann, G., Cunningham, C. (2011). Gamification by Design: Implementing game mechanics in web and mobile apps.

Bull, S., & Kay, J. (2015). SMILI J 9 : A Framework for Interfaces to Learning Data in Open Learner Models , Learning Analytics and Related Fields.

Bull, S., & Kay, J. (n.d.). Student Models that Invite the Learner In : The SMILI9 Open Learner Modelling Framework.

Bull, S., & Kay, J. (n.d.). Open Learner Models.

Kapp, K. (2012). The Gamification of Learning and Instruction, Pfeiffer.*San Francisco*, 480. https://doi.org/10.4018/jgcms.2012100106

KhanAcademy, 2006.www.khanacademy.org

Monterrat, B., Lavou, E., Monterrat, B., &Lavou, E. (2015).Motivation for Learning : Adaptive Gamification for Web-based Learning Environments To cite this version : Motivation for Learning : Adaptive Gamification for Web-based Learning Environments.

Swacha, J. (2013). Gamification - based e - learning Platform for Computer Programming Education, (2012).

Ullirich, C., Borau, K., Luo, H., Tan, X., Shen, L., &Shen, R. (2008). Why Web 2 . 0 is Good for Learning and for Research: Principles and Prototypes. Www 2008, 705–714. http://doi.org/http://dx.doi.org/10.1145/1367497.1367593

Urh, M., Vukovic, G., Jereb, E., &Pintar, R. (2015).The model for introduction of gamification into e-learning in higher education.*Procedia - Social and*

ISBN: 978-1-387-00704-2

Behavioral Sciences, *197*(February), 388–397. https://doi.org/10.1016/j.sbspro.2015.07.154

Zichermann, G., Cunningham, C. (2011). Gamification by Design: Implementing game mechanics in web and mobile apps.

ISBN: 978-1-387-00704-2

www.ingramcontent.com/pod-product-compliance
Lightning Source LLC
Chambersburg PA
CBHW051221050326
40689CB00007B/755